Tex[t]-Mex

William Anthony Nericcio

SEDUCTIVE

HALLUCINATIONS OF THE "MEXICAN" IN AMERICA

Tex{t}-Mex

not Chicano

UNIVERSITY OF TEXAS PRESS   AUSTIN

Copyright ©2007 by the University of Texas Press
All rights reserved
Printed in the United States of America
Third paperback printing, 2016

Requests for permission to reproduce material
from this work should be sent to:
    Permissions
    University of Texas Press
    P.O. Box 7819
    Austin, TX 78713-7819

http://utpress.utexas.edu/index.php/rp-form

The paper used in this book meets the minimum
requirements of ANSI/NISO Z39.48-1992 (R1997)
(Permanence of Paper).

Library of Congress Cataloging-in-Publication Data

Nericcio, William Anthony, 1961–
    Tex[t]-Mex : seductive hallucinations of the "Mexican"
    in America / by William Anthony Nericcio. — 1st ed.
        p.   cm.

Includes bibliographical references and index.
ISBN 978-0-292-71457-1 (pbk. : alk. paper)
1. Mexican Americans in motion pictures.
2. Mexican Americans in popular culture.
I. Title.

PN1995.9.M49N47 2007
305.8968'72073—dc22   2006015013

For Lila, Lorenzo Antonio y Sophia
Alessandra Nericcio . . .

y *para* Mama and Daddy,
Trinidad and William Nericcio,
y *mis hermanas*, Josie and Mary Anne.

and lastly, for Severiana Nericcio, Ana,
my father's mother, in whose house
I learned to love to read and draw and
write; and to her husband, my
grandfather, William Nericcio, né
Guglielmo Nericcio, the old Siciliano,
from Partanna, whom I never met, but
whose ghost forever walks the velvet
corridors of my family's imagination.

Hallucinate \Hal*lu"ci*nate\ v. i. [L. hallucinatus, alucinatus, p. p. of hallucinari, alucinari, to wander in mind, talk idly, to wander; [dream.] 1. To wander; to go astray; to err; to blunder; 2. Specifically: To perceive a non-existent phenomenon; to believe that one is experiencing something which in reality does not exist; to experience a hallucination[2].

CONTENTS

NONHALLUCINATORY PREFATORY PALABRAS...

This will never end. And that's all right—having too many people to thank means I've had some good luck when it came to mentors and friends.

At Blessed Sacrament Academy, 1966–1973, Laredo, Texas, I owe a tip of the hat and a big *abrazo* to Sister Elaine, now Elaine Carter, who taught me to love school, and maybe about love in general, seeing as I had a huge crush on her—*abrazos*, too, to Mrs. Leyendecker, Mrs. Notzon, and Mrs. Martin, who all had a hand in letting me love drawing and writing; a stiff kick to the memory of Sister Cecilia, who used to take bad children (never "little Billy, " *whew!*) into the dark closet to whip them within an inch of their lives with a thick jump rope—can you say "Catholic pathology"? I knew you could!

At St. Augustine School, 1973–1980, Laredo, Texas, wreaths of affection are thrown out to Sister Vivian (eighth grade English and Grammar diva), to Sister Corinne, and to Brother Phillip Degagne as well; Mr. Peter González, who almost convinced me to study to be an oncologist, is wreath worthy as well. Sister Rose, who despised me toward the end and who taught me literature and who, almost, caught me cheating on an English final (guilty!), should get some love as well.

At the University of Texas at Austin (where I finished my BA in English, with a specialization in the literature of Latin America), I am at the knees of comedy-savant Richard Keller Simon, who recently passed away; Larry Carver; Ramón Saldívar; Elizabeth Cullingford; and Elisabeth Segré—all of whom worked in the Department of English while I was there from 1980 to 1984. Lance Bertleson deserves special praise/blame for asking me "You ever thought of becoming an English professor?" during a fateful office hour, the same week I had dropped out of Organic Chemistry. The answer then was "No, Lance . . . what's it like?" and the rest, as they say, is history. Also to be singled out at the University of Texas, though she moved up and out of it and on to bigger and better things, is the outrageously dedicated and drop-dead amazing Gayatri Chakravorty Spivak—more on her to come. Also at UT, but having nothing to do with academe, I want to thank my college roommates and friends Jay Whitley, Efraín Pérez, and Robbie Araiza for not killing me—an existential *beso* as well goes out to *vecinos/amigos* Gerardo "Chore" Longoria (RIP), Ricky González, Alfonso "Poncho" Lozano: thanx for the air-conditioning and free beer!

At Cornell University, I crossed paths with many friends, colleagues, and associates who left tattoos on my soul; these include Oliver Mayer (and Balder, RIP), Beatrice Jamaica, James Guiry, and Andrew Hewitt. I guess I better thank my professors in and around the Department of Comparative Literature as well, who are ordered here in a ciphered manner that I will only reveal to readers of the book who write and ask: Carlos Fuentes (who changed my life—*besos* for the *abrazo* in *Crystal Frontier*), Gayatri Spivak (my diva/guru—I don't care what prose slackers say, you write like a *shaman*), Enrico Mario Santí (who saved my career—*gracias*), Dominic LaCapra, Geoffrey Waite (to whom I owe the birth of my semiotic pathology), Henry Louis Gates, A. A. "Archie" Ammons (who always let me crash the MFA room and chat on his comfy sofa chair—RIP), Edgar Rosenberg, Mary Randall, Wolfgang Holdheim, Mark Seltzer, Walter Cohen (the Marxist with the nicest house on this hill!), John Kronik (who went on to edit the *PMLA* and who chaired my Chicano literature special study when no one else would), Jonathan Culler, Barbara Harlow, and Cynthia Chase. High above Cayuga's waters, love must be sent to the ghost of Vladimir Nabokov that really does still prowl the halls of Goldwyn Smith Hall (don't go to Zeus after midnight) searching for stray butterflies and callow coeds.

After I finished my dissertation at Cornell, I was hired by the stalwart trio of Bill Rosen, RIP; Bill Curtin; and Ross Miller at the University of Connecticut at Storrs. I am forever in debt to Professor Rosen for his support and counsel. Bob Hasenfratz, Jerry Phillips, Marianne Sadowski, Lee Jacobus, Mark Schwartz, David Lynch, and Laura Rossi, colleagues, friends, and more, also made those endless winters palatable for this *hijo de Tejas*.

At San Diego State University, where I have hung my hat since 1991, I am beholden to Emily Hicks, Chicana/o studies *y* English, and Tom Davies, Latin American studies, for being key parts of the conspiracy to bring me to the West Coast—I don't know whether to blame or to praise you for that! At SDSU, I want to signal my undying gratitude for friendship and more to my colleagues Peter Atterton, Harry Polkinhorn, June Cummins, Michael Borgstrom (aka M-bo, who wears Lucky Jeans like a *Mutha* and outs Puritan shenanigans like there's no tomorrow), Adelaida Del Castillo, Larry McCaffery, Phillip Serrato, and Laurel Amtower. But my biggest thanks go to my students—especially Michael Buchmiller (graphics genius), Jason Solinger (brilliant Captain), Linda Gerard, Michael Harper (the funniest man on the planet since Bill Hicks), Jonathan Speight, Rebecca Krzyzaniak (letterpress diva), Estela Eaton (twenty-first-century librettist-poet-writer), Diana Contreras (the next Orson Welles), Jamie Fox (improvmeister), Christine Taylor, Erica Anderson, Marc García-Martínez, Ralph Clare, Darl Biniaz, Eric Wallach and Keith Geller, Jake Thomas, Rosina Talamantes, Kelly Nicolson, Joey Ritacco, Stephanie Hyink, Tomás Riley (taco shop muse), Marisa Fierle, Leon Lanzbom (fellow Ponce's devotee), Nikola Djukik, Taylor Mitchell, La Rae Cunningham, Spring Kurtz, Shelley Scott, Andrew Doub, Crystal Alatorre, Travis Temple, Chip Phillips, Vincent Biondo, Carlos Amador, Robby Borland, Brenda Cruz, and Tricia Almase. Sarah Chávez gets a special thank-you for saving my life from a fall on the Picadilly Line, summer 2005, in London; Jen Halpert, her friend, gets a special *gracias* as well for saving that mysterious sombrero from the wheels of that speeding northbound train—a sign from Tlaloc, no doubt, that this book would come to be. John Gutiérrez, my SoCal student, baseball nemesis, and friend by way of the UK, deserves a little love as well.

Last but not least, thanks go to: Adam Gonzalez, barrister extraordinaire; John Makey, Foundation for International Education, London, for the pints and chats; Michelle Habell-Pallan and Mary Romero, for their generosity; Arturo Aldama, for the faith; Frederick Aldama, for his Hermes-like dexterity; Sharon Willis, fellow Ithaca spelunker and film addict, for the guidance; Djelal Kadir, for the *enduring* faith and mentorship and for giving license to my word-fetish tendencies; Davíd Carrasco, for riding my *nalgas* till I finished this book; Irit Rogoff, for London, San Francisco, and keeping hope alive when hope had no hope for another day; Jorge Huerta, a true *mensch!* for sheer enthusiasm; Marisela Norte, for the good vibe; Michael Ryan, Mr. Marxism and Deconstruction, for Leiden and more; Norma Cantú, for all the little things; Ryan Schneider, at Purdue now, for Las Vegas and the Red Fox Room; Fred Gardaphe, for the Gangsters gig, and his *amico* Anthony Tamburri, for getting this Tejano in touch with his Sicilian side. One last loving *abrazo* as well goes to *mis suegros* Paco y Melva Flores and my *cuñada* Sandra Flores. No doubt there are others; I pray this book goes into a second edition so I can thank all the people who made this sixteen-year project possible.

My father, the great World War II veteran, 29th Division, Omaha Beach, William Nericcio, and my mother, the amazing WWII riveter and Ma Bell operator, Trinidad Nericcio, brought me screaming and yelling into this world December 2, 1961, and I love them with all my heart for making my life and my education possible—all that overtime you worked, Daddy, was worth it for me and my family; and Mama, I know you gave up a plush retirement account to stay and help get us through high school in Laredo—you know I can never pay you back for that; Josie, my sister, cool LA sound editor, taught this *niño* to read (more on that in a chapter below); and Mary Anne, big sister and professor now, showed Josie and me the way out of Laredo to Austin and the University of Texas.

Speaking of Texas, none of the ink and paper that you hold in your hands would have ever gotten near your eyes without the incredible editorial team at the University of Texas Press, located in the finest city on the planet, the Paris of the Southwest, Austin, Texas—in particular, let me single out the oracular editorial magic of Theresa May, the design vision of Lisa Tremaine, and the genius syntactic wisdom of Nancy Warrington.

And Rosalinda Nericcio? She teaches me about love. I am her willfully uneducable student—a rapt, lifelong novitiate; her TAs, Sophia and Lorenzo, have taught me about this as well.

San Diego | August 2006

This book contains revised and extended versions of essays and chapters that appeared (or, in one case, *will appear*) in various journals and books; these include: "Lupe Vélez Revisited: Tales of the Mexican Spitfire in an American Vomitorium," which you'll find in *From Bananas to Buttocks: Latina Bodies in Popular Culture*, edited by Myra Mendible, forthcoming from the University of Texas Press, 2007; "When Electrolysis Proxies for the Existential: A Somewhat Sordid Meditation on What Might Occur if Frantz Fanon, Rosario Castellanos, Jacques Derrida, Gayatri Spivak, and Sandra Cisneros Asked Rita Hayworth Her Name," which appeared in *Violence and the Body*, edited by Arturo Aldama (Bloomington: Indiana University Press, 2003); "A Decidedly 'Mexican' and 'American' Semi[er]otic Transference: Frida Kahlo in the Eyes of Gilbert Hernandez," edited by Mary Romero, Michele Habell-Pallán, and Jaime Cárdenas (New York: New York University Press, 2002); "Autopsy of a Rat: Odd, Sundry Parables of Freddy López, Speedy Gonzales, and Other Chicano/Latino Marionettes Prancing about Our First World Visual Emporium," which launched in *Camera Obscura* (37: 189–237) in January of 1996; "Of Mestizos and Half-Breeds: Orson Welles's *Touch of Evil*" came out in *Chicano Cinema*, edited by Chon Noriega (Minneapolis: University of Minnesota Press, 1992), 47–58. Last but not least, an early version of the rant on the Marquis de Sade and a California sheriff's deputy appeared in a 2002 issue (no. 61) of *Bad Subjects*, and a truncated version of my Richard Rodriguez reverie appeared in *World Literature Today* (69:1) in 1994. I am in debt to the editors of these works and the respective presses for permission to revise, publish, and extend pieces that originally appeared under their auspices. *Gracias, gracias, gracias.* Yadda, yadda, yadda. Let the last *bon mot* go here, and let it be dedicated to the saintly *monja* shade of Reverend Mother Rosalie Hill, R.S.C.J., in whose reading room at the Copley Library of the University of San Diego this manuscript experienced its final proofing, by my hand, William Anthony Nericcio, August 2006.

Tex[t]-Mex

A Decidedly Odd Tale of What Happened When Hollywood Killed Vaudeville, Postcards Boomed, and the United States Invaded Mexico

Tex[t]-Mex Textual Politics

Less a people than a *text*, my prowlings, interrogations, and inquests suggest that peculiar and particular manifestations of the "Mexican" are to be found across the bucolic oases and sprawling wastelands of the United States. These droll *mannequins* appear in photographs, in movies, in newspapers and magazines, and on television.

And, arguably, they are all of a *type*: Chicanos, Latin Americans, Latinas, and "Hispanics"—call *them* what you will—in word and image, curious manifestations of Latino "subject-effect[s]" (to borrow from Michel Foucault) and "subject position[s]" (to borrow from my beloved mentor G. Spivak) have made their way to the U.S. public.[1]

Why "Tex[t]-Mex"? Well, to begin with the obvious: I am from South Texas, Laredo, Texas, to be exact, and if Laredo is not the home, the autochthonous *papi y mami* of Tex-Mex, of Tex-Mex music, of Tex-Mex cuisine, in short, of the Tex-Mex *Dasein*, it must at least be damn close. So the word was always in the air—the music of Johnny Canales (RIP) and Flaco Jiménez; the

For a healthy harvest of fresh examples, tune into the Fox Network's vérité teledrama Cops or visit your local pinball /video-game arcade where Latino types, especially cyber-versions of blood-thirsty, Marx-loving Central American insurgents, are a veritable fixture. Although the Contras of Alzheimer's-victim Ronald Reagan's time have faded from the popular imagination, they remain a fixture of the American adolescent unconscious, only somewhat replaced of late by swarthy "Arab" Islamic radical terrorists.

food from my mother's kitchen; those crazy french fries from the Tumble Inn the size of fingers on a baseball glove, always served with jalapeños and a greasy burger; Cotulla's mariachis; engorged tacos the size of Whataburgers . . .

But I was not writing a book about Tex-Mex; I was writing a book about Tex[t]-Mex, so I turned to that annoying and cloying but necessary bracketed [*t*] in the neologism "Tex[t]-Mex," which is, I admit, a tad precious *and* so very 1980s, but I can make no apologies for that, as that *was* the time when I came of age as a cultural critic and a theorist, and the intrusion of the brackets foregrounds the constructedness of "Mexicans" in movies, advertising, photography, and everything else in a way I pray my reader won't forget.

Time will tell.

A somewhat anticipated note about the terms "Mexican," "Latina/o," "Chicana/o," and other "miscegenated" semantic oddities that parade throughout the corridors of this book: in present, everyday usage, the designations "Latino" and "Latina" refer as often to U.S. citizens, permanent residents, and visitors of Latin American descent (Chicanas/os, Cuban Americans, *puertorriqueñas/os*, etc.) as to Latin American nationals (Mexicans, *salvadoreños*, *nicaragüenses*, etc.) living in the United States.

Most of the rogues' gallery of "Mexican" and "Latina/o" types that appear in these pages are animated mannequins of a decidedly Mexican persuasion.

But stereotypes are not usually too precise when it comes to nationality. The animatronic puppet "Freddy López," for instance, whom you will meet in the penultimate chapter below, might be Dominican, Puerto Rican, Mexican, Chicano, Cuban, "Gypsy," or even (and this may be the most telling coincidence) a Central European Jew—he may even be some odd fusion of them all.

Spanish-language surnames and accents type him as one from a Spanish-speaking land, and his swarthy physiognomy types him as evil and criminal. He and the clever retinue of "Mexicans" and "Latinos" that we will meet in the pages that follow are *Latino*; we *know* that much, or, for the moment, we can presume as much. Someway, somehow, we also know that this ethnocultural lineage testifies visually to said individual's criminal potentiality.[2]

And this "someway, somehow" is, in the end, the subject of this illustrated tome, this bastard bestiary of entirely familiar, utterly seductive (*because they are familiar*), popular hallucinations of "Mexicans" in the cultural spaces of the Americas. Simple words and yet these quoted semantic Hefty Bags hide within their ample elastic recesses answers to the mystery of the profound virulence of what I am tagging as "Mexican" in U.S. popular culture.

Pictured here, ruminating in refuse, are two of Speedy Gonzales's *compadre* mice. The frame here reproduced is a digitized screen grab from Director Robert McKimson's *Cannery Woe* (1961) in *Golden Jubilee 24 Karat Collection: Speedy Gonzales' Fast Funnies.*

More sculpted "subject-effect[s]" (*chapeau* Foucault) or "subject position[s]" (*sombrero* Spivak) than "subjects" (in most cases, even *objects* with the *potential* for subjectivity would be an improvement), Mexicans and Americans of Mexican descent in U.S. popular culture have often resembled ugly marionettes in the service of mercenary puppeteers. One wonders, for instance, how the ubiquitous image of trashy "Mexican" types like this one spreads viruslike into the "political unconscious," or better put (since stereotypes affect the cultural body in ways that are palpably material), the cultural and political body politic.[3]

And lest we, through some momentary brain lapse or some incipient flash of collective Alzheimer's, *underestimate* the capacity of pictures to "infect" the masses against particular ethnic groups, we might do well to pause here and go back a few decades to consider the successes of Adolf Hitler. At one point, this diminutive homicidal imagineer, one of the more important m/ad executives of the twentieth century, is recorded to have ordered his media industry to create a mass of *common visionaries* who will "obey a law they [do] not even know but which they [can] recite in their dreams."[4]

When one thinks of the relative status of the term "Mexican," how it is manifest in the textual record available to us as a register of the collective American unconscious, one realizes that some latter-day inheritors of Hitler's visual ideological mandate are still hard at work. One need not be a devotee of the failed European artist/Nazi potentate to suspect that the rules of the semiotic m/adman game still hold true when it comes to the representation of Mexicans and Latinos in mass culture.

AdAge.com is one of the more important industry Web sites for the advertising aristocracy. "M/Ad Man of the Year," pictured here, wrestles with the ironies implicit in this fast-moving guild.

It goes without saying, but I highlight it for you anyway, that this book-length peripatetic sampling of defamatory "Mexican"/Latina/o portraitures has not been fashioned in a political or aesthetic vacuum. Like Native Americans, African Americans, and Irish Americans (just to name a few indicted ethnic "flavors" from this century alone), Latina/o Americans have represented a subject[ed] population—that is, until quite recently, they have not contributed to mainstream, mass cultural textual and cinematic representations of their own communities; even when they *have contributed*, said acts of art have not dominated gallery space at MOMA or rollicked box office tills from Tulsa to Portland to Texarkana.

One has only to remember how Tarzan films, Zulu Technicolor extravaganzas, and blaxploitation feature films (remarkably enjoying a renaissance in cinema art houses of late) like *Mandingo* (1975, directed by Richard Fleischer and produced by noted schlockmeister Dino De Laurentis) concretized notions of the African and the African American "savage" to sense that this is true.[5] And not least interesting, with specific regard to *Mandingo*, is the way said film, a guilty pleasure of a screening if there ever was one, fuses violence and sexuality, a copulative combo that will become familiar to us in the pages of our Tex[t]-Mex odyssey.[6]

A reproduction of the lobby movie poster for *Mandingo* (1975), an outrageous Hollywood mess that features, among other things, Perry King as Hammond Maxwell, spouting lines like "Pleasure me, you ebony wench."

Of course all this lurid nonsense did not begin with the advent of cinema; sample here, for instance, a couple of pages from my private collection of stereotyped artifacts. Both are pages torn from a nineteenth-century cultural history of Africa by J. W. Buel entitled *Heroes of the Dark Continent*, dating to 1890—I ran across the book in a thrift store in New York City in 1988. The first image treats us to a bestiary of African comic/mythological grotesques. The second image graces us with documentary evidence of commonplace genocides, such as "Arabs hunting unarmed Negroes."

(left) A page from J. W. Buel's effort at anthropology, *Heroes of the Dark Continent* (1890).

Another striking feat of graphic racist madness in a page from J. W. Buel's *Heroes of the Dark Continent* (1890).

What's interesting in this microgallery of curated "African" print artifacts is the way these scandalously attractive monstrosities would evolve as they moved from the medium of print *to* the manufactured excesses of motion pictures and television—in a way, O.J. Simpson's and Rodney King's scandals at the end of the twentieth century owed their popularity and their virulence to patterns of visual indoctrination that were ages old. And what's also interesting and patently dangerous about them is how uncanny they are, how *funny* they can be—funny, "odd," if you are more comfortable with that, or funny, "funny," if you want to be more honest.

Laughter will have always already been part of the symptomology of stereotypes—it is at the scene of the crime because, like the thief or mur-

derer who is always drawn back near to the proscenium of the spectacle, it must needs give in to the logic of a determining narcissism.

Alongside these fading ocular-synapse teasers of the "African," we should place an infamous passage from Henri Bergson's legendary *On Laughter* that brings our interrogation into relief. In a passage both lucid and horrifying, Bergson writes:

> Why do we laugh at a head of hair which has changed from dark to blond? What is there comic about a rubicund nose? *And why does one laugh at a negro?*[7]

Bergson's amiable response, clear in its insight, cogent in its utter corruption, soon follows:

> The question would appear to be an embarrassing one, for it has been asked by successive psychologists . . . And yet I rather fancy the correct answer was suggested to me one day in the street by an ordinary cabby [Is it only me, or does this setup by Bergson give you the willies?], who applied the expression "unwashed" to the negro fare he was driving. Unwashed! Does not this mean that a black face, in our imagination, is one daubed over with ink or soot? If so, then a red nose can only be one which has received a coating of vermilion. And so we see that the notion of disguise has passed on something of its comic quality to instances in which there is actually no disguise, though there might be . . .
>
> But here we meet with a fresh crop of difficulties in the theory of the comic. Such a proposition as the following: "My usual dress forms part of my body" is absurd in the eyes of reason. Yet imagination looks upon it as true. "A red nose is a painted nose," "A negro is a white man in disguise," [!] are also absurd to the reason which rationalises; but they are gospel truths to pure imagination. So there is a logic of the imagination which is not the logic of reason, one which at times is even opposed to the latter, with which, however, philosophy must reckon, not only in the study of the comic, but in every other investigation of the same kind. It is something like the logic of dreams, though of dreams that have not been left to the whim of individual fancy, being the dreams dreamt by the whole of society. (86–87; emphasis added)

Leaving aside for other textual clinicians Bergson's meditations on Africans as sooty white men, let our eyes linger instead on the idea of a "logic of the imagination" that mimics (in blackface?) the "logic of dreams." Here we place our examining hands, our probing eyes, on the nexus of an enigma, the enigma that underwrites our love affair with stereotypes and that explains something even the Nazis, those mid-twentieth-century spin doctors, knew about having the masses blind to something they could see in their dreams (more on this below, with pictures, in the Speedy chapter).

"Mexicans," of course, suffered a fate similar to that of their "African" galle[r]y-mates and are no different in this regard. We will come to see that the dynamics of translation from print to moving image work equally well with our "Latina/o" friends in the Americas. Gary D. Keller's *Chicano Cinema: Research, Reviews, and Resources*, chronicling this history with nuanced focus on "Mexican" and "Latina/o" bodies, concludes:

> Hollywood has produced a huge number of films that depict Hispanic characters, mostly Chicano or Mexican . . . manufactured according to a formula that has overtly provided for the denigration of minorities and outgroups. . . . The Hollywood Celluloid Factory reflect[s] and reinforce[s] the pervasive racial antagonisms that have been the bane of American society from its origins. The initial Hollywood result was the cloning of greaser stereotype upon stereotype: incompetent bandidos, goodhearted simpletons, easy *mujeres*, perfidious criminals . . . and so on, ad infinitum and ad nauseam.[8]

Keller's lucid findings present, for us, implicit questions and a nagging task. The questions?

Where did these stupid things come from? What can anyone, *especially a cultural critic in the pages of a book from the University of Texas Press*, do to stop these nasty beasts?!

The task?

Stop them in their tracks.

Had I a Steven Spielberg–like budget, I think I might stand a chance.

A few years ago, without anyone really noticing, Tejano wizard Roberto Rodriguez *almost pulled it off* single-handedly with his first *Spy Kids* movie—a raging revolt against the legacy of Mexican representation by Hollywood—and, all this, *by* a Hollywood-nestled Chicano.

But we know that we have no choice but to act, even if it is only in the pages of books like this one.[9]

These fountains of creative, racially refracted, stereotyped representations bring with them pathological effects. It is not too much of a stretch to suggest that the operation Génaro Padilla outlined with regard to nineteenth-century proto-Chicanas/os lives on and thrives here early in the twenty-first century: "An established way of life is disintegrating, being rubbed out, erased even at the moment the life was being narrated, transcribed, and textualized [by someone else]."[10] For these reasons, among others, this inquest concerns itself with "Mexicans" and mass culture—it manifests my particular interest in the representation of

"Mexicans" and Chicanas/os in the twentieth century and forms an archaeological project of sorts, trudging through visual "digs" while speculating about telling fragments of a violent, contentious past.

"Contentious past"—the words merit a brief exergue, a tasty supplement: it is worth mentioning here that it has not been so many years since the United States and Mexico were at war; vestigial elements of military engagements always color postwar relations between national entities. More, much more, on this appears in the chapters that follow, where the violence intrinsic to the DNA of stereotypes will be laid bare.

I will also add here that I am not interested in indicting these mass cultural ethnic stereotypes as nasty and oppressive manipulators of the domestic Latina/o *Dasein*, "existence"— though they are rather good at it, wouldn't you say?

As Edward Said testily reminds us in his introduction to *Orientalism:* "One never ought to assume that the structure of [cultural phenomena] is nothing more than a structure of lies or of myths which, were the truth about them to be told, would simply blow away."[11] Many ethnic-studies devotees might be staggered by such an utterance, their plaintive howls of self-righteous injury derailed by Said's gentlemanly *slap upside our heads.*

Actually, the sentence opposite contains a glaring overstatement; the amazing B. Ruby Rich outed Robert Rodriguez's ploy in her May 14, 2001, review essay for **The Nation:** *"Rodriguez knows what he's doing and why: Consider right up front that the name of the Antonio Banderas character is Gregorio Cortez. Huh? The founding film of the Chicano dramatic feature movement, made by the non-Chicano Robert M. Young, was* **The Ballad of Gregorio Cortez,** *starring the young Edward James Olmos as the title character. A legendary Robin Hood, Gregorio Cortez was an honorable man forced into crime by a cruel and unjust posse. His fame has endured because of a corrido composed and sung in his honor. (The* corrido, *or border ballad, is a narrative song that passes on the news and opinions of important events and people, making them legend.)*

"In many ways, Spy Kids *is a Chicano movie writ large, a sort of Trojan horse that smuggles the goods (ethnic pride, family values) into the multiplex disguised as entertainment (spy story, children's movie and supersonically cool paraphernalia, no doubt coming soon to a mall or McDonald's near you). Shot in his own town by a Tejano who's made it big,* Spy Kids *is no doubt the very film that Rodriguez wishes he could have seen as a kid and that he's now determined to give his own children."*

But he was right; and even if we are *in the right* when we author our tomes of deathless prose revealing the horrors of this oppression, the unthinkable nastiness of that expropriation, the living nightmare of our own personal suffering as people of color in a Wonder Bread world, our writing still won't change the ways of the world.

Our tour of the "Mexican" *Tex[t]-Mex* will hopefully leave us with a lived understanding that ethnic stereotypes are a cultural practice *and* a narratological category that make us aware of the potential and likely lie or ruse of humanistic discourse—that by describing or prescribing we somehow control the object before us, that by understanding we dominate.

Understanding ("Reason" with a capital *R*), in this context, reveals its other, often-unacknowledged function as a means to a denial.

Ironically, verbose analysis can become an accomplice of a complacent quiet that allows things to stay the same, allows stereotypes to prosper in the rich, dark confines of our collective indifference. For Marx, political economists were the "sycophants of capital," and intellectual cultural workers in ethnic studies must work to ensure that we are clever adversaries of the culture industry that produces both us and our students—we ought not to ape the moves of our political scientist and economics colleagues that Karlitos M. took to task—and to avoid becoming sycophants of stereotypes and stereotyped thought. Our teaching and writing, if lively enough, might just make a difference. Student by student, mind by mind, imagination by imagination—it is at that crossroads of the pedagogical and the scholarly, on the blackboards and in our handouts, syllabi, readings, and Web pages that the dynamics can be changed.

What obsesses me, what urges me to bring these words to your eyes, is the network of signs in the U.S. mass media that do yeoman's service representing the various peoples, cultures, institutions, and corporations usually totalized, homogenized, and smelted under the classification "Mexican" or "Latina/o."

But these signs (as semioticians, poststructuralists, and others within the cultural-studies mall have taught us) are not representations of anything approaching reality.

Reality is a Utopia, a dreamy conceptual substance favored by politicians, demagogues, and aesthetic-overdosed humanists. In analyses of Mexicans as well as "Mexicans," we are trafficking as much with *mass* culture as *masked* culture—here please call to mind speculations on Mexican subjectivity from the once-lucid Octavio Paz in his *Labyrinth of Solitude*.[12]

So I want to guarantee that we will not spend the time we have here together trying to take off this mask, to resuscitate the essential figure of some "real Mexican." If that were possible, we could just change the channel or turn off the television every time someone like Freddy López or Speedy Gonzales (*or "Manuel" from the BBC's* Fawlty Towers) appears and, by doing so, halt the dissemination of these extraordinary ethnic tropes.[13] "Real Mexicans"? "True Latinas/os"?

We ought not to linger in that snake pit. And we have 1980s Euro-wunderkind Jean Baudrillard, among others, to thank for graciously saving us some ink. Baudrillard's critical "spankings" rate a second glance, especially those moments in "The Precession of Simulacra" where he surmises that "it is always the aim of ideological analysis to restore the objective process."[14]

Good enough. Most of us want little more than to even the score, set things right, heal the rift, "restore" objectivity, and so on. But this will not do.

The germ of this book was a vendetta I had for an animated Mexican mouse by the name of Speedy Gonzales; but, in the end, I had to let the anger go. Baudrillard, holding forth again, says: "It is always a false problem to want to restore the truth beneath the simulacrum."[15] Look behind Speedy or beneath Freddy López and one will not find Mexican-hating illustrators or Latino-loathing puppeteers (ok, maybe one or two; we *are* talking about animated "Mexicans" created *in* California). More often than not, one will find someone working *sine dolo malo*, "without fault, without an intent of evil," as the Romans used to say. But not *always* without fault—the autopsy of a rat that appears within the pages of this book features enough innocent villains and guilty angels to populate a Hollywood B film. And, to be frank, it is not just "Africans" or "Mexicans" that come off badly when it comes to mechanical reproduction of ethnic types—check out these cute *gringo kids* from my private collection of "ethnic" types (in particular, look closely at the boy on the right, who has been digitally processed so much that his "skin" takes on the texture of a Pixar-born(e) computer-generated-image offspring of a CGI wet dream by the in vitro–cloned hybrid child of Mengele, Geppetto, and John Lasseter).

One might venture that Manuel, Basil Fawlty's waiter/bellman/foil on Fawlty Towers, is "Spanish," not "Latino." But are not "Spaniards" the "Mexicans" of English popular culture? I do not have the space to elaborate upon this here, but much of what we understand of "Mexicans" in U.S. mass culture is but a mildly adulterated and transplanted form of English-forged Spanish-esque marionettes.

So, I promise: we will not labor to discover the true "Mexican," nor will we seek to restore the essential and true Latina/o phenotype and *rescue* "our" representation from the clutches of a manipulative mass media; rather, I want to try something much more modest and not at all perfectly organized—my one genuflection to the niceties of organization was to order my chapters somewhat chronologically in the order that they were conceived. This may lead to some grumbling from the peanut gallery regarding Lupe Vélez's entrance in the later galleries of this labyrinth of horrors, when chronology and history would place her first—but doing so would upset the gods that have ordained this critical effort, and it is to them I must pay obeisance even before the needs of you, my gentle, indulging reader.

Found in the trash can behind a toy store in La Jolla, California, in 2004, this piece is now featured in a group of Joseph Cornell–inspired found-object sculptures entitled "Startling Gringo Artifacts." I am still trying to find out what planet the depicted organisms on this torn box cover come from.

In these pages, we, together, will sift through some telling historical artifacts (visual and linguistic, words and images) so as to understand the series of events (historical and aesthetic) that rendered our contemporary "Mexican" and Latino hallucinations meaningful. Where did these ghosts come from? What do they do to us while they hang around? What did they do to the people (Lupe Vélez, "Rita Hayworth") whose bodies literally served as transport vehicles for the ruling Latina/o stereotypes? Where are they going next? And, lastly, in my final chapter on Chicana/o sequential artists: Who's trying to forge for us the Mexican *pharmakon, the cure, at once a poison*, that will make things move and evolve in a different way?[16] If it is the technologies of mass-produced imagery that have fucked things up so royally, is it possible that a means to salvation (ok, recall that your author *is* a recovering Catholic Tejano—idealism and the apocalypse lurk round every paragraph) might be found in images wrought by Chicana and Chicano bodies themselves?

The mission here is truly archival, seeking to track those entertainments that embody the "considerable material investment" in these stereotypes in the United States.[17] How is it that laziness, the siesta, tequila, banditry, sensuality, and other odd sorts of attributes make their way into the U.S. lexicon of Mexican character traits? And how does what can be called the syntax of mass culture work to reimagine and restore (restock, really) these visually charged tropes on a day-to-day basis?

the cock of the gun thrills, and we watch silently, in the dark, mouth agape, blood pressure rising, eyes glued to the silver screen for the end of the story, the bang for the buck, the loving ritual of the telling of the tale.

the gun of the cock, the gunning of the cock thrills, and we watch silently in the dark, mouth agape, blood flowing south, eyes glued to the silver screen for the story of ends, bucks, and banging, the ritualized loving of tails telling tales.

amidst these two tellings is the story of an evil, an enchanting evil, an almost glamorous evil, and a decidedly sexual evil, evident in the history of the representation of "Mexicans" in America.

Postcards and War

The foundation for Hollywood-style Mexicans had been built up in the first two decades of the twentieth century, and it was to have a determinantal impact on the artistic conjuring of Speedy and his universe. Said foundation had been laid in the early and remarkably popular "greaser" film series—some titles of note include *The Mexican's Revenge* (1909), *The Mexican's Jealousy* (1910), *Chiquita the Dancer* (1912), *The Girl and the Greaser* (1913), *The Greaser's Revenge* (1914), and the especially sadistic *The Cowboy's Baby* (1910), in which a "greaser" tosses "the hero's child into a river."[18] Do please note the production dates of these features— they are not without some intrigue of their own.

If motion picture houses from Maine to California were offering a particularly ruthless vision of the Mexican, picture postcards were doing no less. A technological and entrepreneurial hit in the second decade of the twentieth century, postcards became one of the most convenient and visually memorable ways for American servicemen to correspond with family and friends as they travailed at their trade miles away from the familiar climes of home. The e-mail of their day, picture postcards were all the more impressive because of the way they married at least two graphic modes, handwriting and photography. Postcards were a novelty, a marvel, a fad, a must-have *technotextuo* novelty analogous to the World Wide Web myspace.com pages of our current day. Their role in the visual ideological development of the Americas has only begun to be elaborated.[19]

Two representative examples are drawn from Paul J. Vanderwood and Frank N. Samponaro's *Border Fury* and give us a taste of what U.S. post-

"Greasers"

Americans had little sense of the issues in Mexico's civil war. Villista, Carrancista—to them, all Mexicans were "greasers" and were labeled as such on their postcards. (Courtesy Carter Rila Collection.)

(upper left) "Greasers," one of several outtakes from *Border Fury*, Vanderwood and Samponaro's amazing illustrated inquiry into a turn- of-the-last-century form of instant messaging (IM): the postcard. I am no hypochondriac, or, at least, not that often one, but the thought of this photo-laced missive making its way through the U.S. mail conjures for me a collage of Typhoid Mary and Roland Barthes—a semiotic contagion infecting the eyes of all who touched this card with Mexican-loathing affect.

A triple execution—Vanderwood and Samponaro's caption is better than anything I could write.

The triple execution series was particularly profitable for Horne, and he reissued the three popular postcards repeatedly during 1916 to fulfill demand along newly arrived National Guard troops. Francisco Rojas was the first to die in front of the wall of the Northwest Railroad Station in Ciudad Juárez on the morning of January 15, 1916. Captain Javier J. Valle commanded the firing squad. Horne sent this card to Gertrude: "Took photos of three executions today. Here is the first one. The bullets have gone through the man. Notice the dust from the above wall back of him." (Courtesy El Paso Public Library.)

men were frying American citizen's minds with through the mails a tad after the beginning of the twentieth century. I have left their captions intact, as they assist us on our tour. The first image,[20] with its "Greasers" titling helpfully included, allows us to cement the case for a living, almost sexual (incestual) sharing between media when it came to "Mexican" hallucinations in the minds of Americans. The second, the work of Walter H. Horne, underscores the violence that was a staple of the genre. It was one of the best sellers of the time, something analogous to the Viagra spam e-mails we see daily in our cyber in-boxes.

Historians Vanderwood and Samponaro are no mere archive crawlers, no mere vigilant stacks rats; their prose is chillingly telling in its range and command: "The jingoistic patriotism of so many soldiers, frustrated by national policies which precluded their outright invasion of Mexico, also is apparent in the postcards. *These men did not just disparage Mexicans as an enemy; they disdained them as human beings, and the popular literature of the times nourished this bias. Photo images of Germans during World War I, or even Spaniards during the Spanish-American War, were not nearly as sinister or degrading as those of Mexicans during the revolution*" (ix; emphasis added).

The key to this tale is in that last word, "revolution," because why, you may ask, did these "sinister" and "degrading" cybermail ancestors, these grotesque yet seductive postcards, feature representations of "Mexicans"?

The answer can be found in a coincidence of coincidences: at the very moment that new image technologies are mesmerizing an ever-growing, novelty-seeking American consumerate, with motion picture houses dis-placing closing vaudeville showrooms and picture postcards clogging the nation's mails, at this very historical moment, south of the U.S. border, Mexico is convulsing its way through one of the more momentous revolutionary moments in the twentieth century—from at least 1910 to the early dawn of the 1920s Mexico was at war: with itself and with others.[21]

Familiar Scene in Mexico during the Revolution of the Past Three Years.

Pirating was a common practice during the postcard era; no effective defense existed against it. H. H. Stratton was one of the more notorious pirates of the period. In this example he spent a few cents to buy a Walter H. Horne postcard of a hanging in Mexico—the kind of macabre scene that invariably sold well. He made a copy negative of the Horne card and touched it up to eliminate three of the four men stand-ing in the original picture as well as the left hand of one of the hanging victims. He then added a neatly printed caption and sold the product as his own work. (Both courtesy John Hardman Collection.)

Emiliano Zapata to the south and Francisco "Pancho" Villa to the north, near the U.S.-Mexico bor-der, are engaged in popular political and military resist-ance movements that change the face of Mexico in this century.[22] The United States is not indifferent to these activities, events that culminate with Villa's invasion of the United States at Columbus, New Mexico, on March 9, 1916. The U.S. Army's "Mexican Punitive Expedition" (1916–1917), led by the heralded General John J. Pershing, was the talk of the nation.

At the very second all this is going down some 150 miles north of the California-Mexico border, Hollywood and the movie industry are changing the face of the United States, and reinscribing the physiognomies of that nation's peoples. As image technology comes of age and the engines of our American culture industry move into overdrive, the United States finds itself at war with Mexico.[23]

For Mexicans and Latinas/os and Chicanas/os, this is a licentious semiotic marriage—a conjunction/concurrence of events made in a visuo-political hell worthy of Pieter Breughel (Jr.).

Nothing will ever be the same.

The last postcard I sample contains within its body an allegory of the Tex[t]-Mex thesis. Vanderwood and Samponaro's caption is key, so I leave it intact again.

H. H. Stratton's savvy pirating of Horne's wily art allows for the propagation of dead Mexican bodies—the fruits, as it were, of violence south of the border proliferate within the borders of the United States, where odd and inerasable hallucinations of violent, revolutionary, savage "Mexican" subjectivities become de rigueur, and embed themselves in the collective synapses of Uncle Sam's semiotically retarded, scoptophiliac children.

Some of the Why of It

Tex[t]-Mex: Seductive Hallucinations of the "Mexican" in America was constructed in the attempt to make a meaningful contribution to at least four lively, *sometimes* interrelated, scholarly categories: ethnic studies, Chicana/o studies, film theory, and cultural studies. (It adds, as a subplot, various digressive instances of Chicano autobiography that you are free to ignore, as they are the province of my analyst and my progeny.)

A comparative and interdisciplinary speculation on manufactured Latina and Latino bodies in the imagination (and the marketplace) of the United States, *Tex[t]-Mex* assesses the impact of various image and narrative industries on Latinas/os in literature, art, and mass culture. It does so with illustrated chapters on icons of "Mexicanicity" from the twentieth century: greasers in Hollywood's silent films; "half-breeds" in Orson Welles's *Touch of Evil*; Rita Hayworth; Lupe Vélez, the sexy, cantankerous "Mexican Spitfire"; and would-be Latina and eugenics intrigues in Warner Bros.'s Speedy Gonzales animated shorts.

Detail of Remedios Varo, *Bordando el mante terrestre/Embroidering Earth's Mantle*. Artists Rights Society, 536 Broadway, 5th Floor, New York, NY 10012.

The chapters in *Tex[t]-Mex* suggest that "Mexicans," in the imagination of the Americas—North, Central, and South—are less a *raza* than a seductive ruse and maintain that the peculiar and particular apparitions of "Mexicans," "Mexican Americans," "Mexican-Americans," "Hispanics," "Chicanas/os," and "Latinas/os" in the U.S. marketplace are overdue for patient scrutiny. Only the masterly forensics of cultural studies can properly peruse this fuzzy brown mass of familiar and toxic detritus.

These "Latino-esque" hallucinations appear in movies, newspapers, and magazines and on television, among other forms of print and "tele-media." *Tex[t]-Mex* studies the "drift" of these image forms *across* various media—from photography into feature films, from advertising into the novel, from television into public policy. Like some ungodly, miscegenated fusion of the "visual unconscious" and the "political unconscious," these walking billboards act as almost-sentient and ambulatory prostheses. There is always more than *meets the eye* when it comes to Mexican bodies in the eyes of the Americas.

Tex[t]-Mex Rant: A Prayer For and Against, sit venia verbo, Pendejo Mannequins[24]

The Tex[t]-Mex is a tattoo, a mark on the body of America it likes to look at—and it has a right to look at it, be entertained by it, laugh at it, and loathe it:

It made it; it put it there; it is the sum total of its demented vision. And this Tex[t]-Mex tattoo is clever, almost sentient, always salaciously seductive—moving with the dynamics of what Freud called "hysterical identification," it elicits "sympathy . . . intensified to the point of reproduction."[25]

That demented vision haunts all, influenzes all (like an existential halitosis from "our" not-mouth)—leaving the taint of its stain here and there to haunt, perhaps most of all, the Mexican Americans, the Chicanas and Chicanos, the Latinos, who must wear it like a sandwich board scrawled with crude epithets for all to see and wonder at. Or better, like a disguise that won't come off—some aberrant child of Halloween—Latino stereotypes are the mask that can't be pried away, the fabric that becomes skin.[26]

Allow me to suggest a counterpoint, un antítesis, *a negative—recall that epic moment from Homer's momentous epic wherein Menelaus, wanderlust-ful Helen of Troy's "better half," addresses Telemachus, Odysseus's son and heir. Menelaus's words anoint Telemachus in this form:*

> Enjoy yourselves and eat. After supper
> We will ask you who you are—your bloodlines
> Have not been lost in you. You belong
> To the race of men who are sceptered kings
> Bred from Zeus. You're not just anybody.[27]

"Mexicans" in the eyes of Americans, get a different kind of welcome, a very un-Menelausian salutation, the fabric that becomes skin, the text that becomes Mex, or, better put, proxies said Mex, is of a race of men sans scepter.

Tex[t]-Mex. Like we don't already have enough problems with skin—its color, its texture, its smell. Mexican Americans are born through the racist fury of a "Mexican" view of race that is both Spanish (think castes, Empire, Inquisition, slavery) and Mexica/Aztec (think castes, Empire, Inquisition [ask the Cholulans and the Tlaxcaltecans], slavery—oh yeah, and that little thing with the obsidian knives and victims' hearts; the Spanish merely roasted their victims' hearts over a fire).

So the Mexican American, and the Mexican-American, and the Chicana/o (are they the same thing?) are already at a disadvantage when it comes to skin, and yet, in the context of the United States, it gets worse, because our own skin, our own brown-ness (as Richie Rich, er, Richard Rodriguez, weightily intones), brings with it a certain sheen that catches the eye of other Americans (and our own eye as well).

The Tex[t]-Mex is the fabric made by others, worn by ourselves. Recall here the fabulous textile of Mexican emigrant from Spain Remedios Varo in Bordando el mante terrestre/Embroidering Earth's Mantle, *famously rewoven in the pages of Thomas Pynchon's* Crying of Lot 49, *the most famous Chicano novel written by a recluse Anglo-American.*

In it, a captive, knowing seamstress weaves a fabric that bounds out a tower's window, so much so that it makes up the world atop which the tower sits. Such an evocative metaphor, such a provocative conjuring through which to see the body of the Mexican American, the body politic of an ethnic half-breed in its odyssey across America.

Tex[t]-Mex; ironies abound: text-Mex, text minus Mex, as if the text of the Mexican stereotype in the American imagination was allowed to at once exile the bodies of "real" Mexicans. Tex[t]-Mex, the lure and the surrogate, author of an evolving elision of the mexicana *subject. . . .*

SEDUCTIVE HALLUCINATION
GALLERY ONE: AN INTERSTICE

Being the First of Several Summary Interruptions of the Drearily Semantic in Favor of the Deliciously Semiotic, a *Frontera* of Sorts

interstice: [ad. L. *interstiti-um* space between, f. **interstit-,* ppl. stem of *intersistre,* f. *inter* between + *sistre* to stand; cf. F. *interstice* (14th c.).] 1. a. An intervening space (usually, empty); *esp.* a relatively small or narrow space, between things or the parts of a body (freq. in *pl.*, the minute spaces between the ultimate parts of matter); a narrow opening, chink, or crevice. b. *Physics.* The space between adjacent atoms or ions in a crystal lattice. 2. a. An intervening space of time; an interval between actions. Now *rare.* b. *spec.* in *Canon Law (pl.)* The intervals required between the reception of the various degrees of holy orders.[1]

One of the many things this volume purports to accomplish is to begin an ongoing archive of inventive, derogatory stereotypes, and the United States being what it is, the task seems as endless as it does frustrating. I do not have the space for a full catalogue, but a brief optic appetizer does seem in order. Sample the following entries from my rogues' gallery of accumulated visual pathogens.

Tex[t]-Mex: Exhibit A | Genesis

What you are looking at here is, as it were, the spermatozoa of this book—as I am ova-less, I must rest content with this.

It is May of 1990, and I am an assistant professor of English at (of all places for a Laredo-born would-be academic) the University of Connecticut; picture the headlines: "Laredense in Storrs, Conn." (fodder for my autobiography). More to come later.

For our *Tex[t]-Mex* leisure cruise, however, it is crucial to include this document in the opening gallery of hallucinations—not so much as W. A.

William Anthony Nericcio
aka:Guillermo Antonio Nericcio, tipo loco de Tejas
Assistant Professor of English, Comparative Literature and Latin American Studies
The University of Connecticut, Storrs; Box U-25, 06269

The illustration on this page made me angry. Most of all because it made me laugh.
It was only when I asked the question "why does this make me laugh" did I
stumble on the complex world of the stereotype--specifically, the Hispanic American
and the African American stereotype. Fortunately or not, the history of these
stereotypes is wrapped up with the LITERATURE of the United States of America.

I was not taught that when I was your age.

To this day I wonder why.

Photograph of a photocopied handout produced for outreach work in Connecticut while I travailed there as an assistant professor.

(my initials as well: *scary*) Hammond would have it, *as* "evidence of [my] cerebral derangement . . . [a] common phenomena of insanity," though some of my colleagues would surely attest to this as a possibility, but more with the sense of hallucination as "a wandering of the mind . . . a blunder," as that is how I happened upon this oh-so-funny cartoon in the first place.[2]

Journey with me, hallucinogens optional, to 1991. We are on the East Coast and I had been called on to give a presentation to a group of elementary school children, largely *puertorriqueños*, African Americans, and some Anglos, in Willimantic, Connecticut, an old-mill industrial town in eastern Connecticut.

I created the hand-typed handout (left) to distribute to the children. The Aunt Jemima makeover illustration that appears below in my chapter on Speedy Gonzales, and that would eventually become part of a digital art piece, also had that handout as a source. The drawing, by Leslie Starke, originally from *The New Yorker* but reproduced here from *Starke Parade*, still haunts me, as does the memory of laughing my ass off when I first saw it; here perhaps is born the idea of "Mexican" hallucinations—ghosts realer than the real, who move us with their shadowy logic.[3]

Tex[t]-Mex: Exhibit B | Castro Made Me Do It!

This outrageous image appeared on the cover of a scandal tabloid called *The Globe* in the weeks following the urban rebellion in Los Angeles after the Rodney King (beaten March 3, 1991) police trial not-guilty verdicts, handed down on April 29, 1992.

Needless to say, Fidel Castro is a convenient substitute here for a particularly "Latino" strain of revolutionary—nothing but bad news in the U.S. political unconscious. Note that the "le[ader]" of the riots in the photo is also quite willing to get down and dirty with his looting foot soldiers, look-

A glance here suggests why turning to the *Weekly World News* or *The Globe*, staples at supermarket checkout stands, for news about Latinos and Latin Americans can lead to misunderstandings and confusion.

ing on enthusiastically as one of his charges leaps upon the metal fencing of a storefront with simian grace and human guile.

On March 1, 1942, the German propaganda maven Joseph Goebbels, ranting on the niceties of radio and mass communication, had argued that "when necessary, [radio] should raise the hearts and touch the conscience," which is nice enough, even for Goebbels; but his concluding clause is more direct, more haunting, more sinister, conjuring a very different *end* for this engine of communication: "It should attack the enemy wherever he may be."[4] Radio, tabloids, billboards, and television—that ubiquitous stew from which all of us sup.

While the result of the Castro "Photoshopped" *Globe* tale is comical, the portion of the American consumer populace potentially swayed by this image moves us from the terrain of the comic to the tragedy of lemmings leaping off a cliff, of a nation of drunk semiotic-aholics chugging stereotypes like there is no tomorrow.

Tex[t]- Mex: Exhibit C | Pancho Villa: Renegade y Papi!

Pancho Villa was an infamous star, a clever tactician, a ruthless brute, and a banal *pater familias*. The images on the right, of course, are the ones that draw my eye.

The eye tires or, better put, the eye develops habits, bad and good; and the gaze tends to follow the path of least resistance—Mexican as bandit (horse, full gallop, rifle, etc.), more familiar, hence normal.

The other Villa, the other Doroteo Arango, as captured by the Casasola brothers, Agustín and Miguel, might as well be a space alien: posing stiffly with his children; stiff white-starched shirt alongside the missus . . . it's as if someone had run crazy with Photoshop and doctored up the pictures.

A gallery of visual challenges and a taunt: which image makes *you* feel right at home?

Tex[t]-Mex: Exhibit D | José At Your Service, ¡por supuesto!

A digital photograph of a mixed-media installation/altar entitled "The Best and Worst Bodies on the Beach."

"José is a virtuoso at ensuring you always put your best foot forward." A detail (opposite) from two Four Seasons Hotels ads that appeared in the progressive "new" *New Yorker*. Such artistry! Such a talent! All in the service of a loving gringo clientele! The novelty of Latinas/os as (hardworking, honorable, reliable) members of the service sector is subject to some question. These ads work because they are familiar, and they are familiar because the logic that sustains them is reinforced by their very existence. In a nation that fosters such virulent existential and visual tautologies, hope cannot be *seen* or *said* to spring eternal.

Tex[t]-Mex: Exhibit E | Bordered Allegory of Beauty

Brace yourself for another allegory: the collage to the left features—you can see it in the detail—a tale of mirrors and subjectivity as deep and perverse as that to be found in

Oscar Wilde's *The Picture of Dorian Gray*. Intercepted from the pages of the *Laredo Morning Times* and the journalistic eye of Ricardo Segovia, the captioned reverie becomes a page in an attempt to recuperatively challenge the stagnant clichés of a Tex[t]-Mex visual legacy with a bordered Tejano eye that is attuned to the complexities of Tex-Mex subjectivities. Both women look at someone, at something. The beauty contestant eyes herself with an internalized gaze, the facsimile of judge's eyes that will soon paw her waiting figure. More curious, I think, is the other girl—the friend, the companion, God knows? What is she looking at?

It might be ghosts.

Am I hallucinating?

Let's look closer:

No, it is there. A hand. A hand in the foreground.

And the hand is gesturing or pointing.

It is as if the hand said, "Watch what you look at."

Nothing is as it seems.

At Four Seasons Hotels, we know that brilliantly shined shoes can reflect positively on those who wear them. Thus, our valets will unfailingly polish your Oxfords and pumps to mirror-like perfection, make small repairs, if needed, then return the shoes with dispatch to their rightful destination. And not only is the shoeshine worthy of compliments, but at Four Seasons it's always complimentary. Which fits comfortably with our belief that in these value-conscious times, the demands of your trip should demand nothing less than Four Seasons Hotels.

Four Seasons
Hotels·Resorts

MIRROR, MIRROR: A Miss Texas Pageant contestant, left, looks in a mirror during Monday night event, La Chic, at Mall del Norte. A second contestant, partially blocked by the mirror, looks at

Times staff photo by RICARDO SE

(left) What becomes a servant most? Who would *not* want the likes of José outside one's room bringing one one's own shiny shoes to festoon one's lovely feet?

An inset detail blow-up of a section of "The Best and Worst Bodies on the Beach" taken from a June 22, 2004, edition of the *Laredo Morning Times* and featuring a photograph by Ricardo Segovia, who, like Gene Shalit below, reveals his gifts as a would-be Derridean photographer.

The Danbury Mint caught red-handed trafficking in the manufacture and distribution of "Mexican" automatons.

Tex[t]-Mex: Exhibit F
Danbury Mint Latina or María Número Uno

This amazing artifact deserves a book of its own—or, perhaps better, a gallery or altar of its own—so as to afford us the space we need, the time we need, to understand her. "María" looks out at us with winsome eyes. "An adorable Latina," she has "helped her *mamacita* all day." Her "cascading black curls" nicely "accented with a silken rose," Maria's objectified figure cries out for consumer affection.

Now one does not turn to the Danbury Mint, the home of the "Saluting John-John Doll" and the "Guardian of Freedom" sculpture, when one is solicitous of nuanced reflection on ethnic American difference.[5]

Still, I believe it worth our bother to ponder the wonders that are "Maria," to take her pulse, as it were, or comb through her recombinant DNA to fathom the forces at work on culture to make commerce in her exchange a matter of public record—she came to me like manna from heaven in the pages of the *San Diego Union-Tribune* Sunday comics supplement between ads for salad dressing and dog food. Her appearance here in our retarded reliquary of Tex[t]-Mex artifacts signals a

Another mannequin facsimile available through the Danbury Mint.

Patriotic sculpture available from the Danbury Mint.

softening in the heart of your stalwart, rasquache tour guide.

I have to confess that I almost bought her; I should have, as a search I performed on the Internet in August of 2005 revealed she was no longer to be had, even for a king's ransom.[6] Said paucity of "Maria" speaks to a revealing demand on the part of tchotchke-hoarding purchasers of Latino-esque mannequins. It is to be hoped that the humble efforts of our current inquiry go a way toward explaining this covetous fetish in ways that are both illuminating and entertaining.

Tex[t]-Mex: Exhibit G | María Número Dos

José's companion, no doubt, from Exhibit C above—the Four Seasons was doing quite well by its help in the early 1990s when these ads appeared in the *New Yorker*. Note that Maria is a miracle worker! Within an hour, your unsightly wrinkles disappear through the "magic" of her nimble workings. I love the look on her face—an almost defiant subservience manifests itself in a smile that just won't quit and a hand-on-the-waist erectness that gives "starch" a new meaning.

(left) José's sidekick, "María," pictured here, gives the old shoe shiner a run for his money. The irony of ironies in this particular image is that the "Mexican" in the photograph is as real as the figure inside the coat "she" is holding. "Wait," you are thinking, "that's a hanger! There is no one *in* that suit." Exactly.

A Tex[t]-Mex allegory of a "Mexican," "Latina" pillow fluffer.

Tex[t]-Mex: Exhibit H | María Número Tres

Now this is getting plain ridiculous—yet another "María," yet another smiling servant, this time at Leona Helmsley's Park Lane hotel. For eight years this smiling automaton, this ridiculously happy, seductive hallucination or hallucinatory mannequin (you take your pick) has been doing what? Fluffing pillows? "When you fluff a pillow for eight years, you can imagine it's rather soft"—in my dreams, I picture myself cornering the copywriter of this ad (my research failed to track her or him down) for some mad, banditlike harassment, channeling in one mad fury the energy of all Latino stereotypes past, present, and future.

Tex[t]-Mex: Exhibit I | Can I Put the Hallucination on the Walls of My House like a Stripped Pelt; or, "No More Marías"

Assorted 1950s wall ornaments collected from thrift shops in New York, Connecticut, and California.

These lovely decals/appliqués were popular with children during the 1950s. The Duro Decal company markets exotic, cheery accent decorations to spruce up the antiseptic confines of I LIKE IKE–era suburban households. The bucolic peace of our sombrero-wearing youth jars tellingly with the site it will ostensibly ornament. "Mexicans" and other "Latin Americans" take a break from their usual roles as rogues, thugs, and harlots; here their exoticness lends a wall the lure of the eccentric, the pleasant allure of the pastoral native savage.

CHAPTER 1
HALLUCINATIONS OF
MISCEGENATION AND MURDER

Dancing along the Mestiza/o
Borders of Proto-Chicana/o Cinema
with Orson Welles's *Touch of Evil*

It is now almost impossible . . . to remember a time when people were
not talking about a crisis in representation. And the more the crisis is
analyzed and discussed, the earlier its origins seem to be.
> —*Edward Said, Foreword,* Selected Subaltern Studies, *1988*[1]

"I don't speak Mexican."
> —*Detective Hank Quinlan (Orson Welles) complains as accused bomber
> Manolo Sánchez and Pan-American Narcotics Commission officer Miguel
> Vargas (Charlton Heston) converse in Spanish during an interrogation
> sequence in* Touch of Evil, *1958.*[2]

To betray betrayal, transgress transgression . . .
> —*Severo Sarduy,* Written on a Body[3]

half-breed: [Americanism] n. a person whose parents are of different
races; especially, an offspring of an American Indian and a white person—adj. half-blooded, sometimes regarded as a hostile or contemptu-
ous term.
> —*Webster's New World Dictionary of the American Language*

Reel One: [B]ordering Film[4]

Given recent developments in critical theory, in particular the increased
market share now being solicited under the rubric "cultural studies," this
seems an opportune moment to engage two critical projects that, until
recently, have for historic, institutional, practical, and political reasons
not had much to do with one another: film theory proper and Chicano
critical theory.[5] Perhaps under the tolerant auspices of cultural studies,
the overlapping interests/origins of these once-disparate practices will
become more clear.

Of course, if you think about it carefully, film theory should always have been a part of an overall Chicana/o critical project—no critic of Mexican-American, Mexican American, Chicana/o, Latina/o, or Hispanic culture[6] would want to ignore the very real tensions cinematography and its sister visual technologies (photography, postcards) helped foster between U.S. citizens and Mexican nationals since the turn of the last century—think here of the greaser films and scandalous postcards noted in the introduction above.

But in practical terms and until quite recently, the two have had little to do with one another: the Mexican American critical community was hard at work unearthing a textual, hence cultural, legacy destroyed, erased, or just plain lost over the last four centuries—picture here the groundbreaking work of titans like the late greats Américo Paredes and Gloria Anzaldúa, as well as the more recent findings of Génaro Padilla, Norma Cantú, and the Saldívar clan, etc., etc.; when you are embroiled in culture wars and the pitched intellectual battles that went into the formation of our field (can you say "strategic essentialism"?), there's little time, at times, for the niceties of cinematic semiotics. Film theorists, meanwhile, were busy in other ways, working here and there spelunking the intricacies of filmed art and pursuing their endless inquiry into the dynamics of film-subject interaction, although smoking Gauloises, flocking berets, polishing their Kenneth Cole boots, and haunting the National Film Theatre on the South Bank took up some time as well.

"Quinlan Frames Mexico," digital mixed media, © copyright 2006 Guillermo Nericcio García.

I am joking.

Maybe.

The problem here has to do with the "divide and publish" mentality of the humanities. How, after all, do you reconcile the needs of readers and scholars who consider themselves experts on Chicano studies with those of others who call themselves film theorists—as far as I can tell (and at least until a thaw, of sorts, in the 1990s and early part of the twenty-first century) the members of these groups tended to avoid each other rather than benefit from each other's findings.

I think Welles's movie provides an answer of sorts.

This critical vignette, obsessed as it is with *Touch of Evil*, then, embodies at least two things: a rereading of Orson Welles's 1958 film *and* an attempt to reconcile the interests of competing areas of theoretical discourse. At best I hope to satiate the needs of Chicanophiles and cinephiles everywhere; at worst, to annoy both to the point of anger.

Reel Two: Speaking "Mexican"

What does "speak[ing] Mexican" mean in the unnamed Mexican bordertown across from Los Robles, U.S.A., which, if we are to believe the comforting words of Mexico City narcotics-officer-with–"cabinet status" Miguel Vargas, "isn't the real Mexico." A second later he tellingly adds the following to his perplexed hottie gringa newlywed: "I told you that . . . all bordertowns bring out the worst in a country."

Mexican narcotics agent Miguel "Mike" Vargas (Charlton Heston) and new gringa wife, Susan "Susy" Vargas (Janet Leigh), share a rare moment of intimacy on a fateful drive out to the Mirador Motel (think Hitchcock's *Psycho* with Chicana biker dykes, the desert, and pachucos, and you are ready for Welles's *frontera* "Odyssey").

Orson Welles's noir mystery/thriller *Touch of Evil*, set on the Mexican-U.S. border, attempts to answer this fundamental question of what it means to speak Mexican; or, perhaps better put, it attempts to engage the question, answering it somewhat but also indicting its problematic in the process. This makes Welles's late-fifties masterpiece an integral piece of the Tex[t]-Mex equation—to "speak" Mexican can be seen, in another sense, to enact a scenario wherein the very fabric of Latina/o stereotypes is woven and unravels, at once, before our eyes.

Long lionized by filmgoers, film lovers, and film theorists (at times mutually exclusive clans), Orson Welles's film has all but been ignored or forgotten by the Mexican American popular and critical communities, even though said communities represent the palate for Welles's project. For various reasons itemized below, the film proffers an appropriate arena for an intersection between something that might call itself Chicana/o discourse and that other guild named film theory.

Reel Three: The Scene of the Crime

Edward Said's words above provide the keynote for this essay—what can a close reading of a motion picture be other than a serious meditation on *representation*?

Orson Welles's *Touch of Evil* supplies our point of departure.

This 1958 Universal Pictures film cinematically renders Mexican and U.S. communities on either side of an international border.

The film is about narcotics, about love, about desire, and about murder. It is a movie crafted between two murders—one seen, one that occurs seventeen years before the action starts.

Both murders involve individuals of mixed cultural and national origins, what Welles as Detective Quinlan calls a "half-breed" and what I call in this essay "*el mestizo*." Few commentators, in fact, remember that an unseen, unnamed half-breed (*el mestizo*) is at the center of *Touch of Evil*.

Film theorists' ongoing devotion to Welles's *Touch of Evil* becomes easier to fathom when one realizes that one of the more influential founding articles for the practice of film theory was a complex two-part 113-page essay by Stephen Heath entitled "Film and System"—an opus from the pages of the journal *Screen* that used Welles's bordertale to ponder the fundamental dynamics of film, Subject, and culture.[7]

There is always the chance, of course, that something slipped in the back door when it came to the dynamics of learning how to watch a movie—read Ellen Strain's fascinating essay "Exotic Bodies, Distant Landscapes"; these bon mots cut to the quick: "What may be less evident from examining the short history of film, however, is the notion of touristic viewing as an historically-specific phenomenon which developed in the decades immediately preceding cinema's inception and which was imported into cinema in a developing form" (72). Touristic viewing of "exotic" natives in the nineteenth century—think zoos today sans PETA-fed upgrades—provides a template for stereotype consumers in the here and now, "the world a quarry of sights and sounds" (75).

This is a Tex[t]-Mex moment of epic proportions.

We are witnesses at the scene of a ~~crime~~ birth.

The birth of a field of study in the intellectual history of the American academy: film theory.

And what film provides the space for the creation of that field?

Touch of Evil.

Something quite similar happened in 1915 when D. W. Griffith unleashed *Birth of a Nation* on an unsuspecting horde of American film viewers. It is breathtaking, one of those "watershed moments" that historians are known for noting.

Something very big is going down in America! Technology—motion picture cameras are evolving along with their audiences; Griffith produces *the film* that galvanizes public attention, translating technological innovation in image technologies into a consumable narrative for the masses.

Popular Culture—motion pictures are becoming more and more *the* favored mode of mass entertainment. Vaudeville houses are shuttered more and more; itinerant circuses are reaching their zenith and beginning their decline, so it is to the movie palaces that Americans turn in their search for popular distractions.

And they turn to Griffith's "masterpiece," Griffith's ugly meditation on the fibers of racial hatred as they function in the spaces of America. But more than a meditation, Griffith's visual treatise functions also as an inoculation, not *against* the virus of racism, but as a less virulent, but still potent, inculcation *of* racism or, at the least, a license to *think* racism and be *racist, within reason*, in America.

It is another one of those nasty coincidences in which a hypersexy quantum leap in visual entertainment technology finds itself fused with some "influenzal" [influential + influenza = influenzal] element of our country's racist legacies.

With Heath, it happens all over again, but differently. Here, the domain is smaller; after all, we are talking academia here.

But it is a birth.

A key birth.

Film theory. A big baby. An influential baby.

And the body on the table at its birth? Orson Welles's *Touch of Evil*.

Let us look at the body! Probe its spaces—Heath will help us to know this film. But not all of it. Some of it won't show, won't make itself known or be presented.

Touch of Evil.

It is a remarkable thing. A provocative and monstrous body. In *Touch of Evil*, spectators confront the bordertown and the half-breed, *la frontera y el mestizo*.

The bordertown. Think Laredo, El Paso, San Isidro (U.S.A.); Nuevo Laredo, Matamoros, Tijuana (Mexico). Welles fuses them all together, forging a pastiche communicated to our eyes via the streets of Venice Beach, where he had to shoot his scenes.

The lurid title splash from the Universal International Pictures trailer for *Touch of Evil*, 1958.

Bordertowns are uncanny. By definition, they both *are* and *create* spaces of cultural fracture; individuals who grow up in these spaces both suffer *and* enjoy (can these two words stand together in a clause *without* somehow also enfolding the dynamics of a Marquis de Sade?) geoculturally split, oft-bilingual subjectivities in which identity is not "fractured" but is *fracture* itself—a place where hyphens, bridges, border stations, and schizophrenia are the rule rather than the exception.

Reel Four: Ménage à Trois Synopses

Before proceeding any further, it seems the proper moment to provide three synopses of Welles's *Touch of Evil*. I do this as much to introduce the story to readers who have not seen the film, and to refresh the memory of viewers who have not screened it in some time, as to remind ourselves of the problems intrinsic to something as innocent as a synopsis.

Discrepancies between the versions have as much to do with the places where they appeared and the interests of their authors as they do with chance or caprice. Here, then, follow Heath's "minimal account" from "Film and System"; Gene Shalit's entertaining summary lifted from MCA's (now Matsushita—1993; now Geffen—2005) "Gene Shalit's Critic's Choice" video series back cover; and lastly, my own half-breed or mestizo gloss:

1. During a murder investigation in a border town, Quinlan, the American detective in charge, is discovered by Vargas, a Mexican Official, to have planted evidence framing the chief suspect. Despite attacks on his wife culminating in Quinlan's attempt to frame her for a murder he himself commits, Vargas manages to expose the crooked policeman. (Heath, "Film and System, Part I," 12)

Quinlan's menacing cane looms across "Mexican" Vargas's face during an interrogation scene in *Touch of Evil*.

2. [In *Touch of Evil*,] the whale-like Welles, needing a cane to support his enormous girth, is a morally corrupt police official in a squalid town on the Mexican border . . . The story starts with a murder that ensnares a narcotics agent (Charlton Heston, Ramón Miguel "Mike" Vargas), his wife (Janet Leigh, Susan "Susy" Vargas), a seedy manipulator (Akim Tamiroff, Uncle Joe Grandi), and a web of elusive figures, including Marlene Dietrich, Joseph Calleia, Eva Gabor, Joseph Cotten, Dennis Weaver, Valentín de Vargas, and Ray Collins. Welles' cane is so vital to the elaborate plot that this could have been subtitled "Citizen Cane."[8] The mesmerizing mystery builds to an intense confrontation in which the sinister Welles schemes to destroy Heston and Heston is determined to prove that all's well that ends Welles. . . . *Touch of Evil* reverberat[es] with Welles' touch of genius.

3. An obese, recovering alcoholic detective, Quinlan, obsessed with the strangulation of his wife years earlier by an unnamed "half-breed," does battle with an officious, sexless Mexico City federal drug agent, Miguel Vargas, and his newlywed Anglo wife, Susan. When an explosion destroys an American bordertown industrialist and his attractive "showgirl" from the Mexican side of the border, Quinlan arrives on the scene to investigate the crime and verbally abuse the all-too-helpful Mexican agent. Meanwhile, Vargas's frustrated Anglo wife does detective work of her own after being accosted by a host of Mexican American ne'er-do-wells (including leather-jacketed, rock-'n'-rollin' Chicanos; proto-dyke Chicanas; and one

Spanish-mangling Chicano wannabe[9]) led by a Chicano-Italian boss, Joe Grandi. This gang of half-breeds runs "business" (marijuana, heroin, etc.) on both sides of the border.

With the help of a bottle of booze, Uncle Grandi connives with Quinlan to bring Vargas down, kidnapping his by-now-utterly-sexually-frustrated newlywed wife and subjecting her to a simulated gang rape/drug fiesta, *gracias a los* previously mentioned Chicana/o pachucas/os. All of this is window dressing to Quinlan's true obsession, the "half-breed" who strangled his wife. (Curiously enough, after years of living in Los Robles, Quinlan does not speak Spanish—what he calls "Mexican"—nor, apparently, does he understand it.) The movie climaxes with Quinlan's strangulation/revenge masque

played out on the unfortu-nate body of the eager-to-please Mexican-American-Italian, Grandi. The movie closes on a bridge, not liter-ally one between the United States and Mexico, but one that functions as such via synecdoche. Under said bridge, not unlike a troll in brownface, a wetbacked, eavesdropping Vargas

"Andala, andala" (*sic*). Instructing a terrified Dennis Weaver to hurry up in the office of the Mirador Motel, this particular gringo Chicano thug tells the sexophobic Weaver, "Andala, andala," presumably his version of the Spanish phrase *Ándale, ándale.*

obtains the info he needs (via Quinlan's partner, Pete Menses/Menzies, and a recording device) to nail Quinlan's reign of terror. Quinlan shoots Vargas's proxy, Menses, who in turn shoots Quinlan before Quinlan can rub out Vargas. As Quinlan's body floats in a decayed, trashed-out river of scum, Tanya (Marlene Dietrich) bids him and the film viewer *adiós.*

Synopses akimbo, we are now well positioned to enter some of the more "Tex[t]-Mexually" suggestive elements of this odd tale. But before we do so, another pesky neologism.

Reel Five: Cinematext

Touch of Evil.

A cinematext if there ever was one.

What is a *cinematext*?

The neologism "cinematext" reflects a critical attempt to "read" motion pictures with some *post-Althusserian* sensitivity to the dual role these commodities play in the production and representation of culture.

More than a summary of cultural and counter-cultural invention, the elaboration of the American cinematext suggests that relations between word, image, nationality, and culture are much more complex than is often perceived.[10] The term also reflects the attempt to produce a tolerant common ground where the interests of film theorists and ethnic American critical theorists might engage in dialogue.

But why go back to Welles's *Touch of Evil?*

What, after all, is left to be said that Arthur Pettit's *Images of the Mexican American in Fiction and Film*, Gary Keller's comprehensive *Chicano Cinema*, and Terry Comito's collection of essays *Touch of Evil: Orson Welles, Director* have not already said?[11]

Especially daunting (and especially notable in the polite but conspicuous short shrift given it by Comito's collection) is Stephen Heath's "Film and System," Parts I and II, which, in addition to providing an exhaustive reading of *Touch of Evil*, also attempts to remake/invent the discipline of film theory. After all this commentary, what is left to be said?

Curiously enough, the answer to that question is *plenty*, because Pettit's critique and Keller's survey omit Welles's film altogether, and Comito's volume turns out to contain an uneven hodgepodge of materials—some quite valuable, others of questionable use. Heath's essay, on the other hand, is assailable for other reasons, not the least of which is his problematic usage of the referent "Mexican," discussed more fully below.

Reel Six: Bring Your Own Tequila to the Next Crashed Party

We should hesitate before allowing recent interest in this piece of border-town Americana to blind us to the fact that the film opened to little interest in 1958.

As Barbara Leaming, the writer of Welles's most readable biography, recalls, "Notwithstanding the acclaim with which *Touch of Evil* was garlanded at Brussels, and elsewhere in Europe, where almost instantly it became a cult classic, it was mostly overlooked in America."[12] This reaction may be seen as symptomatic, Chicano hooligans, sexuality, bordertowns, and Mexican-U.S. relations being low on the list of post-McCarthy-era American interests. More than filling the idle time of Americans from East Lansing to Portland, from Miami to Crystal City, were Castro's total war on Batista, Alaska's joining the Union, Vice-President Nixon being spat upon on a

Central American tour, the South's desegregation of schools, and learning the intricacies of the cha-cha.

Also, to be fair, it is easy to understand producer Albert Zugsmith's and Universal Studio's own uneasiness and unwillingness to promote Welles's latest project; it may well be that it was beyond their intellectual capacity to appreciate the dynamics of the product their own capital had financed. Then again, it is also very likely that they were just fed up with dealing with the eccentricities (legion!) of Orson Welles.

The lukewarm reception to the film in the United States led fellow director François Truffaut to declare in June of 1958, four months after the film's release in February and one month after its arrival in Europe in May 1958, that "if the brotherhood of critics finds it expedient to look for arguments against this film, which is a witness and a testimony to art and nothing else, we will have the grotesque spectacle of the Lilliputians attacking Gulliver."[13]

Later, other critics with other interests and, not surprisingly, other institutional affiliations (the newspaper business does not often share intimate space with the academic set), would move in another way toward Welles's opus.

Consider, as well, how the activities of scholars invested in the journal *Screen* in the mid-seventies supplemented the practice of film theory in the United States.

In one of the landmark pieces of criticism from that critical moment, Heath opens his treatise with the following disclaimer—words that make clear the general, incipient status of the body of words that follow: "The following piece has nothing definitive about it; it is offered for discussions in an area—the analysis of film—where, for a variety of reasons, little of real importance has yet been achieved" (7). He adds that his project "seeks to examine and work through some of the problems surrounding 'film analysis' (the reading of films), and to introduce and discuss, provisionally, one or two theoretical concepts of use in the resolution of those problems" (8).

Why should these preliminary moves, a subtle dance perhaps of interest in a retrospective history of American film theory, be of the least interest to Chicana/o scholars? or make the executors of a Tex[t]-Mex the tiniest bit curious?

The answer is clear. Heath reads *one film* in his dense 113-page study, and that film is *Touch of Evil*—Welles's vision of that space where Mexicans, Unitedstatesians, and Mexican-Americans (a half-breed or mestizo subcategory of the Unitedstatesian übergroup) interact. Trends identifiable here at the outset (as Heath would have it) are important; they are harbingers of that which is to come—to the degree that Heath's work has impacted on that discipline called film theory, we might also say that border issues or obsessions are at its origin. Call it the D. W. Griffith paradigm: if race and ethnicity are present at the birth of the modern motion picture, then they appear again in walk-on cameos at the birth of film theory. Who better than we, readers with great affection and sensitivity for the workings of race, to attend this inquest?

Heath's incipient musings on "Mexicans" in Welles's film become a very important issue in our reading of *Touch of Evil* and in our understanding of issues Tex[t]-Mexual. This, especially, when we are dealing with characters in a film who "don't speak Mexican," when we are dealing with a space that is not the "real Mexico."

Might it be that Orson Welles has given more thought to the Tex[t]-Mexual status of Mexicanicity at the border than Heath? Heath, in a sense, invites Chicano theorists to a film theorists' party, a "mixed party," to echo Joseph Cotton in his uncredited appearance as the coroner in *Touch of Evil*. And as we crash this party, we may have to be bad guests at times. We may have to suggest to Heath, for example, that we are not at all content with the spread or the party favors. I am no fan of bad manners, but sometimes they prove necessary.

Janet Leigh, as newlywed Susy Vargas, struts her stuff in a key scene from *Touch of Evil*—a scene of would-be sadism and mutual voyeurism.

Things have come to a head. Let's get the party started and the disciplines mixed. Like some unholy chimera, some unthinkable fusion of beasts, film theory and Chicana/o studies find themselves conjoined.

And why not? It is altogether appropriate, in an essay assessing a film set in a fictional bordertown, Los Robles—where cultural, sexual, and political fracture/difference is commonplace—that we fuse these growing disciplines along that line Susan Vargas (the bullet-bra-wearing, sarcastic, and demanding Janet Leigh) calls "your terribly historic border."

We are, in short, ready to begin our *mestizo* critical inquiry by a *mestizo* critic about a film with an absent, alleged *mestizo* murderer.

Reel Seven: What Becomes a Legend Most

As this essay is a survey of critical treatments of *Touch of Evil* as well as a reading of the film itself, it seems essential to briefly gloss the kinds of interpretations *Touch of Evil* has engendered. What *has* been said about this film to this date?[14]

Predictably, criticism ranges in quality and topic. Terry Comito captures Welles's sensitivity to the conventions of cinema, stating succinctly that *Touch of Evil* is "about a nice couple from Hollywood movies who stumble into a film by Orson Welles" (12). Then there are the critics who use their critical energies to champion Welles's "genius," like Andre Bazin (all the time); Jean Collet and Barbara Leaming (often); and Frank Brady (more often).[15] A sampling:

> Brady: "At an age when most children are still mastering the rudiments of language, Orson already spoke like a miniature Brahmin and could enter into discussion on most World topics"(5).

> Collet: "This colossus does not accept obstacles as a salutary constraint: he pushes them about until they prove to be stronger than he is" (251).

> Leaming: Her auspicious first chapter leaves no room for doubt: "Chapter One: The Genius" (5).

Andre Bazin's form of cheerleading deserves special scrutiny if only for its implicit, hence all the more conspicuous, ethnocentrism. Consider the following: "[Hank Quinlan] is, at least in certain respects, above the honest, just, intelligent [Miguel] Vargas, who will always lack that sense of life which I call Shakespearean" (124). Oh brother!

But here again, one finds support for these sustained critical applauses in Welles's own vision of himself. At the ripe old age of twenty-one, Welles had begun an autobiography tellingly entitled "Now I Am 21" (Leaming, 112).

Years later, over lunch at the obnoxiously elite restaurant Ma Maison in Hollywood, Welles confesses to Leaming (perhaps after a bottle of Gallo premium): "I am the absolute technical master of the medium. I have no shame in saying it. So if people say something doesn't work, they don't know any better. That's all I can say" (294–295).

Even Welles's weight gain proved beneficial to Welles's monumentalization of his own worth: "How did you get so fucking fat?" commercial director Harry Hamburg once asked, to which Orson glibly replied that, "having created works of art when he was a young man, he'd finally decided to make himself a work of art" (Leaming, 550).

Of course, regardless of the views of Welles's critics or Welles himself, it is a mistake to assign *Touch of Evil* solely to Welles, to speak of it as *his* project alone. Though he was director, star, and screenplay adaptor, other key figures were in on the finished product.[16] It is both telling and deliciously curious that the film about Hank Quinlan's obsessive search for the murdering "half-breed" that strangled his wife is itself a half-breed. As we will learn below, Orson Welles was not present for the final cut of the film he had helped bring to life. The resulting exquisite corpse of a film is a mixture of at least two different philosophies of narration—as

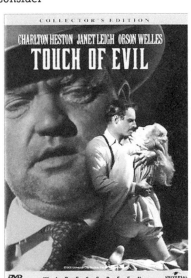

The DVD cover from the Welles's "wishes" edition of *Touch of Evil*, Universal Studios, October 31, 2000.

Leaming observes, "Where Orson had been editing for pictorial and rhythmical subtleties, [Ernest] Nims[, Welles's assistant editor on the film] set about telling a straightforward story." Janet Leigh's choice of terms as she describes Charlton Heston's and her own reaction to the reediting and reshooting of Welles's film seems particularly noteworthy in this regard: "We both resented changing it and *bastardizing* it . . . because what they did made it almost normal" (524, emphasis added).

Predictably, Albert Zugsmith, the producer, underplayed the postproduction team's tinkering with Welles's work: "All that Universal did to the film, beyond what Welles might have wanted, was to sharpen his grammar, dot his 'i's' and cross his 't's'" (Brady, 512).

Bastardizing. Leigh's right.

Absolutely right—and this bastard project, bastard father/mother of film theory, has even more surprises to yield in our exposé of a very American filmed Tex[t]-Mex.

Reel Eight: Amid Ethnicity and Race
Critics Critics Everywhere and Not a Thought to Think

When Heath stated a couple of decades back that "all the habitual paradigms of discussion of film (content/form, content/technique, content/cinema, signified/signifier even) are locked in this positionality—hence the obligation of film analysis to pose its object differently" (70), he showed some very good sense. But it won't be easy.

And thinking about it another way, maybe he has not shown very good sense thinking this way for work that is to take place along *la frontera*, since the film he chose to focus on for over one hundred pages of painfully complex essay is *set* on the U.S.-Mexico border, where sidestepping the niceties of positionality will prove to be a very hard gig.

We come to loggerheads over theoretical tactics and geography—theoretically, with Heath (and, additionally, with Derrida's ghost leering at us from the corner), we want to be one with our poststructurally adept brethren in eschewing the banalities of conventional binary opposites; but in terms of geography, we are always already fixed in binary positionality when we wish to carefully treat with the consequences of two nations once at war: Mexico and the United States.

It is a conundrum.

So let us turn to the words of a literary critic who knew a little bit about the conundrums of the geopolitical and the theoretical, our late, departed teacher, Edward Said: "I am impressed that in so many of the various writings on anthropology, epistemology, textualization, and otherness that I have read, which in scope and material run the gamut from anthropology to history and literary theory, there is an almost total absence of any reference to American imperial intervention as a factor affecting the theoretical discussion."[17]

Said's comments seem engineered for discussions of a borderland where American imperialism and cultural conflict are fundamental parts of recent history.

Even better, given the needs of our study, Said also foregrounds for us the tack to take with regard to Welles's *Touch of Evil*, for Welles's movie is as much about the contamination of the United States by Mexico as it is about the contamination of Mexico by the United States. It is the specific character of that interaction and of that charged and contentious history that is the target of this interpretive essay.

What is obvious in previous commentaries, including the altogether excellent and provocative readings by James Naremore, John Stubbs, and Stephen Heath, is that the "Mexican" contribution has remained unproblematized; it has, in fact, remained *in the dark*—synonymous with the exotic, the dark, the sordid, the sexual, the decayed—with almost predictable regularity.[18]

How bad does it get?

Anywhere one reads an account of Welles's *Touch of Evil*, one should begin to anticipate the antithesis of hermeneutic sophistication; instead, brace for incoming, extended paragraphs of dis-ease and awkwardness. If my experience in researching this film provides any example, then it takes no real stretch of the imagination to conclude that hermeneutical shortcomings of the theoretical set are legion when it comes to speaking of the dynamics of the border.

The critics, like Quinlan, don't speak Mexican; but they are fluent in "Mexican," in repeating the stereotypes typical of the Latina/o Tex[t]-Mex.

But don't be so hard on these poor gringos—few cultural "heterospectacles" are more dense, overwritten by years of conflict, fear, and, not incidentally, several invasions and wars, than the relationship of the United States and Mexico.

Of Touch of Evil *and Hellish Bordertowns*

Critics contemporary with Welles's *Touch of Evil* provided later commentators with ~~racist, ethnocentric~~ *colorful* guidelines.

Howard Thompson's wit in the *New York Times*, May 22, 1958, is typical: "[Janet Leigh's] siege by some young punks in an isolated motel—should make any viewer leery of border accommodations for a long time to come. . . . And why, Mr. Heston, pick the toughest little town in North America for a honeymoon with a nice morsel like Miss Leigh?" Recent commentators pick up and develop the conceit of border space as something other than desirable: Naremore speaks of the "hellish Mexican bordertown of Los Robles," and William Johnson notes that the film is set in a "nightmare world behind everyday reality."[19]

Of course, it is not just the bordertown but also its inhabitants who are something less than desirable, as we see with Joseph McBride's clever description of the "Grande (*sic*) family . . . [as] the scurviest group of misfits this side of [Luis Buñuel's] *Los olvidados*."[20]

It is as if our commentators have taken Miguel Vargas's apology to his annoyed wife, Susan, at face value and incorporated his shame, his outrage, his self-loathing into their own critical essays: "This isn't the real Mexico, you know that . . . All bordertowns bring out the worst in a country . . . I could just imagine your mother's face if she could see our honeymoon hotel." Welles's savvy crafting of Heston's lines as Vargas begin to reveal their depth here; the bordertown as anathema, the bordertown as offal—these are typical Dallas, Texas, attitudes toward Laredo, Texas; typical Monterrey, Nuevo León, attitudes toward Piedras Negras, Coahuila. Mexico City and Chicago are coequal in their disparagement of Tijuana, Baja California del Norte. Welles outs this disdain for the periphery as only an artist adept at cultural intrigue on both sides of the border can; his critics, oddly, are much more provincial.

Akim Tamiroff as Uncle Joe Grandi, licking his lips with lascivious intent, and Valentín de Vargas as the silent and intriguing Pancho, menace gringa hottie Susy Vargas in an early scene from *Touch of Evil*.

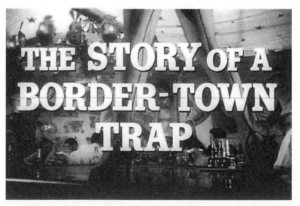

Another telling frame from the trailer for *Touch of Evil*. The film's trailer is one of the extras included on the 2000 DVD release of the film by Universal Studios.

But Vargas is not the movie critics' only guide. Surprisingly, maybe even predictably, Anglo U.S. critics seem enchanted, almost hypnotized (*influenced* would be putting it plainly), by the grotesque Hank Quinlan's "enlightened" view of bordertown citizens.

Note critic Joseph McBride's tone in his assessment of the Mexican shoe clerk Manolo Sánchez (ably acted by Víctor Millán) from his Viking Press book *Orson Welles*. It begins simply enough: "In *Touch of Evil*, Manolo Sanchez is a shoe-clerk, *and* the kept-man/lover of Marcia Linnekar, daughter of the man, Rudy Linnekar, whose explosion ends the most famous opening shot of a film in

Hollywood history. Sanchez is also Quinlan's number one suspect for the explosive crime."

Shortly, things take a turn for the worse: let's listen in as would-be critic McBride reveals his inner-demon, "Mexican"-ophobic soul, channeling/proxying both Marcia Linnekar's Mexican-hating father and half-breed-loathing Hank Quinlan; for an odd second we are spectators at *The Tempest* redux, with critic McBride, as Prospero, sharing Marcia Linnekar's father's repulsion at the thought of his Anglo daughter (Miranda) shacking up with the dark-skinned Mexican *zapatero* Manolo (Caliban):

Manolo Sánchez, played by Victor Millan, pleads for some *mexicano* solidarity from "Mexican" narcotics agent Charlton Heston, aka Miguel Vargas, in *Touch of Evil*. Quinlan, who does not "speak Mexican," leers on the left, contemplating the genius of his evidence-planting schemes.

> The Mexican is silly, smug, absurd . . . Quinlan is brutal, unreasoning . . . but the Mexican offends us by being a fool, and Quinlan makes us admire his godlike insouciance . . . If we are to agree with the Mexican that he is being persecuted, we must do this not through facile sympathy with a noble figure of defiance; we must sympathize with a clown.[21]

Amazing rhetoric, worthy of Hank Quinlan—film criticism becomes a means to an antiseptic slur, refined, but a slur nonetheless. Of course, readers might have a right at this juncture to summon another Quinlan epithet to deal with this type of reading.

> Hank Quinlan [to Vargas after Vargas has discovered Quinlan's planting of the dynamite in Sánchez's shoebox]: "You people are touchy . . . Folks will bear your natural prejudice in mind."

This revealing exchange—revealing as much for the projection of racist attitudes (what William Ryan named "blaming the victim") as for its defensiveness—might well apply to Chicano studies commentators. Given the development of our literatures and our cinema through a rhetoric and practice of resistance, McBride et al. might even make a case, might even make the charge of intellectual and cultural bias stick if brought before the adjudication of a hermeneutic court of law.

Are we, then, merely "touchy" when it comes to *Touch of Evil*, or is it that the film, and Welles through it, provokes the critical agenda, forces us, in an unusual way, to redress the uncanny logic of the U.S.-Mexico border?

Idle speculation. Let us put this to one side and continue with our "reading" of the film.

Frustrated with his encounter with the Mexican narcotics gumshoe, maddened at the upbraiding delivered from the well-dressed, well-spoken Vargas ("he don't talk like a Mexican"), Quinlan dismisses the value of his Mexican adversary by calling the narcotics agent and his offscreen colleagues "Vargas and his Keystone Kops."

The confluence of Hollywood slapstick and the Mexican agent yoked together in this dismissive epithet gains significance when surveying the representation of Mexicans and Mexican Americans in Hollywood cinema—it takes on greater meaning when I argue, as I do below, that *Touch of Evil* systematically and unsystematically challenges many of the stereotypes of Mexicans, Americans, and Mexican Americans.

Touching Race

What happens when film commentators tackle the problem of race in *Touch of Evil*?

The results are mixed.

James Naremore's reading serves as a good example of what happens when commonplace attitudes remain unquestioned in essays that are otherwise quite sensitive to issues of race. After a notable passage itemizing "the sexual psychology of race hatred" in *Touch of Evil*, Naremore concludes: "Los Robles . . . *is quite true to the essence of bordertowns*[:] . . . strip joints and prostitution, a few ragged Mexican poor, and a couple of men trundling fantastic pushcarts . . . the town . . . exists by selling vice to the Yankees, functioning as a kind of subconscious for northerners just outside their own boundaries where they can enjoy themselves even while they imagine the Mexicans are less civilized" (188; emphasis added). Now, you and I can debate our shared experiences in both Mexican and U.S. bordertowns, but there does seem to be evident here a tacit, shared view that border cities suck.

Perhaps Naremore should have written *"true to the essence of bordertowns seen in Hollywood movies."* For all its useful moments, Naremore's critique devolves into a catalogue of bordertown stereotypes.

Other critics lack Naremore's *feel* for the border; Comito's work, following some eight years after Naremore's, seems particularly disturbing:

> To our discomfort, Welles engineers our complicity in violent fantasies, sexual and racial, of the most devious sort, at the same time he appeases the liberal in us with safe homilies on the evils of prejudice. But the crucial border, in spite of the swarthy rapists with whom Welles teases us, is not the one between Mexico and [the] United States . . . The most precarious boundary is one overseen by no friendly customs man. It is the boundary between the apparent solidity of our rational daylight world and the dark labyrinth in

which, if we yield to its solicitations, we will lose our way. Welles's "Mexico" is a place of the soul, a nightmare from which a lost Hollywood sweater girl begs mostly in vain to be awakened.[22]

What Comito forgets, seduced perhaps by the neatness of his polarization (not U.S.-Mexico, but rational daylight world/dark labyrinth of the soul), is how it is not one or the other but *one and the other* who are explicitly complicit, complicitly explicit in this uncanny cultural space—the ease with which abstract existential order is informed, indeed shaped, by the exclusions and misrepresentations we necessarily assign to the other. It is cliché, it is commonplace, to assign Mexico this "darkened" status—a space of the night, of the illicit, of the id.

And so our interpreter, cooing Comito, reads away, forgetting something Welles at least had the foresight to suspect: that the sweater girl suffers not in Mexico but in the United States, in the Mirador, at the hands of Americans, albeit of Mexican-Italian-American origins.

It Gets Worse

Welles's commentators attribute to Welles an unproblematized positive humanism even as they do the opposite in their readings of the film.

So John Stubbs finds that "in Welles's hands, [*Touch of Evil*, adapted from Masterson's novel *Badge of Evil*,] became an extended piece *against* American racism."[23] I would be more comfortable with the assertion that the film is a *representation* of American racism, a masque that meditates on the complexities of ethnicity and race on, at, and over the border, rather than saying it is an extended piece *against* it. *The danger in being against racism is that it is all too easy then to erase yourself from the picture of racism, elide yourself from racism's eloquent utterances in which we participate, through which we are formed.*

If we read *Touch of Evil* more as a representation of racism than an attack on American attitudes on race, we are then more sensitized to that which, as Said suggested above, we are most likely to be blind to—U.S. imperialism and its legacy.

The term "representation" implicitly reminds us that complicity is an ever-present, ever-possible tendency of narration, cinematic or otherwise.

If Welles, as Stubbs contends, speaks against racism, what of Stubbs himself? Again it seems wise to read slowly and quietly the commentator's words themselves. This passage is particularly "loaded" with humanistic doublespeak:

According to the odd double standard of Anglo-Saxon racism, the venturing forth of the Anglo-Saxon male into the more "primitive" or "libidinous" Latin race may be seen as a sexual proving ground of sorts, but the encroachment by the male of the "primitive" race into the Anglo-Saxon world for a partner is usually taken as a move threatening to Anglo-Saxon virility. In this case, Vargas is a challenging figure despite the "social acceptableness" of his government position.[24]

What? Vargas as Caliban—out with it, Stubbs, out with it!?

Even the quotation marks around "primitive" and "libidinous" do not prevent this commentator from questioning the stereotypes (albeit nuanced, sanitized, and academified) in the preceding lines.

The original movie poster distributed in 1958 by Universal Studios; *Touch of Evil* was released that year as the tail feature of a double feature with *The Female Animal*, starring Heddy Lamarr and directed by Harry Keller.

Who, after all, is uncomfortable with Vargas marrying and having sex with a white woman? The border guards at the outset of the film? Perhaps. Quinlan? Surely. Vargas? Most certainly, as Welles is at pains to show throughout the film, exhibiting the Mexican's uncomfortableness with his sexual self. The most ironic aspect of some of the promotional material created for the film is, and this is not uncommon in Hollywood, that the images have nothing to do with events or scenes as they unfold in the film—so that the Eros and passion seen in the original movie poster for *Touch of Evil* features an intimacy and a hot-blooded Mexican sexuality that is nowhere in evidence in the film.

Mexicans in *Touch of Evil* are *in need of* Viagra *and* Levitra (cf. Vargas); it is the godless, bastard, half-breed Chicanos, floating between hetero-normative and homophilial scoptophilia, who provide most of the sexual threat to sweater-girl Susy Vargas—who is a threat herself, as will be seen below. This is part of Welles's genius, part of the reason why he, in a decidedly peculiar way, can be made to be seen as a precursor to Luis Valdez when the history of Chicana/o cinema in the twentieth century is written.

Stubbs's prose cited above might have been stated with greater economy: *Anglo racism against Latinos works two ways: Latinas are a hot test of tepid Anglo sexuality, and Latinos threaten Anglo tepidicity with their self-assured bravado. Though Vargas is a bureaucrat, he still scares the Anglos (Stubbs?) with his hot brown tamale.* I might add that there is the further problem in that Vargas is a Latino simulacrum, painted mustache, brown face, and all.

A second selection from Stubbs's essay shows a similar implicit reading that oddly fuses nationality and sexuality: "The . . . menace comes when a Grandi boy, probably 'Pancho,' shines his flashlight on Susan through her window . . . the act has sexual undercurrents, for the male invading the privacy of the Anglo-Saxon woman is a Mexican."[25]

Would the act not have "sexual undercurrents" if the "male invading the privacy of the Anglo-Saxon woman" were Anglo? The *simile*-zation of "Mexican" for the sexual is worthy of future scrutiny because of the way Welles's characterizations both explode and reinforce this all too easy stereotype—consider here, again, Miguel Vargas's problematic sexuality. As one will have gathered from the foregoing, we remain firmly entrenched with the problem of representation. We really are reprobing the arena of the subject, or "*subject-effect*," and the representations to which *it is subjected* in *Touch of Evil*.

Prowling the Shadowy Heath

Stephen Heath's work is much better than most of the quoted passages above, and that makes it that much more difficult to read and interpret. For instance, the paragraphs where Heath reads a split subject, reading between Welles's camera and pen, are some of the best renderings to date of how this system functions in cinema; describing the indeterminacy of racial/cultural purity, Heath writes:

> Vargas is Mexican but not really (Quinlan: "You don't talk like one—a Mexican, I mean"); the real Mexicans are Grandi or Pancho or Sanchez, or more importantly they are hors-la-loi, half-breeds, sexually dubious. The film uses the border, the play between American and Mexican, the passage from country to country in the motions of exchange . . . at the same time as it seeks to hold that play finally in the opposition of purity and mixture which in turn is a version of law and desire. ("Film and System, Part II," 93)

In Naremore's view, "Heston gives a remarkably believable, unstereotyped portrayal of a Mexican . . ." (184). How do we address this statement? We meaning us, not them. Makeup notwithstanding, Heston embodies a remarkable Mexican simulation, to appropriate Jean Baudrillard's useful reissue of the term. The biographer Brady's account of Heston's transformation seems useful here: "Heston was brought to a Mexican tailor, and two suits, exactly the kind worn by most Mexican businessmen, were made for him. His hair was dyed black, his skin was darkened, and a mustache was pinned on his lip" (502).

Desire and the law, eugenics and corruption: Heath had touched on this earlier in the essay in his description of how the camera bisexualizes Joe Grandi: "The comedy of Uncle Joe's person is a focus on a mixed body, male and female, and this focus, and hence the loss of the hair-piece, is to be climaxed in the scene of his strangulation by Quinlan" ("Film and System, Part I," 46–47).

Somewhere in this meeting ground of sexual difference (male and female) and sexual purity (corrupt acts of miscegenation versus the policing of sanctioned acts of fucking: Mexican/Anglo, bad; Anglo/Anglo, good) comes the best part of Heath's accomplishment as a writer and "father" of film theory—that he somehow sustains in the midst of a close critical analysis of a film the wherewithal to also engage with those fundamental attributes of human culture that find themselves both memorialized and inflected *by* motion pictures.

The term "half-breed" discussed above (here translated as "mestizo") takes on an added valence, signifying racial, national, cultural, and now sexual heterodoxy. Even Naremore, whom I took to task above, is not above a telling gloss, reaching a conclusion similar to Heath's regarding *Touch of Evil*'s depiction of the relationship between cultural self and sexual self, with racial and sexual indeterminacies playing themselves out across the silver screen: "If we are going to accept the film's vision of a racist society, we first have to rid ourselves of liberal complacencies. Just as we are made to acknowledge the humanity of the bigot Quinlan, so we are made to experience the sexual terror which lies behind his racism."[26] These passages show that prior critics have not ignored the delicate and vulgar dance of race in *Touch of Evil*. But there are limits to their discussions.

This might be the right moment to return with some patience to what the word "Mexican" signifies in *Touch of Evil* and how it figures in the criticism the film has produced.

The following passages selected from Heath's challenging two-part theoretical tour de force are significant in this regard. This segment appears in one of his extended synopses:

> Character: Introduction of Pancho, marked with 'Mexican-ness' and a certain foreboding of sensuality (pose, manner, expression, leather jacket, insouciance, Susan's reaction). ("Film and System, Part I," 38–39)

First question: what is this "'Mexican-ness,'" and should Heath's use of inverted commas slow our critique? The inverted commas here are the punctuation equivalent of Quinlan's "touchy" comments above. By letting us know *he* is in the know, Heath halts our progress, releases our suspicions.

Let us look at what Heath is looking at: actor Valentín de Vargas as "Pancho." The character's name is not even his, but we will get to that shortly.

"[P]ose, manner, expression, leather jacket, insouciance, Susan's reaction," Heath has written; he puts his critic's hand to the pulse of a living synecdoche, a pulsating metonym: "'Mexican-ness' . . . a certain foreboding sensuality." No, it is more than that; it is as if Heath has captured the very orgasm of a metonymic moment—to steal from the world of pornographic cinema, Heath films a come-shot: the term "Mexican" splooges, comes, shoots, as it reveals itself as *the* signifier in American cinematic history that "stands in for" incipient sexual latency. We are amid the textual and the sexual, call it the *s/tex[t]ual*—somehow this neologistic excess relates to our ongoing study of a Chicana/o Tex[t]-Mex.

I need a Kleenex.

A couple of pages later, Heath writes, "Grandi speaks Spanish with Pancho [and is] endowed with 'Mexican-ness' in his appearance" (41). There it is again: "'Mexican-ness.'"

What exactly, does the sign "Mexican" signify? It is as if we had happened upon the only item that goes unquestioned in Heath's otherwise critically adept praxis, where every other instrument is subject to analysis, every other thought rethought.

This question is particularly critical, as these are evaluations of a cinematext that is set outside the "real Mexico" at the margins. If "Mexican" means anything in this context, where does that meaning come from? Let me assure you that these are not abstract, inconsequential questions, particularly since our terrain is twentieth-century U.S. cinema—responsible perhaps more than any other media for collective cultural perceptions of the "Mexican" and, in turn, the Mexican American subject-effect.

Valentín de Vargas, "Pancho," surveys the coming "orgy" at the door of Susy Vargas's room at the Mirador Motel in a late scene from *Touch of Evil.*

Heath's most bizarre moment comes toward the end of his piece (i.e., the end of Part II). Here, discussing clean and dirty, family and incest, chastity and sexuality, the subtext of his own narration becomes apparent (by the end of this we will be needing a trench coat and brown paper bag!):

> There can be no question of trying to fix the film in a single reading . . . the purpose of the present analysis is merely to suggest the mechanism of the film, its functioning, its system, the terms of its production . . . the narrative action is not obliged to be clear . . . Vargas can be played as Mexican or American (*or* rather than *and*: Vargas is outside the sense of confusion), one way in respect of Susan, another in the conflict with Quinlan (in fact, the latter— good Mexican versus rotten American—serves as a cover for the disengagement of Vargas), *Charlton Heston as pure, hence non-Mexican*, in the face of the *dirty sexuality* by which Susan is *contaminated*; we need to follow through in the *film the patter round Susan of Vargas's identification by Quinlan with Sanchez* . . . and his own identification with Schwartz (Schwartz is Vargas's "friend" and associate, the dis-

trict attorney of Las Robles played by Mort Mills); from Susy to Sanchez, from Sanchez to Schwartz, from Schwartz to *Susan*, Vargas gets things back in line. ("Film and System, Part II"[95]; emphasis added)

Heath's view here is complex and multivalent. But even as it questions its own deployment of the terms "Mexican," "pure," and "sexuality," it reintroduces the terms in ways consistent with popular perceptions of the Mexican as impure (the greaser; the rapist) and of miscegenation as dirty.

One does not evade the pejorative nature of the conceptual space demarcated by the term "bastard" by noting its *bastardicity*. For Heath cannot escape the fact that Heston is a clean Mexican because he is Heston—the celebrity of the player translates itself, however so unpredictably, to the light dancing on the silver screen.

I am curious (and even no doubt flattered) that Mexican-ness becomes shorthand for sensuality and sexuality (if it be impure and dirty, so be it); but I am simultaneously curious about how this came to be, how Mexicanicity became shorthand for what the Anglo critic calls sexual.

As I suggested above, discussions of the "Mexican" subject, or of any subject, need not languish in the airy confines of abstract reverie.

Perhaps this is the moment to remind ourselves that any discussion of the subject necessarily introduces the category of the half-breed or mestizo: one cannot exist without the other.

And this is the conceptual intersection where ethnic studies and film theory meet—let us hope, just to overdetermine the metaphor, that this meeting is not some TV version of Oedipus redux, some awkward replaying of that chance, yet oracle-fated encounter of Laius and his son, from which only Oedipus emerged alive. Is film theory the father? Is ethnic studies the son? Are we always already merely reasking the question, "Who's your Daddy?" Bastards indeed.

Understand here that it is not that Heath got it wrong or that we as Chicano discussants can "get it right," but that by reading *à côté de*/alongside each other, critics more closely approximate the web of threads composing that fabric of culture named *Touch of Evil*.[27]

In the history of American cinema, who was the most uncanny "Mexican" of them all? Charlton Heston, as Miguel "Mike" Vargas, in Orson Welles's *Touch of Evil*. This particular screen grab underscores Welles's playful c/sinematic eye: "Welcome Stranger to picturesque Los Robles," yells the billboard in front of which Vargas (Heston), in spatula-applied brownface, and his shadow appear. This billboard wars in a dynamic way with the postcards sampled in the last chapter.

*   *   *

Critics more closely approximate.

I should have written, "Critics embody."

Because, ultimately, that is what these acts of criticism ask you to enact, dear, patient, indulgent reader.

That by writing about this film and rereading what others have said about it, we can, through some sort of metamorphosis worthy of Ovid (more on this below in the interstices), become the Tex[t]-Mex, become that knotty mix of threads and histories that make this conversation possible. Or, if we can't *be* the Tex[t]-Mex, then we can be something else, something more transparent, more permeable—its rival, its nemesis.

We are trapped in an increasingly complex scenario—a history of American culture, the forging of an American cultural study that would become a history of *photokinesis*, a history of our movement under the influence of light; usually it is biologists and, even more often, botanists who use this term, but what really happens to us in the dark corridors of a motion picture palace? In the dark, hypnotized by the light, photokinetic forces influence us, *influenze* us.

And how to counter this attack, this intrusion, this seduction (for some a rape, for others a welcome partner).

pho·to·ki·ne·sis (fō′tō ki nē′sis, -kī-), *n. Physiol.* movement occurring upon exposure to light. [PHOTO- + Gk *kīnēsis* movement; see KINETIC] —**pho·to·ki·net·ic** (fō′tō ki net′ik, -kī-), *adj.*

Analysis?

No, *analysis, ana+ lysis, a loosening throughout*, will not do.

Photolysis?

No, no room for a constructive neologism, as the term already exists, also within the realm of biology and chemistry.

Photolysis: "decomposition due to the action of light."

In the dark, with *too much light*, Tex[t]-Mex is a monster subjecting us to photolysis—breaking us down in the act of subject-formation.

No wonder the Chicana/o *movimiento* was nothing more and nothing less than a series of beautiful effervescences; light against light, hope against hope, in the minds and bodies of the movement, in the mouth and pen of figures like César Chávez, Luis Valdez, and Gloria Anzaldúa, there was found respite, a moment of peace against the gnawing maw of decomposition.

* * *

Theoretically speaking, Heath seems beyond reproach—this is especially true of his interlude on "the split/and/or fractured divided subject." In these dense, complex lines, Heath conjures a "drama"—an almost traumatic scene (shades of Freud's Wolf Man) in which the critic seeks to "maintain a violence, a heterogeneity, from the position of the subject." This subject, or subject-effect, or subject-position, or even "Mexican" subject, if you prefer, becomes crucial here. Heath knows this all too well and writes: "the position of realism is the position of intelligibility and the guarantee of intelligibility is the stability of the subject." Heath's climax now follows, as film narrative and, implicitly, the critic's analysis "becomes the fiction of reality, the form of realism." What we call the "real" and what we name as "enunciation" are subsumed at once "into a whole" at "the *order* of the subject." Heath's denouement? "The paradox of such a narrative is then this: aimed at containment, it restates heterogeneity . . . if there is symmetry, there is dis-symmetry."[28]

Heath is right on target: but *not only* with regard to the film he ostensibly critiques; his findings may aptly be applied to his own dazzling essay. Because this Heath-forged subjectivity of the "Mexican" (picture Heath here as Prometheus, but with a sombrero and a paste-on mustache, playing with mud from the banks of the Rio Grande), his linkage of it in *Touch of Evil* with the orgiastic, with the sexual, with the dark, with the mixed-blooded, with the half-blooded, is worthy of question, especially since in the film itself, *Welles works constantly to refigure these stereotypes.*

For if "Pancho" embodies sexuality, it is not that of the sort usually attributed to him and his Latino ilk.

Let me be clear.

In what may well be called a *sympathetic transference*, or, if you will, a fit of racist cross-dressing, that is, humanists cross-dressing as racists, critics of *Touch of Evil* have internalized Hank Quinlan; they have also taken Susan Vargas's position to heart, to crotch, and transferred onto themselves Susy's fears and anticipations of what constitutes the Mexican American at the border.

Let us turn to the first meeting between the young "Pancho" Grandi and Susan in the first minutes of *Touch of Evil*:

Susan, rushing back to her hotel room on the Mexican side of the border, makes her way through a dense, diverse crowd of visiting sailors, salesmen, and local citizens. Before crossing a dangerously busy intersection, she is stopped by a handsome, leather-jacketed young man (an unnamed Grandi nephew played by Valentín de Vargas). Both characters pass under a neon sign reading "paradise"—Welles's irony at its best.

> *Grandi: Tengo un mensaje por usted . . .* [pause as Janet Leigh struggles to understand his meaning] *no me entiende* [directed at a passing stranger]
> *Stranger:* [translating for Grandi] Lady, he say you don't know what he wants.
> *Susan Vargas:* I know very well *what he wants.* [(emphasis added)]
> *Stranger:* He saved your life, lady.
> *Susan Vargas:* Tell him I'm a married woman.

[Leigh discovers that the leather-jacketed young man wants her to follow him back across the border to see Uncle Joe Grandi.]

Susan Vargas [deciding to follow him]: What have I got to lose? . . . [She directs her answer to her own question at a somewhat leering, interested stranger whose face she reads] . . . Don't answer that . . . [to the young man] Lead on, "Pancho!"

Note how, in this scene, it is Susan who *reads* "Pancho's" advances into the text at hand.

Now I don't want to play coy, stupid, and cute and *pretend*, after watching Welles's film, that "Pancho" is not at all aggressive to Susan—that Valentín de Vargas does not loom over Leigh's Susy with an air of impending menace.

What I am saying is that a large degree of the sexual tension that derives between the two is not so easily assigned to the "'sexual'" Mexican American.

"Mexican" and what this signifier has meant for a generation of critical commentators/explicators of Welles's film is here both pertinent and useful. In Welles's film, at least, Mexicanicity is not equal to sexuality; and *if there is an equation between the two, between the figuration of the Mexican and of the sexual*, it is one that questions the identity of each other element.

After a diligent screening of *Touch of Evil*, one is less likely to work with valorized or concretized notions of what constitutes the *Mexican* or the *sexual*.

Welles's film, tellingly set on the U.S.-Mexico border, represents a perfect example of what we can call *la quiebra* (from the Spanish verb *quebrar*, "to break").

La quiebra—a break in the order of things, is also, significantly, the moment when prior understandings of the order of things lose value and are subject to bankruptcy.

It is one of the oddest coincidences of language, of English and Spanish, of the United States and Mexico, that "to break" and "*quebrar*" translate perfectly both literally and figuratively. Both terms mean an act of fracture in their literal embodiments; and both mean "bankruptcy" (I'm broke = *estoy quebrado*).

In a series of crosscuts that open the film, Welles purposely and purposefully blurs the line between the United States and Mexico. One of the commonest complaints of freshmen in my classes where *Touch of Evil* plays is that they can't tell by a certain point whether they are in the United States or in Mexico. Contrast that with Welles's inferior directorial counterpart Steven Soderbergh, whose touted film *Traffic* (2000) works to underscore and reinforce stereotyped views of the United States and Mexico in a way that is much closer to the greaser films and postcards of 1910–1920

The screen grabs figured here are from the Academy Award–nominated film *Traffic*, directed by the Academy Award–winning (for Best Director) Steven Soderbergh.

than anything to be found in Welles's offering.

Even as *Touch of Evil* represents images and events seemingly in sync with prior representations of the borderlands, of Mexicans, of Chicanos in word and image, it also plays upon (preys upon) these expectations, taking spectators to another place, to another understanding.

Consider the following *quiebra*.

"Pancho" Grandi is no simple leering, dangerous "greaser."

"Pancho" (we *never hear his real name*) represents both a problematized Mexican subjectivity (he is a Grandi, and as such he is Mexican, American, and Italian) and, particularly in his relationship with Susy Vargas, a problematized sexual subjectivity.

In the scene transcribed above, it is Susan who reads desire between the lines of a simple communication of information—"*I know very well what he wants*." In addition, all their future "sexual" (Mexican?) encounters are mediated, and multivalent.

The picture they take together is sweet, with both parties smiling—at a baby no less.

"Pancho's" note accompanying the picture (signed "a souvenir with a million kisses—, Pancho") is written in a florid, almost feminine script.

In a later scene, "Pancho" attempts to simultaneously harass and caress Susan—with an ardent flashlight beam splashed out of his flashlight (Freudians, calm down!), penetrating her dressing room and spotlighting Susy as she dresses.

Intriguingly, Susy Vargas does not respond as one who is haunted, harassed, violated, or even intimidated; in fact, Susan Vargas, almost like a "Mexican," responds in kind, turning on the main lights in her room to assist her would-be voyeur with his scoptophiliac project (shades of Michael Powell's *Peeping Tom*, released the next year, 1959) and afford

"Pancho," whom she herself has renamed, a clear shot at her special mix of Anglo action.

The ballet of light and dark, of penetrating flashlights and spotlighted breasts, ends, as it were, with a bang, with Susy returning "Pancho's" gift" of light, his teasing *photokinesis*, his piercing *phototaxis*, quite violently by *unscrewing* (!) the *naked* light bulb in her hotel room in Mexico and throwing said castrated source of light right at him through *his own window*.

Welles authors an epic "sinematic" (sin + cinematic) allegory of displaced "Mexican" sexuality; "Pancho's" castrated flashlight, his eviscerated phallus, comes back at him through his window, through his open cave (look at the still closely; the shadows conjured by Welles's director of cinematography, Russell Metty, figure an architectural pudendum, a shadowy world of personal sexual space that Susy's bulging ~~penis~~ bulb attempts to enter. In short, the girl/Anglo's "cock" penetrates the silent "Mexican's"

body, and in one fell swoop, Welles recasts the figuration of the "Mexican" in the history of Hollywood.

Okay, perhaps I have exaggerated the point, belabored the allegory—that's showbiz. But then again, conceivably, my own light has hit the target. Time will tell.

To continue: the proposition on the floor is that Welles's "Mexicans" don't behave—they

don't behave as "Mexicans" manufactured in Hollywood, seductive hallucinations with an unambiguously sexual and decidedly violent inheritance, usually behave.

Even in *Touch of Evil*'s climactic, violent, and disturbing would-be rape of Susy Vargas, where Welles foregrounds "Pancho" leering in King Kong–like proportions (picture to yourself the close-up shots of the tragic, horny, leering, primate beast in Merian C. Cooper and Ernest B. Schoedsack's 1933 classic) into the camera and licking his lips, "Pancho" does not, in fact, touch Susan, or, at the very least, Welles does not let us see him touch Susan. Instead, "Pancho" barks out his predilections and has his gang's biker/dyke women (let Mercedes McCambridge's line "I like to watch" echo through our synapses) and other young pachucos, Anglo, "Mexican," and Mexican-Italian alike, "hold her legs" as the door closes, as the scene ends, barring Welles's spectators' voyeuristic "enjoyment" of the scene. Grandi sexuality is a problematized sexuality, and these Mexican-American-Italian wonders, miscegenated beasties worthy of

Mercedes McCambridge and Arlene McQuade as Latina, leather-jacketed, heroin-using, lesbian thugs from the Susy Vargas "rape sequence" in *Touch of Evil*. The mise-en-scène of this landmark Wellesian nightmare goes on to permanently trace the eyes of late-twentieth-century and early-twenty-first-century directors like Quentin Tarantino, Darren Aronofsky, Vincent Gallo, and Neil LaBute.

Cortés's letters to the Spanish Crown, are evidence of both Welles's imagination *and* his ability to *figure the border*, if not *figure it out*.

I find it both curious *and* symptomatic that previous generations of Welles biographers and film critics and theorists have focused more on the threat "Pancho" poses to Susan, blinding themselves in the process to Valentín de Vargas's complex performance, a walking anti-allegory of "Mexican"icity.

Heretofore, in Hollywood, for the most part, Mexicans, Latinas/os, and all other species of Hispanic mannequins parading across the silver screens of American movie palaces are of a type: *corpus sine pectore*, "a body without a soul"—Horace will forgive me for lifting his concept from his *Epistles* 1.4; another translation for the original Latin? "Brainless trunk"!

"Pancho" is no such automaton—no walking puppet. Consider this last sweet touch, this last key character detail: "Pancho" introduces himself to Susan Vargas as a monolingual Spanish speaker incapable of speaking English, when he is, in reality, or at least in the reality of the film, a fluent, bilingual manipulator of both Spanish and English—his smooth FM-radio-DJ Anglo-esque voice when he impersonates the front desk clerk at the Mirador is particularly and acutely funny and ironic. Given imperialists' and critical theorists' traditional failure to note that duplicity is not the talent of the Empire builder/cultural anthropologist alone, it seems a glaring and perhaps predictable turn of events that "Pancho's" complex role in Welles's project has yet to be elucidated. It may well be safe to assume that the mestizo/half-breed represents an intrinsic *quiebra* in any narration within which s/he is placed.

Welles, struggling in Hollywood since his incipient epic, *Citizen Kane* (1941); beloved by his loyal troupe of Mercury Theatre players (including Everett Sloane, Joseph Cotten, and Agnes Moorehead); and beleaguered by an insider Hollywood fed up with Welles's arrogance and vision, gets his chance to work his magic one last time for the established studio system—at Universal. If *Citizen Kane* forever transformed the domain of cinema in the United States, extending palettes of representation by forging new syntaxes of visual expression, so too does *Touch of Evil* transform the cinematic/sinematic spaces of the Americas, problematizing Latina/o representation in ways that have yet to be articulated.

One is used to reading of Welles as a genius, albeit a genius whose wisdom peaked with *Citizen Kane*. One is used to reading of how Welles's vision is championed and copied in film schools across the country and across the globe—indeed his name is usually found in the company of Godard, Buñuel, and Hitchcock. For this reason alone, Welles's contribution to the dissemination and problematization of the "Mexican," Mexican American, and Latina/o stereotype/subject-effect in *Touch of Evil* seems worthy of pursuit.

But before we join the gaggle of critics standing in line to lionize Welles in print, let's hold on a minute.

Let's leave our critical survey momentarily to inquire into the particularities and peculiarities of citizen Orson Welles—not the director of infamy, not the enfant terrible of Hollywood, but George Orson Welles, the man.

Are there, for instance, any materials that allow us to better situate Orson Welles on matters of race, on the issue of ethnicity? The answer, perhaps predictably, perhaps annoyingly, is yes and no.

One would have to begin by mentioning the circumstances that first brought Welles to national fame in the American theater: his fabled directorial turn at the head of an all–African American cast for a production of *Macbeth* (with the setting moved from Scotland to Haiti) by the Negro People's Theatre of Harlem, part of the Federal Theatre Project of 1936.[29]

But further inquiry into Welles's oeuvre yields vexing problems. To read his biographies, works, and statements is to encounter contradiction upon contradiction—contradictions, moreover, that we must sift through, if not live, if we are to read *Touch of Evil* with any sophistication, with any sensitivity to its *mestizo* complexities. Because this is a film whose center, whose weighty protagonist, Hank Quinlan, *acts* because of *acts in the past* committed by an unnamed, racially impure, racially heterogeneous "half-breed," the man who strangled Quinlan's wife. This murdering mestizo, Quinlan's nemesis—the source of his tragedy, his alcoholism, and his monomaniacal, if not fascist, understanding of law along the border—must now come to the front of the stage. But to do so, we must, for the present, return to Welles.

To read critical summaries is to believe Welles a champion of the oppressed—as is commonplace in John Stubbs's essays—which is, perhaps, typical of these accounts? "Of course, abhorrence of any form of bigotry had long been a part of Welles's social and political liberalism" (Leaming, *Orson Welles*, 183).

But alongside Stubbs's evocatively positive ululations, we might rightfully want to place contrapuntally the scene of a boisterously energetic Welles bragging about his powers of impersonation to Barbara Leaming: "They'd say 'eighty-year-old Chinaman'; they'd hand me a script, and I'd do it" (147).

Later, we read that the multifaceted actor's/radioman's/director's views on minorities and the downtrodden were part of what made him attractive to women, what made him elusive Hollywood eye candy, as when Leaming reveals how "Rita Hayworth's inherent altruism made her especially receptive to [Welles's] views on racial injustice" (341)—per-

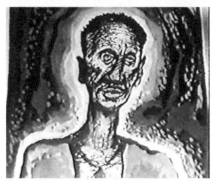

Sketches from the set designer's sketchbook, a climactic voodoo sequence, and crowds of supporters in Harlem, NY, 1936—a tableau of visual artifacts from Welles's production of *Macbeth*. The last figure, a close-up of an "Afro-Caribbean" man, is the most interesting artifact, as it is a sketch from the hand of Orson Welles himself. In 1955, on the BBC, Welles hosted six episodes of *Orson Welles's Sketchbook*. Episode 2 focused on his memory of his work on the all-black version of *Macbeth*. Welles's words here add to the tapestry of our chapter: "Let me assure you that there was a Negro Macbeth, that is, a production with Negroes, of *Macbeth*, that we did in Harlem, some years ago, in a government sponsored theater, a Negro theater. And our purpose was not as capricious and foolish as it may sound, because we were anxious to give to Negro artists who are so very talented, an opportunity to play in the sort of thing that's usually denied them. *As you know, the parts that fall to Negroes are too often old mammies with bandannas and watermelon eating pickaninnies and Uncle Rastuses and so on, so we did quite a number of shows from classical repertory*. We began with a Gilbert and Sullivan . . . *Hot Mikado* we called it. And encouraged by that success, we went on to Shaw and then backwards into literature, and finally dared a production of *Macbeth*" (emphasis added). Welles's words here are food for further thought when served with his bon mots on half-breeds noted in this chapter.

haps, too, it was her own status as an on-the-rise "Mexican" automaton, but that is fodder for our next chapter.

Welles's position, stated in print, is almost too clear for even your *touchy* mestizo critic to ignore—in a political journal named *Free World*, Welles writes, "This is our proposition: that the sin of race hate be solemnly declared a crime" (cited in Leaming, *Orson Welles*, 346).

So why bother? Race in Welles, then, is far from problematic. Aside from a quip about a "Chinaman," his record was unimpeachable.

"Leave him alone, already," readers in the peanut gallery rightfully proclaim.

But I can't—Welles won't let me.

Let's return to *Touch of Evil*.

And to the scene where a slurring Hank Quinlan, drunk and still drinking at the Grandi Rancho Grande cantina on the American side of the border, confronts his partner of decades, Sergeant Pete Menzies.

Menzies—Menses? For the moment, we will hold our tongue, maintain in reserve our rant on the feminine archetypal patronymics afoot in *Touch of Evil* . . . ~~Menses~~ Pete Menzies orders a drunk Quinlan some java as the nostalgia-obsessed, chocolate-, cigar-, and booze-laden detective reflects on the moment that changed his life forever—the moment when a mysterious mestizo interrupted the glory that was his life:

Menzies tries to sober up a melancholic and nostalgic Hank Quinlan; here Quinlan utters his slurred soliloquy on the "half-breed" that strangled his wife.

Quinlan: . . . dynamite's no way to kill . . . did I ever tell you the smart way to kill, Pete?

Pete: Sure, sure, strangle . . .

Quinlan: Mmmm . . . clean, silent. . . .

Pete: You told me all that. . . . [pause] come on, finish that coffee.

Quinlan: That's how my wife died. . . . [mumbling] I don't usually talk about my wife.

Pete: Never when you're sober.

Quinlan: . . . She was strangled, Pete.

Pete: I know, I know . . .

Quinlan: . . . binding cord, she was working out at the packing plant. . . . So the killer had it right to hand . . . you don't leave fingerprints on a piece of string. . . . the half-breed done it of course, we all knew that. . . .

Pete [to the bartender]: La cuenta, la cuenta

Quinlan: . . . I was just a rookie cop . . . I followed around after him, eating my heart out trying to catch him . . . but I never did. . . . and some mud hole in Belgium, 1917, the good Lord done it for me . . . [Action: Quinlan forgets his cane at the bar; as they exit, Pete hands the forgotten cane back to Quinlan.]. . . . Pete, that was the last killer that ever got out of my hands.

Even Welles's early commentators were on to the significance of this slurred soliloquy as it relates to the host of racial epithets Quinlan throws around in the course of the film. Andre Bazin sees how Quinlan's "professional ignominy is . . . exacerbated by a sickening racism which the *mixed population* gives him the occasion to exercise."[30] More recently, Stubbs describes how "certainly a major part of Quinlan's moral twistedness is his intense racism[, using] every chance he gets to insult or deprecate Mexicans."[31]

Alas, these are age-old operations.

Earlier last century, sage father of ethnic American cultural studies Américo Paredes had spoken of these attitudes toward mixed-bloodedness and "Mexicans" in his history of the *corrido*: "Thievery is second nature in the Mexican, especially horse and cattle rustling, and on the whole he is about as degenerate a specimen of humanity as may be found any-where. . . . *[This degeneracy] is due to his mixed blood, though the elements in the mixture were inferior to begin with. He is descended from the Spaniard, a second-rate type of European, and from the equally substandard Indian of Mexico, [who] must not be confused with the noble savages of North America.*"[32] Most pointed here in Paredes's summary of attitudes toward Mexicans, with the old Tejano's signature irony firmly in place and his probing eye utterly acute,[33] are his conclusions that suggest that the proliferation of "Mexican" hallucinations one finds in the Southwest are "not found in the cowboy-ballads, the play-party songs, or the folk tales of the people of Texas." His meditation on the origins (and virility) of "Mexican" stereotypes then shifts into overdrive; listen carefully: "Orally one finds it in the anecdote and in some sentimental verse of nonfolk origin. *It is in print—in newspapers, magazines, and books— that it has been circulated most. In books it has had its greatest influence and longest life*" (16; emphasis added).

As an out-of-the-closet Derridean, I should not render the following words, but when it comes to "Mexicans" in the imagination of U.S. mass culture, the ancient Roman sages got it right: *verba volant, scripta manent* "spoken words fly away, while the written word remains."

Etched into the collective synapses of "Americans," *estadounidenses*, from the Anzo Borrego desert to the

The monstrance, or ostensorium, *is the vessel that holds the Holy Eucharist on display in Roman Catholic churches; no need to footnote my research here, as I was a lector and altar boy at Blessed Sacrament Catholic Church in Laredo, Texas, from 1968 to 1972, and I had to carry the heavy things to and from the back altar. "Monstrance" comes from the Latin* mon-strare—*a word also lurking in the skeleton closet of the somewhat innocent word "demonstrate," as well as, for the purposes of this chapter, the more sinister term "monster." "Half-breeds" are both monsters and monstrous to the extent that they carry, hidden in their blood, illicit and untoward mixtures and speak to the corruption of the body and the most latent fears of the body politic. (A very interesting review of the monstrous history of mixing and its semantic manifestation and consequences can be found online in Blair Shewchuck's "Mulatto and Malignity" for the Canadian Broadcast Company at http://www.cbc.ca/news/indepth/words/mulatto.html (January 11, 2004).*

windy streets of Chicago, *"Mexicans" circulate "in print"—[in] "books,"
they have "great[. . .] influence" and a "long[. . .] life"* (emphasis added).

Welles, rendering Quinlan, summons those most ancient and tragic of
antipathies: the fallen, stolen, murdered woman, killed by a "half-breed";
perhaps, one imagines, she has been violated by her long-dead mestizo
strangler as well. Off-camera, never seen, never envisioned within the
semiotic/synaptic space of *Touch of Evil*, Quinlan's wife's murderer is a
latter-day chimera (that deliciously mixed-up Greek beast: lion/goat/ser-
pent), a latter-day sphinx, a latter-day minotaur—this destroyer, who is
also a monster, if not a *monstrance,* evil in deed and contaminated by his
blood, must die.

But World War I intervenes and, as Quinlan laments, "the good Lord
done it for me."

God steals Quinlan's thunder—proxies the act that would restore
order to a *mestizaje*cized new world order.

But mixedness must still be erased, vengeance must still be enacted,
so Hank Quinlan's frustrated, intercepted violent climax must be relieved,
worked out another way: cue Akim Tamiroff as Mexican, American,
Italian, "Uncle" Joe Grandi.

As we watch Hank Quinlan strangle Uncle Joe near the end of the

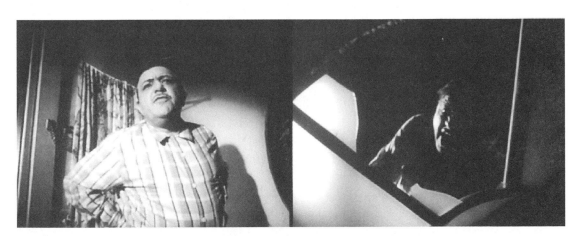

movie, we see as well a *prosthetic ejaculation of hate* that reestablishes
calm and provides the denouement in anticipation of Quinlan's own
death—a sacrifice the entire trajectory of the film anticipates.

But this, then, is Quinlan. How do we approach Welles's position on
the question of race, on the matter of the mestizo, of the enigma of the
"half-breed" to which he refers, in character, and to which he will refer,
sans costume, soon.

The place to begin is with what Welles and his cinematic alter ego
have in common—obsessions with, interests in, and desires for subjectivities South of the Border. For as Naremore suggests, quite rightly, I

Akim Tamiroff as Uncle Joe
Grandi—shot 1: prestrangu-
lation; shot 2: during strangulation. Grandi's role as the
Mexican-Italian-Border-Verged
proxy "half-breed" for
Quinlan's raging, murderous
bent is the stuff of cinematic
legend.

believe, "Welles may be the only German Expressionist who is authentically attracted to Latin cultures, and who is able to appropriate their 'feel' to his style" (205).

Of course, it was always more than a "feel" that drew Welles's interest (though *feel* he did, if his various biographies provide any evidence). Latino culture had always been attractive to Welles—in particular, Latina women and bullfighting.

For example, at the tender age of seventeen, in an incident instructive as much for Welles's incipient *latinophilia* as well as megalomania, we find that "in Seville . . . Orson studied bullfighting with a matador, and then turned over a considerable portion of his earnings from [his] pulp

The death of Hank Quinlan by a bullet shot from the gun of a dying Menzies/Menses.

magazines to an impresario who booked him in a succession of pitiful bullfights in which he had himself billed as 'The American.' But the 'hot-blooded' spectators were perhaps predictably unamused by the incompetent's having bought his way into the arena, and showered him with beer bottles (from which he . . . bears a slight scar on his upper lip)" (Leaming, *Orson Welles*, 74).

I should have said, bulls, Latinas, and cinema, for much of Welles's work on film had a distinct Latin flavor; for example, in "February 1941 Welles does pre-production work on *Mexican Melodrama* starring Dolores Del Rio, who intercedes on his behalf with the Mexican government when they get edgy about the plot—Nazi spies in Mexico" (267). Welles's various affairs with the leading ladies and chorus girls of Hollywood is now common knowledge in Tinseltown folklore: two of his longer-lasting relationships and, in one case, a marriage are pertinent to this survey: Welles's long affair with "Lolita Dolores Martínez Asunsola López Negrette," aka Dolores Del Río; and Welles's marriage to Rita Hayworth (née Margarita Carmen Cansino), who had worked in Tijuana and Aguas Calientes in a Dancing Cansinos act with her dad, an alleged "Spaniard." Welles, with predictable candor, corrects this lie: "She's half Gypsy, not half Spanish" (322).

This sensitivity to half-lineages will resurface later, as we shall see.

Later, Welles is again able to fuse these Latina-filled predilections nicely: "Among his latest projects in late 1944 was teaching Rita [Hayworth] to bullfight" (369). In addition to these lifelong fetishes, Welles was apparently also professionally ready to tackle the role of the racially obsessed/possessed Quinlan at the time of the movie's shooting. As Naremore notes, *Touch of Evil* owed "a good deal to the appearances Welles had made recently as an actor." In *Man in the Shadow* (a 1957 drama directed by Jack Arnold in which Welles starred as Virgil Renchler), Welles "had been cast as a southwestern rancher who exploits Mexicans" (198).

Now we must bring the last evidence to bear on this question of Orson Welles's relationship with Hank Quinlan, of Welles's relationship with subjectivities from South of the Border, and with American cinema's relationship with the Latina/o in general. The disclosure comes from a joke, a confession shared in the posh digs of Ma Maison in Hollywood between an aging, fat white director and, as *accomplice*, his aging white biographer:

> At 6:30 in the morning [Welles] had arranged in advance to have someone drive him to Lake Mercer. He was very glad he had changed his plans when at Woodruff he found a drunk "cross-eyed half-breed" waiting for him in a Model-T. His new destination, Lake Falambeau, was in the midst of the Ojibway Indian Reservation, where Orson promptly hired several "squaws and a few antiques in the neuter gender," as he wrote . . . to build a birchbark and deer-skin wigwam on a parcel of land . . . his hosts had offered for this purpose. (Leaming, *Orson Welles,* 64; quotation marks within the set-off quote signal Leaming's direct quotation of Welles's words)

A smoking gun! The birth of a phrase; the conception of a notion in the head of a young actor.

Here Welles's description of his Native American laborers takes on added significance when we remember Quinlan's description of his wife's alleged murderer as a "half-breed." Through Welles's words, we are brought to a place where the actor/director and Quinlan come together, if only for an instant—the puppet and the puppeteer fuse, merge, mate (Charlie Kaufman and Spike Jonze's *Being John Malkovich*, works here as a cinefied allegory of Welles's displacement with his own protagonist).

One begins to piece together a hierarchy in the Wellesian order of things; one suspects that individuals of mixed inferior stock do not rate highly on that list. Welles gives further evidence of his attitude for those of suspect or divided stock when he assesses the lineage of his renamed wife Rita Hayworth: "I wasn't smart enough to know [Rita's jealousy] was neurotic. *I just thought it was Gypsy, and I said, this is that Gypsy kick and I've got to cure her of that*" (325).[34] It is through an interrogation of the pejorative cultural space of the Gypsy and the "half-breed" and by our hermeneutic manufacture of this enabling, contentious mongrel/ethnic lens that we set the stage for the most comprehensive methodology with which to reexamine *Touch of Evil.*

Reel 10: Of Racist Epithet Hurlers and Proto-Chicano Activists

Having isolated Welles's problematic attitudes toward ethnic impurities (the "half-breed," the "Gypsy"), your average ethnic American cultural theorist, armed with the self-righteous authority of ideologically sensitive poststructural high-minded rhetoric, might just be willing to say "Ah hah! Welles the racist" and be done with it.

But nothing in the work of Orson Welles and nothing in the life of Orson Welles was that simple.

Now we must turn to an action that will be of special interest to Chicana/o scholars, an incident that reinforces the ties between Welles's scholarship, film theory, and Chicano studies: the Sleepy Lagoon Case or the Zoot-Suit trials.[35]

In Leaming's version of this series of events (known well to anyone vaguely familiar with Mexican American history or Luis Valdez's play and film *Zoot Suit*), we hear about the murder of José Díaz on August 2, 1942: "The police harassment of the Mexican American community in Los Angeles that followed the discovery of Díaz's body (he had been run over by an automobile) was symptomatic of the intense wartime racism in the United States. The next night as they left local dance halls, young Chicanos were confronted by police who tore into their zoot suits with razor-tipped pokers. As many as 600 . . . found themselves hauled in by the police for questioning" (*Orson Welles*, 334)

These and other related events led to what came to be called the Sleepy Lagoon murder case, "constructed by the press in Los Angeles, anxious to invent a Mexican American crime wave . . . in particular . . . among the so-called zoot suiters" (333–334). Perhaps predictably, given the nature of propaganda, the Axis powers seized on the opportunity to exploit this "Yankee persecution" via radio broadcasts beamed throughout Latin America that ranted eloquently against the "concentration camps of Los Angeles."[36]

So we are between the years 1942 and 1943, when the United States is at war with the Axis forces and is increasingly wary of Nazi overtures to the Latin American nations, particularly Argentina and Mexico. Leaming continues the tale: "During this period . . . a political group calling itself the Citizen's Committee for the Defense of Mexican American Youth asked Orson [Welles] to act as its spokesman[; . . . this marked] his public debut as a serious political activist, a role he would increasingly seek to cultivate" (333). Welles's friendship with then president Franklin Delano Roosevelt as well as other interests brought him on board the project. Leaming leaves Welles's rationale less ambiguous than it is: "Welles's association with Roosevelt's Good Neighbor Policy, as well as his inherent hatred of racists and Hearstian yellow journalism, caused him to become intensely interested in the case, and he agreed to pen the foreword to a political pamphlet about the trial and its international implications, which was published in June of 1943 with his name displayed prominently on the cover" (335).

Why did Orson Welles commit himself to the defense of Mexican

American youths? It seems the time is ripe to explore the various individuals involved in securing Welles's involvement on this project—especially given the way his career intersects at this moment of American history with the interests of a Mexican American community that had not even renamed itself Chicana/o yet. Welles's intimate association with the interests of Los Angeles Mexican Americans caught up in the national struggle for political subjectivity gives *Touch of Evil* analysts one more thing to worry about as they produce their readings of Welles's bordertown chronicle.

Lest we think too highly of the cinematic master-cum-genius, let us eavesdrop one more time on a conversation between Leaming and Welles at that special private table at Ma Maison as Welles reminisces about that time in 1945, at the end of the war and the founding of the United Nations, when serious thought was actually given to having the film director/celebrity/actor/personality represent the United States at that influential body.

Leaming writes: "[In 1945] a singular plan was to put forth as a candidate for the Secretary General of the United Nations the name of Orson Welles" (372). Welles's memory of this speculation seems noteworthy: "I wasn't very keen about it . . . I was in on the founding of the thing, and at the founding it was apparent to me that all the limitations we know now were inherent in it, and that we were eventually going to be imprisoned by what is now called the Third World. So I had a dim view of its future" (372).

With or without knowing it, we have returned once again to the domain of the problematized "subject"; this anxiety of corrupted subjectivity is evident in the film *Touch of Evil*, in the work of that film's analysts, in its director and star, and, perhaps, in this summary of the field circumscribed by all those listed above. The "half-breed" is more than the culprit responsible for Hank Quinlan's unceasing obsessions; it is also the term that best characterizes the incongruities and contradictions at play in the texts surveyed for this act of critical inquiry.

Welles knows "Mexicans" and produces a film that problematizes their figuration—and all this in a Hollywood milieu that had successfully worked for decades to simplify their figuration. And he is a champion of exploited Mexican Americans; yet he is leery of "half-breeds" and "Gypsies," and won't run the United Nations because he fears it will imprison the United States at the mercy of Third World wardens. Oh yes, and he likes bullfighting and Latinas—a lot!

What a mess.

It is worthwhile to return to the problem of the subject, especially as elucidated by one Stephen Heath, whose findings have been appropriated and indicted in the course of this reading.

Heath is at his best when he circumscribes the domain of film analysis within the larger body of activities and phenomena now most commonly gathered under the rubric of cultural studies:

> It is precisely the figure of the subject as turning-point (circulation) between image and industry (poles of the cinematic institution) which demands study in the analysis of films. The hypothesis, in short, is that ideology depends crucially on the establishment of a range of "machines" (of institutions) which move—transference of desire—the subject ("sender" and "receiver") in a ceaseless appropriation of the symbolic into the imaginary, production into fiction. In film, it is narrative that has served as the mode of that appropriation, the very mirror of the instance of the subject in its reconstitution. ("Film and System, Part I," 8)

That Heath himself leaves unproblematized the figure of the "Mexican" (of "'Mexican-ness,'" quotation marks notwithstanding) does not undermine his otherwise complex and rewarding practice (so complex that Comito and other popular chroniclers of Welles's career give Heath a rather wide berth).

It merely reminds us of the pitfalls of cultural commentary: that which goes unexamined, that which is self-evident, is that which one can *least* rely upon as one moves through a carefully crafted critique. That, after all, may be the most we can hope for from our dedicated efforts as we place pen to page, finger to keyboard. As Edward Said laments with regard to the writing of history, which is, after all, what the interpretation of texts ultimately amounts to, "If there can be no actual taking of power in the writing of history, there can at least be a demystifying exposure of what material interests are at stake, what ideology and method are employed, what parties advanced, which deferred, displaced, defeated."[37]

Final Reel

> "This isn't the real Mexico . . . all bordertowns bring out the worst in a country, you know that. . . . [Later that day he adds:] 1,400 miles without a machine-gun in place . . . I guess that sounds kind of corny."
>
> —Miguel "Mike" Vargas, *Touch of Evil*

This chapter's obsession with borders (between nations, between races— what is the "half-breed" but a slur attributed to an individual or community that has transgressed lines of difference?)—is underwritten by the cinematext named *Touch of Evil*. Renato Rosaldo's reminder of the conflict along one part of that border in his *Culture and Truth* is worthy of calling to mind here; Rosaldo writes: "Military conquest transformed the Rio Grande from a fertile place of gathering together into a barbed line of demarcation."[38] Gloria Anzaldúa aptly describes that same border as *"una herida abierta"* (an open wound).[39]

The internalization of this fracture, of this open wound, of this determining *quiebra*, has often colored the development of narratives and strategies of reading that call themselves Chicana/o. It seems essential that we *retain that schism*, but that we simultaneously also recognize that evolving sutured *cosa* as one of our strengths—otherwise, monsters lurk ready to out our failure.

The easiest mistake? That we fall prey to an empty nostalgia for an orderly, solid, homogeneous origin that never existed, even if it is named Aztlán.

Rosaldo's conclusion seems right on target: "These continuities and changes in Chicano narrative forms reveal shifting conceptions of culture. Once a figure of masculine heroics and resistance to white supremacy, the Chicano warrior hero now has faded away in a manner linked . . . to the demise of self-enclosed, patriarchal, 'authentic' Chicano culture."[40]

This is not something to be lamented—it places a Mexican American cultural studies, a strategy of Chicana/o discourse, at the forefront of pedagogical/political developments. Edward Said's writings speak to this confluence: "Exile, immigration, and the crossing of boundaries are experiences that can therefore provide us with new narrative forms or, in John Berger's phrase, with other ways of telling."[41]

The border, border/ed narrative named *Touch of Evil* takes on added significance in this context.

* * *

Gary Keller's "Image of the Chicano" in his collection *Chicano Cinema* seems worthy of further scrutiny and a careful rereading—I have learned much by carefully reviewing its pages. Drawing largely upon works by Arthur G. Pettit, Blaine Lamb, Cecil Robinson, and George H. Roeder, among others, his solid overview of Mexican and Chicano cinema coupled with his innovative rhetoric—a sort of academese *estilo Chicano* with strategic weaving of idiomatic Spanish throughout—is useful to anyone interested in Chicano discourse and film history.

If Keller's summary of Mexican American and Mexican representation in the United States is accurate, and I believe it is, then it is worth considering Welles's film as one that ultimately alters the trajectory of all other Hollywood-borne stereotypes that precede and follow it in 1958, repeating to ourselves as we do so the mantra from Blaine T. Lamb's writings: "Celluloid Mexican stereotype[s are] almost as old as the film industry itself."[42]

In Welles's opus, one *mexicano* (Vargas) does not lie, does not steal, is not amorous, does not use a knife, does not wear a sombrero, does not look or sound like a Mexican, and runs not from battle but to his wife—*movidas* (extramarital liaisons) being totally absent from the scene.

Touch of Evil works against what Keller aptly calls "the requirement of assembly-line produced celluloid, the establishment of minor variations on familiar themes instantly recognizable to the moviegoer, the emphasis on depictions of America at the most cliché, banal level, the need for formulaic and painfully simplified conceptions of plot and conflict (heroes versus villains, them versus us, Americans versus aliens, Happy Endings, "good" always wins out, and so on), and a production philosophy of films keyed to a star system predicated on Anglo conventions of handsomeness and winsomeness."[43]

Miguel "Mike" Vargas, "Mexican," speaks Spanish sooooooooooooo bad, that even Welles had to laugh at the farce of gringo Charlton Heston as a "Mexican." Late in the film, as Vargas busts into the Grandi bar and confronts the Grandi Boys/Thugs, things get messy and ugly fast—Valentín de Vargas, our beloved, pretty boy "Pancho" (Susy's light-bulb love thang) ends up with his gorgeous head pushed through a jukebox, killing the buzz of everyone in the Rancho Grandi nightclub. But "Mike" is not done; Heston as Vargas grabs Risto, played with surly acerbic detachment by the late Lalo Ríos (b. 1927, Sonora, Mexico; d. 1973, Los Angeles, CA, U.S.A.), and demands to know where Susy (drugged and kidnapped by the Grandis) has been taken. "Háblanse, háblanse" (Speak, oh elder respected ones; **my translation**) *the deranged-by-anger and jealousy-mad "Mexican" narcotics dick demands, in lieu of the anticipated* "Dígame" *(Tell me [where she's at];* **my translation***) one might reasonably expect from an irate Mexican. Risto's response is priceless as Vargas/Heston insists on mangling the Spanish mother tongue: "Oh talk English, will you please."*

I do know that one can find and document how Welles's *Touch of Evil* reinforces predictable stereotypes of the *mexicano* subjectivity and of the Anglo subjectivity. Closer scrutiny reveals, however, that these expressionistic archetypes are mined with nuances of difference, which derail the archetype. These characters accomplish this even as they reveal our need (evident in much of the commentary surveyed above) for the reassuring logic the stereotype "Mexicans" and "Mexican Americans" provide for a U.S. critical community enchanted with diversity and difference as aesthetic categories, not material, breathing realities.

Welles's work is a true border text—it does not hide the wounds evident at the border; if anything, he visualizes them in a way that is hard to forget. His inheritor in this regard is David Lynch, especially in his lauded teledrama *Twin Peaks* (1990–1991), another border tale/bordered tale (Canada and the United States) championed for its eccentricity that centers around a murder perpetrated by a psychic/psychotic "half-breed." Both tales abound with detectives, prostitutes, "half-breeds," grotesques, and failures.

In the Lobby: Mestiza/o Blindness

Mundus vult decipi.
[The world desires its own deception.]

—Old Roman *dicho*

—Pity about her, says the citizen. Or any other woman marries a
half and half.
—How half and half? says Bloom. Do you mean he.
—Half and half I mean, says the citizen. A fellow that's neither fish
nor flesh . . . A pishogue, if you know what that is.[44]

—Mestizo Leopold Bloom, an Irish and Jewish pastiche/monstrosity

in the eyes of his attack-
er, the superpatriot,
Irish, nationalist, drunk
"Citizen" from the
"Cyclops," *Ulysses*.

I will close with an anecdote
lifted from Leaming about
what happened when the
time came for the final editing of those film reels that
eventually became *Touch of
Evil*. In short, one sees a marvelous and significant series of events come
to pass. Leaming reveals how "over Orson's strenuous objections, [post-
production head Ernest] Nims and [production head Ed] Muhl decided
that it was time to inspect the picture. Whereupon Welles left for Mexico;
while it seemed to Nims that he had stormed off in anger, actually Welles
had planned to go even before this, to work on a sort of "home movie" of
Don Quixote he had been intermittently fiddling with since 1955 in Paris,
and which he hoped to work on while wrapping up *Touch of Evil*" (*Orson
Welles*, 523).

Did you catch it?

Welles leaves *Touch of Evil* to work on *Don Quixote*, Miguel Cervantes's
seventeenth-century evocation of the delicious pathologies of narration
and representation, of an obsession with a literary chivalric tradition that
comes to overwrite the "reality" of its crazy main character.[45]

Don Quixote, *a film project Welles never finished*—a *quixotic* gesture if
there ever was one.

Life imitates art imitating life: the poststructural commonplace of
life imitating literature drops to the next spiral of an endless labyrinth.

The result of these series of events, these Jorge Luis Borges–like

Read the sign opposite
Heston/Vargas, arguably the
blindest bat in this asylum
of a film, and you begin to
appreciate the irony of
proto-Chicano Welles.
Heston/Vargas's sightlessness
is cinematically showcased
by Welles's twisted wit and
Russell Metty's clever camera.

Tex[t]-Mexual details, is that commentators are left with a text in dispute, a mestizo-like "half-breed" of a finished product whose lineage will be subject to endless debate.

Leave it to the old gringo Welles to have produced a mestizo film, a proto-Chicana/o masterwork, to have *figured* the border out, to have represented it, and then to have parodied that representation in the material work of realizing and distributing the film.

Touch of Evil. The quintessential Tex[t]-Mex.

CHAPTER 2

WHEN ELECTROLYSIS PROXIES FOR THE EXISTENTIAL

A Somewhat Sordid Meditation on What Might Occur if Frantz Fanon, Rosario Castellanos, Jacques Derrida, Gayatri Spivak, and Sandra Cisneros Asked Rita Hayworth Her Name at the Tex[t]-Mex Beauty Parlor

by William Anthony Nericcio, Guillermo Nericcio García, and Margarita Carmen Cansino

Electrolysis Primer

No art can possibly comfort her then, even though art is credited with many things, especially an ability to offer solace. Sometimes, of course, art creates the suffering in the first place.

—*Elfriede Jelinek*[1]

Ever since Gayatri Spivak's English-language edition of Jacques Derrida's *Of Grammatology* appeared in 1976, critical inquiry in philosophy, literature, and the arts has been in a tizzy about the category of the name.[2] All right, perhaps names have never been that out of vogue among the so-called intelligentsia, but Derrida, via Spivak, certainly did hand us a novel rhetorical armature we have yet to trade in or throw out. In this vein, the pages that follow can be read as a donation to a hermeneutic vault called *name theory*, examining how different writers deploy the category of the name in their writing while also, and not incidentally, touching upon the nature of stereotypes. What are "stereotypes" but the ready *names* we apply to S/subjects with differences somehow beyond the scope of our understanding or our experience?

One might be moved by the utterance of Derrida's over-alluded-to name (especially those silly twerps who never understood our late, departed guru's brilliance) to remark at this point, "so what?"

I agree.

For that reason our discussion moves rather quickly from the theoretical to the particular, scrutinizing *two* particular names and *one* particular person: Rita Hayworth—born into this world as Margarita (or Marguerita, depending on your sources) Carmen Cansino.

In the process of reviewing "Hayworth's" metamorphosis, we will begin to attune ourselves to the particular and peculiar phenomena that are engaged when we consider the relationship of names to people and words to subjects.

One important phenomenon is "violence," to the psyche, *por supuesto*, and to the body as well. Without giving too much away here at the outset, I do think it obvious enough to note and important enough to underscore that a simple inquiry into the history of names shows an undeniable connection to those histories that concern themselves with violence. And we need not trot in Siggy Freud here in the footnotes to submit that the repercussions of name changes can have an uncanny impact on the psyche at the level of the unconscious.

The story of Rita Hayworth will teach us this and more. That her literal body changed (hair follicles are, after all, a noteworthy feature of our lovely corpus) alongside her name makes her case all the more curious. But I am getting ahead of myself and I need to introduce our costars.

"Rita's Existential Guillotine,"
Guillermo Nericcio García.

To retell the story of Rita Hayworth I have brought together extracts from Frantz Fanon's *Black Skin, White Masks*, Rosario Castellanos's "Woman and Her Image," Jacques Derrida's *Limited Inc.*, Gayatri Spivak's "Who Claims Alterity," and Sandra Cisneros's *House on Mango Street* so as to provide points of entry (some mutually exclusive) for our reexamination of the life of Rita Hayworth.[3]

Our magnificent psychiatrist from Martinique; Latin-spewing, word-wizard *diva* from Mexico; departed, dashing philosophical deity from France; sari-/mini-skirt festooned fashionista and polyglot postcolonial Bengali–Ivy Leaguer; and nasty, sharp Chicana eccentric from Chicago (though of late Cisneros has been cross-dressing as a Tejana from San Antonio) all have generously agreed, through the magic of citation and the occasional footnote, to assist us on our quest.

With friends like these, one might imagine that the success of our exegetic enterprise is a given, but *I* wouldn't be too sure about that!

Allow me to confess that the last thing I want to do is to restore dignity, personhood, and wholeness to Margarita Carmen Cansino. My theoretical point woman, the late Mexican dramatist/novelist/poet/theorist/ambassador (!) Rosario Castellanos, cured me of that urge in "Woman and Her Image." Here one finds a disturbing if sobering warning

This chapter has coauthors: Guillermo Nericcio García and Margarita Carmen Cansino are to be heralded in the credits. Here's the story: had I been born a mile or so south of the old Mercy Hospital (Laredo, Texas, U.S.A.), in Nuevo Laredo, Tamaulipas, about eleven blocks south of the casita *at 1609 Hendricks where my father, William Nericcio, and my mother, Trinidad Nericcio lived, my name would likely be very different: not "William" but "Guillermo"; not "Nericcio" but "Nericcio García," following the practice in most Latin American families whereby the maiden name of the mother follows the last name of the father. (The next time you are in a bookstore, check where they stock Gabriel García Márquez; I am not saying the proprietors are barbarians if you find his oeuvre listed under Márquez, but they do need some cultural retooling—then again, said stocking practice may also be positively viewed as a bit of gyno-driven resistance to the name of the father, chapeau* Irigaray.*) But to return, the peculiarities of my Laredo/Nuevo Laredo border space suggest the degree to which naming, geography, and bicultural territorialization mark the self who lives within that border, supplementing somewhat Deleuze and Guattari's overcited mouthful of a concept. Postscript (January 2002): When* Romance Language Annual *(Purdue Monographs, Winter 1992) published an earlier version of this chapter, they removed my second name, written in Spanish. And while I am forever in debt to those generous* gente *at Purdue, especially Anthony Tamburri, that decision, that "matronymic scalping," is not without significance, given the discussion that now follows. When a tweaked version of this chapter appeared with Indiana University Press, in Arturo Aldama's edited collection* Violence and the Body, *Margarita Carmen Cansino's name was chopped from the credits—editors, with their pencils, are like electrologists gone gaga with their charged pincers; so this second scalping, too, has a significance not to be ignored. My thanks to the University of Texas Press for allowing this final version of this chapter to appear with the proper opening credits.*

to critics seduced by the romantic *jouissance* of their own righteousness: "Let us not allow ourselves to fall into the old trap of trying to change, by a syllogism or magic spell, the mutilated man—who according to St. Thomas is a woman—into a whole man" (243).

Justly chided, firmly repositioned, we are freed: establishing that the *whole woman must not be our objective*.

As if!

Moving from the theoretical delicacies of Mexico to a perhaps more familiar offering from France, we find Castellanos's censure echoed years later in the words of cyber-quotable French maven Jean Baudrillard in *Simulations*, where the prince of simulacra urges us to avoid "retrospective hallucinations." Let us re-cue our Baudrillard loop from the introduction: "It is always the aim of ideological analysis to restore the objective process"; and let us now add to it Baudrillard's next line, the clincher, as it were: "It is always a false problem to want to restore the truth beneath the simulacrum."[4]

As "Truth" is not our issue, nor *my* specialty, so I will leave "truth" or its absence, the aporia of the indeterminate, for *Paul de Man's* acolytes to debate.

In any event, to restore the objective woman Margarita Carmen Cansino would not heal the body of a dead woman—healing Rita Hayworth is beyond the scope of a piece of critical film theory, no matter the verbosity and good intentions of this or that theoretical pundit. In the end, a monomaniacal focus upon alienation (the retrieval of the tortured star's alienated body) would merely reproduce the most annoying academic fetish: that we can, via prose, recuperate and restore alienated subjects—Spivak, as I suggested in the last chapter, quite rightly calls them "subject-effects." Her canny hedge is bracing. One would never take the wake of a boat for the boat itself, yet it is quite commonplace to presume a subject-effect to be a Subject (nautical tropes from a Laredo boy: go figure).

It is at moments such as these that Fanon's declaration that "intellectual alienation is a creation of middle-class society" (*Black Skin, White Masks*, 224) cautions those hoping to effect change from the ivory tower. We "institutionally placed cultural workers"—the long, if accurate, name Spivak conjured for us ("Who

Readers ought not to allow my saucy tone to throw them here. Alleged Nazi fetishism notwithstanding, I was as moved as any other theorist of my generation by the theoretical stained-glass windows to be found in Paul de Man's essays. But as I argue below with regard to Derrida and the Pillsbury Doughboy, something definitely happens as ideas move from the mouth of the "priest" to the soul of the writing "acolyte." On another topic, fans of de Man mournful of his current leperlike infamy should patiently wait a decade or so. Late-twentieth-century and early-twenty-first-century recuperations of Richard Nixon ("Nixon" logo T-shirts were all the rage in Southern California in the mid-1990s) and Henry Kissinger (the noted Nobel Prize–winning genocidist) show just how forgetful and forgiving the collective unconscious of a given Western state can be. Our more recent deification of criminal president Ronald Reagan—the telepageants for "Ronnie" on Fox News were worthy of a pope's funeral—as well as the George W. Bush reelection, in the shadow of the Abu Gharaib prison scandals and his invisible weapons of mass destruction farce in Iraq, show that it takes very little in the United States to move from the ignominy of war criminal to the ethereal heights of a demigod.

Claims Alterity," 280)—should not overestimate the impact of our textual labor.

After all, can a commentary on a movie ever hope to impact with the force of the movie itself? Of course not. Many of you reading these words would just as soon plunk down one hundred dollars for drinks and dinner with Paris Hilton, Bernardo Bertolucci, Spike Lee, Edward James Olmos, or Robert De Niro as have a free twenty minutes with Jonathan Culler, Cynthia Chase, or Jürgen Häbermas, no offense intended.

So this is no time for hubris. Especially when even our best-intended actions (like, say, multiculturalism's embrace of all things diasporic or, even, recent Chicano paeans to the transnational) may be, as Spivak suggests, in and of themselves suspect: "Heterogeneity is an elusive and ambivalent resource (except in Metropolitan 'parliamentary' or academic space), as the recent past . . . [has] shown" (280).

So we will show some caution and continually attempt to underestimate the importance of these proceedings as we, *estilo* Michael Taussig, run away from "High Theory, while preserving its haughty suspicion of the obvious."[5]

None of this means that I will avoid passing judgment on the weave of texts or of media (film, film fanzines, film reviews, and film theory) informing mass cultural manifestations of "Rita Hayworth."

I have noted that some recent forays in critical theory have led to erudite, if disappointing, intrigue where critical caginess devolves willy-nilly into borderline wishy-washiness. Sample, for example, a *position* statement by the redoubtable and usually quite excellent Richard Dyer in his gyno-noir piece on Charles Vidor's Hayworth vehicle *Gilda:* "I am not aiming to produce a definitive reading, nor yet a 'counter-reading' in the spirit of [, citing Eco,] 'semiotic guerrilla warfare.' Rather, *I am interested in indicating some of the readings that the film makes possible.*"[6]

Now I am a big fan of Dyer's, and yet even *I* can't always stomach this kind of hermeneutic hedging—though I will certainly try to get away with murder, as would any writer, especially one like myself, haunted by the shades of Derrida, Borges, Sarduy, and Castellanos.

In a sense, this is my way of warning you that your time in these pages will be a bit more *vulgar*—in the best, most Antonio Gramsci-doused sense of the term. For, ultimately, each frame in the *text* of a given piece of cinema can be subjected to an infinite number of readings—recorded images are the epitome of what our aforementioned nineteenth-century Viennese cigar-smoking entrepreneur Freud called *overdeterminacy* in his dissection of the *dreamwork*.

Seeking to avoid this attractive, if only momentarily satisfying, open-endedness, this reading of the life and times of Rita "Hayworth" aspires to a somewhat less cagey statement of position: Rita Cansino got screwed both figuratively and literally, and the way this screwing "functions" speaks eloquently to ethnicity and gender as lived and living categories; further, it sheds light on the way these categories have been impacted upon by motion picture technologies in the twentieth century.[7]

Other Rita chroniclers have taken a somewhat different tack than Dyer with regard to the late Hollywood legend, and they are anything but inconsistent. Pity us readers and visual aficionados of Rita Hayworth as we endure the repeated droning of her commentators and biographers. Like some drugged-out chorus chained to a merry-go-round, they speak time and again to the tragedy of Hayworth's "love goddess" life, the tragedy of the fallen princess. All this schmaltzy shedding of tears masks the more crucial, less ~~marketable~~ tasteful issues.

For instance, I find it more profitable to see Rita Hayworth as a *proto–Richard Rodriguez,* a proto–Michael Jackson (*dig* that new *cara,* damn!), or as a proto–Clarence Thomas—that is, as one of those tortured and homogenized ethnic-esque types, endlessly prowling the hallways of celebrity and government in search of solace for their wounded souls—souls scarred by ethnic, gender, and sexual warfare. Condoleezza Rice, secretary of state in the George W. Bush administration (¡diosito mío!), and Albert Gonzales, attorney general, are new members of this wretched gallery.

Visit Seductive Gallery 2, below, for a picture of Dorian Gray Richard Rodriguez; since I spend a few paragraphs in this book bitch-slapping poor Richard, let me point out that he authored a quite useful piece on Native Americans and animation (can you say "Pocahontas") in a newspaper special—"The Real Pocahontas: Disney's Revisionist History Perpetuates the Myth of the Dead Indian," San Francisco Examiner, July 16, 1995. Additionally, the interview he did for Nepantla 4, no. 2 (2003), 269–282, with Claudia M. Milian Arias, is not without its good moments.

These souls, moreover, are willing to manipulate the way they materially *display* their subjectivities in public—here we are speaking of self-authored monstrances/monstrosities.

While many (Kobal, Ringgold, Morella, Leaming, et al.) have documented Rita Cansino's transformation into femme fatale, love goddess, alcoholic, senile Alzheimer's victim Rita Hayworth, few have probed the cultural artifacts that remain from this grand ~~ca~~metastrophe; few have poked through the traces to understand the significance of this de-evolution in the cultural legacy of the United States.

A Star Is Form[ed]

"So we don't have another dame with big boobs on the [studio] lot. So what? . . . We'll make one."

—*Harry Cohn, Columbia Pictures Studio Chief*[8]

Of all stars, why Rita Hayworth in this Tex[t]-Mex catalogue?

For at least two reasons.

Though many think they know about this "Latina" Hollywood "glamour girl," few have inquired into the sordid processes that brought about her metamorphosis from an incestuously violated dancing vaudevillian by the name of Margarita Carmen Cansino to a Tinseltown celebrity, Rita Hayworth. Her name change, at Columbia Pictures mogul Harry Cohn's suggestion ("Cansino was too . . . well . . . Spanish sounding"), was only the start of her material translation from one mode of being to another, her de*latina*ization—an event that makes concrete and *brown* Fanon's lament that "what is often called the *black* soul is a white man's *artifact*" (*Black Skin, White Masks*, 14; emphasis added).

Latino/a souls are just as susceptible to this "artif[r]acture." For it was not *just* a name change Ms. Cansino endured. As we will shortly witness, Hayworth/Cansino suffered months of painful electrolysis on her hairline so as to assure her "attractiveness," to ensure she would not look like a "Spanish dancer": it is a lurid scene, you have to admit—some grotesque pastiche where eugenics and beauty parlors meet.

The second reason for discussing Rita Hayworth is to bring various interlocutors of critical theory back down to earth.

What is more basic to *estadounidenses* than cinema?[9]

Too often, theory languishes in the airy heights of abstraction and pretension—this is especially so in the hands of secondary commentators seduced into replicating jargon they neither relish nor understand. You only have to call to mind the watered-down, mutated versions of Derrida's *deconstruction* stalking the halls of academe here in the United States—my own experience at Cornell and my travels in the late 1980s to Yale, Harvard, and Princeton suggest that the East Coast was suffering from an epidemic of these fawning, insufferable American wanna-bes.

Pity poor Derrida as his slippery anticoncepts (*déconstruction*, *différance*, *pharmakon*, *hymen*, *marge*, *supplément*, etc.) enter the commodifying context of corporate culture U.S.A., the academy included.

A decidedly odd black and white, ebony and ivory Pillsbury Poppin' Fresh Doughboy augurs Derrida's domestication in the space of American academe.

Urban African American and Latino/a rap artists from the metropolises must have shared Jacques's sentiments when they saw the pudgy ultrawhite Pillsbury Doughboy rapping in prime-time television commercials late in the 1980s.[10]

Something had definitely been lost (silenced?) in the translation. So as to avoid diluting any of the theoretical sophistication we have come to expect of our cultural commentators, but at the same time open up the field of play to a greater range of players, I have in these pages assembled an unlikely grouping of costars—unwitting celebrities, really—and will bring their voices to bear on Rita Hayworth's name change.

As we consider the violence perpetrated upon the body and the psyche of Margarita Carmen Cansino, we are reminded of how the dynamics of cinema and the dynamics of self increasingly overlap in twentieth-century Western mass culture. We see again how the legendary silver screen *disseminates* particular versions of ethnicity and gender to its passive spectators, to *la cultura estadounidense*.[11]

Had Castellanos remained alive and writing, it's frightening to think (exhilarating is the better term) how the course of American (in the best sense said palabra *can be used) intellectual history might have been changed. Castellanos is every bit as theoretically adept as Irigaray and Kristeva, surveying in the 1960s terrain similar to that of the French dynamic duo that began to appear in the 1970s. She also had an eccentric and delicious wit. The dramatic horror of her death (she was electrocuted while turning on a lamp after taking a shower) is just one of those ugly events you have to get used to on this damned planet.*

Before we congratulate ourselves on the New World Order, or guzzle champagne as we celebrate the success (aesthetic?) of multiculturalism, we ought to bother to recall, along with my much-cited postcolonial *maestra*, that when "we 'remake history' only through [the] limited notion of power as *collective validation*, we might allow *ourselves to become instruments of the crisis-management of the old institutions, the old politics*" (Spivak, "Who Claims Alterity," 270; emphasis added)—in other words, *sell-out, status-quo, conservative flunkies in the guise of intellectual progressives*.

We will have to be diligent about this, and even then the outcome is uncertain.

What *can be* forwarded for the moment is the following: this comparative analysis, linking avatars of cultural critique with a manufactured Hollywood goddess, reveals a bitter, alienating matrix where Cansino becomes Hayworth, where "Mexican" or "Latina" becomes *latinesque*, and where, curiously enough, victim becomes both worshiped deity *and* commodified fetish object. Lupe Vélez had walked on these waters before Cansino/Hayworth, yet let her specter be held in reserve for the time being.

Daddy Dearest

Two citations prepare us for the story of Rita Hayworth, the story of how a fractured self goes on to become a superstar. They are recent revelations and come from the pen of Rita's (that's what I'll call her for now) latest biographer, Barbara Leaming, a good writer, Orson Welles's biographer as well, and a biographer with a penchant for armchair psychiatry.

The revelation concerns young Rita Cansino's introduction to the world and to the world of sex. We begin with Leaming quoting Eduardo Cansino, Rita's father, with a statement attributed to him upon the birth of his child: "I had wanted a boy . . . *what could I do with a girl?*"[12]

Unfortunately for Rita, Eduardo came up with a startling answer to his own question some fifteen years later, an answer Rita only revealed to

"her second husband Orson Welles." Save for Leaming, no other biographer or commentator has even hinted at it. *"What could I do with a girl?"* Leaming answers the father's question directly: "during this period her father . . . repeatedly engaged in sexual relations with her."[13]

This incestual *anointing*, this clandestine invocation of that most sordid of taboos, provides the *key* (shades of Freud's *Dora* and Nabokov's *Lolita*) to the puzzle of Hayworth's emotional volatility for Leaming, and her greatest contribution, if accurate, to Hayworth archaeology. The urge to read Rita as victim may well overwhelm us before we reach the end of the story, but there is so much more left to see and to tell, so we're just going to have to put that urge on hold.

An early publicity photo of Rita and Eduardo Cansino, aka "Daddy Dearest," reproduced from the pages of Gene Ringgold's *Films of Rita Hayworth*.

Haircuts

"Rita Hayworth gave good face."

—*Madonna (Ciccone)*[14]

"Screwed" (the verbal keynote I deployed above to characterize actions taken at Rita's expense) is a "saturated" term with references to tools, sexual practices, and acts of injustice bouncing about its semantic domain. We shall have to look about for better, more precise terms.

Again, and especially with regard to Rita Hayworth, *Rosario Castellanos's* words come to mind. Listing a gaggle of male philosophers, scientists, and know-it-alls from centuries previous, Castellanos relents and allows the terms of one Moebius to serve as emblem for Western intellectual attitudes toward women: "Moebius found women physiologically retarded."[15] Castellanos's essay establishes that this *retardation* is anything but a "natural" state; rather, it is the work of dominant cultural elements on what we can call, quite literally, a woman's *body politic*.

If one were to need further, graphic illustration of this *retardation* (manipulation, amputation, decapitation—call it what you will), the life of Rita Hayworth provides painfully eloquent testimony. Take the problem of Rita Hayworth's hairline.

Yes, hairline.

It boggles the imagination the degree to which the placement of hair-bearing follicles on the forehead of a young actress impacted the course of film history in the United States. As we will see in the next section, the bloodline and cultural lineage of Rita Cansino led to quite a debate early in her career: was she Mexican, was she Spanish, or was she a Gypsy (Orson Welles's favorite designation for her)?

But it was her hairline that initially drew the most attention and labor. This was no small issue for Rita's early handlers (Ed Judson, her first husband; Winfield Sheehan, the man who *discovered* her—echoes of Cortés, Colón, et al.—in a Tijuana nightclub; and Harry Cohn, the studio boss at Columbia), and it was resolved with the electrically charged pincers of a Hollywood electrologist. These reproductions (opposite) from Cansino/Hayworth publicity glossies capture the dimensions of Rita's *offensive-for-some*

Harry "Guapo" Cohn, Columbia Studio boss, with Rita, left.

hairline for posterity and her transformation into a more semiotically palatable Hollywood commodity.

As our eyes drift from photo to photo and back to the page, from the gorgeous low-brow swarthiness of "Rita Cansino" playing opposite her detective "Chinaman" (brilliant, but still, really, a "coolie" in a White Suit[16]), to the almost-Aryan ideal excess of her post–World War II, post-baby glossy shot in *Motion Picture Magazine*, we might want to recall how Rita began her show business career—as her father's dance partner in nightclubs (some posh, some not) in northern Mexico and southern California. There, apparently, Rita's father worked to *accentuate* her "Latina" looks for her captive Tijuana audiences—too much, *way* too much, so it

Pre-electrolysis. Portraits of Rita Cansino before electrolysis and before the name change in 1935. The poster promoted *Charlie Chan in Egypt* (1935) from the Fox Film Corporation, directed by Louis King and starring Warner Oland. These detailed, minimally enhanced scans derive from an original movie poster from the personal collection of the author.

Post-electrolysis. Pictured here at the height of her stardom, post-pincers, is Rita Hayworth in all her *electrolytic* existential glory. The first image, of Rita in full *Lady from Shanghai* mode, is from a circa 1947 issue of *Silver Screen* that I lost out on in an eBay bid. The second image, of Rita with her daughter, Rebecca Welles, by way of Orson Welles, is from a January 1946 issue of *Motion Picture Magazine*.

appears, for her future boss, the formidable Mr. Cohn at Columbia. For that reason, it was suggested and then decided by the studio that Rita needed a haircut and a tint.

The ironies here abound. For the moment, consider this: an American girl, both Irish and "Gypsy," becomes a local celebrity in Tijuana, Mexico, partly because her incestuous-sex-loving father has dyed her hair black to appear more, here it comes, more "Mexican"—there in TJ, however, she is *discovered* by Hollywood moguls and their assistants and she is shipped north to Tinseltown, where she looks *way too* "Mexican."

Holy Pinocchio, Batman.

We find ourselves in a hallucinatory whirlwind of representational paradoxes—a veritable wet dream of ethnic simulation and dissimulation. Again, however, we are getting ahead of ourselves.

After all, there is nothing particularly objectifying, "amputating," or alienating about getting a haircut, but Rita's was of a special nature. Ed Judson, Rita's aforementioned first husband, and Helen Hunt, Rita's hair master at Columbia, conspired to "Americanize" Rita by performing electrolysis on her forehead—this apparently would serve to de-Mexicanize the would-be mestiza features of Rita Cansino.[17]

John Kobal, citing extensively from a letter written by Hunt, details the particulars of the process: "I worked with the electrologist, drawing lines on a still picture showing the line we wanted . . . *this lasted another year until the work was finished*" (*Rita Hayworth*, 77; emphasis added). Hunt continues her narrative with great energy and excitement—but before I cut to the Hunt quote, picture here Pygmalion and Geppetto sharing a martini, grinning; one wonders whether it is a woman or the raw materials of a taxidermist being discussed—now, cue Hunt: "achieving a new design for Rita's forehead entailed a long and very painful process. Each hair had to be removed individually, then the follicle deadened with a charge of electricity" (77).

In the creation of this Tex[t]-Mex movie star, in the transmutation of "Margarita Carmen Cansino" to "Rita Hayworth," we witness an example, in the flesh, of our aforementioned coconspirator Jean Baudrillard's familiar scribbled flourishes, those places where he struts his proto-SimCity knowledge: "Simulation is the generation by models of a real without origin or reality: a hyperreal." But he's not done; he then reminds us how this hyperreality is "the product of an irradiating synthesis of combinatory models in a hyperspace without atmosphere" ("Precession," 23). For the purposes of our Tex[t]-Mex exposé, the "real without origin" may well be the term "American" implicit in Kobal's term "Americanize." Post–*Happy Days* Ron Howard notwithstanding, what, after all, is particularly "American" about a large forehead?—even Sir Francis Galton, the father of eugenics, might find that one hard to swallow. One would be hard-pressed to discover the origin of this aesthetic/cosmetic ideal, though I am sure SS clinical archives would provide a host of ever-so-useful guides.

Rita wasn't thrilled with the year-long ordeal and, according to Leaming, "desperately wanted to avoid the agonizing treatments" (*If This Was Happiness*, 41). But she needed this electricity-charged regime as part of her transmutation from *Mexicanesque* dancing girl/incest victim to American Hollywood Star—*so* "American" that her image graced the first atomic bomb (she wasn't too thrilled about this *honor* either).

Curiously or predictably (your pick), Cansino/Hayworth's biographers often reenact the roles of her hair-plucking handlers. Kobal, writing about critical disregard of her early films, notes that in "these little known films . . . her work is usually written off because of her hairline" (65)—critics as well as studio bosses, husbands, and hairstylists seem to find something wrong with the young actress's hairdo.

Pity the "pure" Mexican starlet looking for jobs in Hollywood, California, with the wrong acreage of forehead. Some years after Cansino's *erasive* encounters with these hairkeepers-from-hell, Frantz Fanon chronicled the psychological fractures accompanying similar processes in *Black Skin, White Masks*, where, describing the "inferiority complex of the black man," he notes the "internalization—or, better, the epidermiliza-

tion—of . . . inferiority" (11). Altering the terms but not the spirit of Fanon's findings so as to better understand the trials of Rita Hayworth, we might speak of a "defollicization," a dehairing, of difference that blanches perceived defects. The physical operation is different; the psychological result is the same. And it is permanent—no existential Brazilian wax, electrolysis is forever.

Rita's hairline, her hair in general, was not just an issue of taste with regard to fashionable and unfashionable ethnic traits; it was, of course, a matter of money—capital and ethnicity have always shared structurally significant positions in that transparent matrix called ideology. Rita, after all, was an investment of great consequence for Columbia Studios—as Leaming so pithily puts it, "It wasn't just hair, it was a studio asset, a valu-

A none-too-delicately augmented screen grab from *The Lady from Shanghai* highlights the haircut that drove Harry Cohn through the roof. Early in her career, like some monstrous revision of *Rapunzel*, Rita Hayworth's life crises seemed always to revolve around her follicles.

able piece of property" (*If This Was Happiness*, 135). No shock, then, to read of Columbia president Harry Cohn's howling reaction to Orson Welles's cutting and tinting of Rita's hair for her role in *The Lady from Shanghai* some years later. Cohn: "Oh my God! What has that bastard done."[18]

The studio was to make much of Rita's transformation, and many were led to believe that "like some latter-day Athena, Rita had sprung fully formed from the head of a Zeus-like Harry Cohn" (Kobal, *Rita Haworth*, 59).[19] This is objectification in its vulgar form, and it is good for spectators and critical theorists alike to see it as such. Cohn, Hunt, Judson, and others are players in a horrific drama—Rosario Castellanos serves as our fetching, aspiring applicant for the role of dramaturge: "The antithesis of Pygmalion, man does not aspire, by means of beauty, to convert a statue into a living being, but rather a living being into a statue" ("Woman and Her Image," 239). And she gets the job—I am tempted to make her the queen of Tex[t]-Mex, I have learned so much from her writings. For here, via minimal extrapolation, Castellanos pinpoints for us the dynamics of a mass-reproducible statue, produced with *great profit* accruing to the sculptor—in this case, Cohn and Columbia Studios.

These are not, let me repeat, *hard-to-understand concepts of high theory*. Rita's ne'er-do-well first husband, the inimitable "pimp" (as Welles called the dastardly Ed Judson), appreciated the investment his "sculpting" of Rita represented. When confronted with Rita's reasonable request for separation, he threatened to "toss acid in her face" and, in doing so, hoped to destroy the product he felt he had helped fabricate (Leaming, *If This Was Happiness*, 64).[20]

Watching Rita's films again recently in preparation for this investigation, I was brought back time and again to Castellanos's excellent description of the way patriarchy retards collectively and individually the psyches and the bodies of figures folded into the term *woman*: "In the course of history . . . woman has been a myth . . . and the cumulative myth-making process manages to conceal its inventions with such opaque density, insert them so deep in the recesses of consciousness and at such remote strata of the past, that it obstructs straightforward observation of the object, or a direct knowledge of the being that has been replaced and usurped" ("Woman and Her Image," 236). Castellanos's words here provide a spur of sorts, for if woman is myth, and cinema is the site extraordinaire of twentieth-century Western myth production, then the body of events shaping the intriguing story of Margarita Rita Carmen Dolores Cansino Judson Hayworth Welles et al. may well provide us with a working model to better define a late-twentieth-century paradigm shift: a move from the inwardly introspective (the existential) to the outwardly spectatorial (the ocular)—an ocular economy of the self by and large determined by advances in image technology.

Our internalization of a Hollywood-fashioned "Self," our collective forced and willing consumption of various "Mexican" and "Latina/o" Tex[t]-Mexes, makes public our ancestry as "photophilous" beings—photophilous (fo-tó-fi-lus) organisms love light, flourish in light; botanists and their ilk are apt to use the term to speak of certain plants.

But we are not speaking here of plants; here we confront the specter of an organism, *Americanus* ~~moronicus~~ *cine-sapius*, who does not himself or herself thrive or burgeon in the shining light of the silver screen, but whose optically borne pathologies, especially those prone to the seductive hallucinations of stereotypes, multiply exponentially after these serially imbibed (through the eyes) potions, these tasty, visual concoctions.

The movies. And, all too often, we are willing, chained slaves to the shadows dancing on the pretty, shiny wall—shut up, don't think, and pass the popcorn.

The result of Hayworth's hairline renewal, her "subject-effect" manipulation, was that she began to internalize the divide between her living and her cinematic self. So it is that Leaming speaks of "the familiar 'Rita Hayworth' mask Rita was apt to wear" (*If This Was Happiness*, 100). Shifra Haran, Welles's secretary and later Hayworth's assistant, confides that "Miss Hayworth herself said she was two people . . . the star on the screen and the person" (122). Here, we might with some benefit imagine ourselves on a terrain much like that which Argentine seer Jorge Luis Borges surveyed in the oft-cited poem "Borges and I." Borges, writing on "Borges," describes how "it's to the other man, to Borges, that things happen."[21] Rita's saucy paraphrase of the testy, blind Argentine's lyric autobiography? "Men go to bed with Gilda, but wake up with me" (Leaming, *If This Was Happiness*, 122).[22]

Borges and Hayworth share an analogous space, and an unhappy one at that. Somehow, involvement with the production of narrative and the mass distribution of the same creates a special sort of alienation as *celebrity* (outside recognition/adoration) barges its way onto the scene. Rita's longtime friend, the *makeup artist* (almost *too* appropriate!) Bob Schiffer, describes the degree to which she internalized the desires of her artist/keepers: "[Rita] reflected what the men wanted. Unfortunately, that's the way she thought it should be" (Leaming, *If This Was Happiness*, 39). In short, "Rita Hayworth, gave good face," but which one it was and whose it was to give remain items ripe for additional inquiry.

If we, in the dark of the theater, reveal our tendency to ethnocentrically flourish in the harsh, sexy light of motion picture palaces, desirous addicts of *photophilous* processes, then perhaps said pleasure comes at a cost to the body providing the source of all those photons—*photolysis*, "decomposition due to the action of light," may be the price Rita had to pay for becoming a star, for fueling the delicious photophilous fires of our cinematic Tex[t]-Mex.

¿Spic?

We began with the apparently inessential: haircuts. We learned quite shortly that hair was a central issue with Rita Hayworth. Now we move to a more obviously charged arena. Anyone the least bit politically erect understands that *ethnicity* in cultural studies is a category with few peers, and given the politico-cultural history of this country, this ought not to come as a surprise.

It goes without saying, but I'll say it anyway, that the question of Rita's hairline was really a question of ethnicity. Having danced in Mexico and thus been Mexican identified, Rita Hayworth was too "Mexican" for her investor/handler Harry Cohn—how could he pour money into her when, in his own words, "Latin [*sic*] types are out" (Leaming, *If This Was Happiness*, 34). It was not only the general public that apparently feared the monstrous presence of Cansino's "Latin[a]" visage gracing the contours of the silver screen; critics (surprised at Hayworth's meteoric rise) also harbored latent Latina-phobic tendencies. In this regard, Gene Ringgold speaks condescendingly of "the creation of Rita Hayworth from *the unlikely foundation* of one Marguerita Carmen Cansino" (11; emphasis added).

Not only critics are to blame. Fanzines and popular rags contemporary with the *electrolysized statuette* did their bit to play up the unlikely rise of Rita Hayworth-born-Cansino. These sources depict her as the *pièce de résistance* of a "Hollywood know-how that could transform just another dirty-faced Mexican kid into an all-American dream" (Kobal, *Rita Hayworth*, 50). And pre-electrolysis, if we are to believe *the published record* (and Paredes's words above should have cured us of that), "she certainly looked Mexican," with most maintaining that "the Mexican look was good for the [Tijuana dance] act [with her father]."[23] The critics and biographers all make some mention of her apparent Mexicanicity, with even Leaming chiming in that Cansino "passed for a Mexican" (*If This Was Happiness*, 26).

Rita's breeding becomes a topic for extended discussion and conjecture in many of these biographies—Morella and Epstein are particularly scrupulous, evincing a dedication that would have made our eugenics poster child Josef Mengele proud. Readers of *Rita: The Life of Rita Hayworth* know from the first sentence of the book that Cansino's parents were "well-bred": Volga Hayworth, her mother, had stalwart, upstanding Pilgrims and Irish-born luminaries *stocking* her genetic closet, and Eduardo, equally "well-bred," was the son of entertainers from Madrid (13–14). Other biographers are not quite so sure of this purity of lineage; Leaming casts doubts on Eduardo's claim to a gloried bloodline: "Although in America Eduardo liked to claim his father was descended from the Moorish kings of Granada, in Spain, others called [his father, Antonio Cansino, nicknamed "Padre,"] a Gypsy" (*If This Was Happiness*, 2).[24]

I'll conclude these notes on Rita Hayworth's ethnicity by following up on this last piece of Leamingian speculation: not everyone was sure that Cansino was indeed Latina, or even Spanish for that matter. Conjecture abounds that she was, in fact, part or all Gypsy. So it is that Hermes Pan, Rita's choreographer, whispers to Leaming that "she always reminded me of a Gypsy" (*If This Was Happiness*, 55); Jack Cole, yet another choreographer, echoes these sentiments, concluding: "She was just a dancing Gypsy girl who would have been very happy working in a chorus happily married" (Kobal, *Rita Hayworth*, 183). Biographer Leaming herself seems moved by the testimony attributing a "dark Gypsy pessimism" to the young star (*If This Was Happiness*, 81). Leaming's views seem particularly informed by her close friendship with Hayworth's second husband, Orson Welles, and it is worth noting that she came to Rita via Welles, having first written a biography of the "mighty Orson"— I can just picture Leaming and the aging Welles, holding forth after a couple glasses of Pinot Noir at Ma Maison.

Welles, never short of words on any topic, speaks endlessly of Rita's "Gypsy blood" (Leaming, *Orson Welles*, 80). When moved to describe Rita's growing neuroses during the course of their marriage, Welles goes to familiar ground, offering up the following confession, which I repeat here from the *Touch of Evil* chapter you just finished reading: "I wasn't smart enough to know [she] was neurotic. I just thought it was Gypsy and I said, 'This is that Gypsy kick and I've got to cure her of that'"(85).

Rita Cansino as an exotic Argentine "Gypsy" in *Under the Pampas Moon* (1935).

This catalogue of Gypsy-centered commentaries concludes with Rita's friend Ann Miller's description of an older, more volatile Rita Hayworth, a woman who reflects the psychological impact *statuification* (to adapt Castellanos's statement above) had on the star. Miller: "[Rita] was really . . . a dual personality . . . [she] was a very shy person. But when she drank, *out came this spittin' Gypsy*" (Leaming, *If This Was Happiness*, 334; emphasis added). In the end, husbands, lovers, secretaries, hairdressers, fans, and critics alike all seem to have focused their energies on ferreting out the ethnicity of this particular star—me included.

Gypsy, Spaniard, Irish, English, or Mexican? Let's allow Cansino/ Ha[y]worth to mouth the last speaking part of this section via Ringgold's recorder. Noting the ironies of the first time her form inflected the silver screen in a "Spanish-language . . . Columbia quota quickie film" made in Mexico by director Fernando de Fuentes, Hayworth never stopped getting a charge out of alluding to this film and the fact that de Fuentes assumed she was, in her own words, "just another dirty-faced Mexican kid."

Name[s]

But where do we go from here? To what use can we put this mildly entertaining, certainly disturbing information about a star from yesteryear? What is our context? Our aim?

One of the things I want to do is unravel the fabric binding ethnicity, celebrity, and show business, and I want to do this in that rarified well-armored quadrant called *theory*, with specific emphasis on what more and more people call cultural studies.

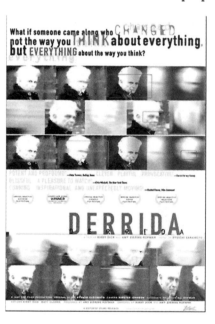

This is serious business, but the last thing I want to be is too serious.

So many self-proclaimed theory-heads (those comfortable using the word "deconstructionism" (*sic*) in mixed company) are all too serious. This is somewhat puzzling. All one has to do is read Derrida's *Limited Inc.* to understand the very real seriousness of taking yourself too seriously. And the late, great Derrida himself knew how to have fun (without electrolysis)—all you have to do is rent the DVD of Kirby Dick and Amy Ziering Kofman's (2003) *Derrida* documentary masterpiece to get a feel for his clever, mischievous play and his playful, clever philosophical mischief.

This is why our focus, though ostensibly that of ethnicity and manipulated bodies politic, also uses materials with which the reprehensibly conservative Mary Hart of *Entertainment Tonight* fame would herself be comfortable. For although the masses are not comfortable with the verbose, highfalutin armaments of poststructural critical theory, they are, for the most part, at home with movies. DVD sales and rental receipts provide material testimony in support of this position.

So how will we now use Rita Hayworth? For now, we continue by talking about her name. And, perhaps, we will also use the history of her particular *patronymic/matronymic* manipulation; in doing so, we might arrive at a lexicon that would somehow successfully unpack the political and existential issues at stake in her renaming.

This is not a simple task, but neither is it at all hopeless, as, returning to the pages of Derrida's *Limited Inc.*, I have found a statement that prepares us for the job at hand. Cue Derrida: "The structure of the area in which we are operating here calls for a strategy that is complex and tortuous, involuted and *full of artifice*: For example, *exploiting the target against itself by discovering it at times to be the 'basis' of an operation directed against it; or even 'discovering in it' the cryptic reserve of some-*

thing utterly different" (55; emphasis added). I love that last part—finding the "cryptic reserve of something utterly different" in the target of hermeneutic ramblings. It is exactly what happened with Speedy Gonzales, as will unfold in the chapter that soon follows, exactly what happened with *Touch of Evil*, where I began with a vendetta to out Welles's racism and ended up finding one of the first "Chicano mestizo" filmmakers of the twentieth century.

Back to Rita. If we allow a figurative gloss of Derrida's words and apply said interpretation to what has preceded, we find a version, a summary, or an echo here of Rita Hayworth "herself."

Derrida describes Hayworth's body, her psyche, and yes, her utility—for in the end, even cultural commentators are mercenary, though perhaps not so bad as those Spivak calls our enemy outside the academy, "the real racists."[25]

In the story of Rita Cansino, in the play enacted upon her body, one does find a "cryptic reserve of something utterly *different*," a semantic residue with which to mildly assault the culture industry that did her damage even as it profited gloriously from its actions.

Given that we are about to discuss the renaming of Margarita Carmen Cansino, it is no little accident that I have prefaced these proceedings with Derrida's *Limited Inc.*—a delicious diatribe that shows just how *real* a subject's investment in his or her signature can really be. In this instructive text, Jacques, the European/North African guru *mestizo* (the Algerian Jew living the dialectic Albert Memmi captured in *The Colonizer and the Colonized*), plays Virgil to our Dante: "No signature is possible without recourse at least implicitly to the law, the test of authentication is part of the very structure of the signature" (Derrida, *Limited Inc.*, 133).

That is, we can discover in the various events surrounding the renaming of Rita Cansino and the alteration of her signature/self laws governing the manufacture of the relative value of various individuals and communities in the United States of America (circa 1940–1950)—especially with regard to the relative value of Latina and Latino citizen/subjects. These peculiarities of naming, along with the pleasures and pathologies that come with "Mexicans" trying to *pass*, continue into the present, as the postscripts appended at the end of this chapter succinctly attest.

So what *is* the history of Rita's name? At birth, October 17, 1918, she was named Margarita Carmen Dolores Cansino. Later, when she *passed for/served as* father Eduardo's wife in Tijuana nightclubs, she was billed as "Marguerite Cansino," perhaps so as to add an "exotic" Frenchness to the name—anyone publishing in critical theory knows the value of a Gallic bon mot here and there.

Oui?

¿Cómo que no?

Later, 20th Century Fox production chief Winfield Sheehan *discovered*

Rita in one of those aforementioned nightspots, and he shortened her name. Morella and Epstein re-create this scene: "The next step [for Rita] was a new identity. Margarita Cansino is too long a name for the marquees, decreed Sheehan . . . [so] *Rita Cansino was born*" (*Rita*, 25; emphasis added). But they were not done with her yet. Despite the fact that Rita's new name fit on the marquees of film houses across the country, there was still room for improvement.

Enter Columbia bossman Harry Cohn.

Cohn, as was noted above, had a ready eye on the bottom line (not to mention the marshaled desires of his Columbia motion picture consumers) and was not at all content with Rita's new name. Leaming provides a somewhat timid play-by-play: "Cohn declared that she really ought to change her name. Cansino was too . . . well . . . *Spanish* sounding" (*If This Was Happiness*, 36; emphasis added). I should have had the typesetter print ". . . Spanish" [*(sic)*, Anglo Southern California code/patois for "Mesican"].

Morella and Epstein's version of the event seems more representative of Cohn's *wit*—Cohn: "She sounds too Mexican" (*Rita*, 25). It is at this very moment that soon-to-be ex-husband (he of the tossed acid) Ed Judson pipes in something to the effect of "how about her mother's maiden name, Haworth." Cohn grumbles, says add a *y* so the spelling will match the pronunciation—don't want to confuse the ticket buyer—and the now-familiar refrain appears again, slightly altered: "*Rita Hayworth was born*" (34; emphasis added).

Having reviewed this curious history—where the mother's maiden name, Haworth, elides the patronymic, the incest-laced patronymics of Cansino—it seems the right moment to return to the theoretical informant who penned *Limited Inc.*, our beloved Jacques, whose own intimate and complex relationship with his mother is more than intriguing—sample *Memoirs of the Blind*, and *Jacques Derrida*, written with Geoffrey Bennington, if you have your doubts.

Derrida's skewering of John Searle is one of the more eloquent public spankings of an intellectual colleague to be seen since the Encyclopedists drew quill-and-ink swords. Throughout *Limited Inc.*, Derrida defends himself from Searle's would-be assaults on the French philosopher's reading of J. L. Austin. One of Derrida's wittier moves, and critically devastating at the same time, is to rename Searle as Sarl, an acronym for *société à responsabilité limitée*. When Derrida intones at one point that he "hope[s] that the bearers of proper names will not be wounded by this technical or scientific device" (36), he is only too well aware of the rhetorical, personal, and intellectual violence he is perpetrating, calling into question not only the unity of his adversary's attack, but also the stability of the person masquerading under the copyright "© John R. Searle."

This is a terrain not limited to brilliant French innovators, nor to theorists in general—not for nothing have novelists labored in the past and in the present to expose the intersection of identity, ethnicity, and names. Chicana/o artists, living within the borderline of culturally diverse origins, are among those contemporary figures who most eloquently speak to the problem of names—as such, they add texture to our tour of all things Rita.

Sandra Cisneros is only most notable and, perhaps, most eloquent chronicler of this connection. So it is that *The House on Mango Street* monumentalizes, in an apparently minor incident, the hit-and-run death of "Geraldo no last name" (65), an undocumented worker killed after a night of dancing. The lack of a proper name underscores the pathos of this unidentified, unacknowledged victim who perishes between territories, between cultures.

Cisneros's narrator, Esperanza, a gifted young writer guiding us through her development as a young artist in urban Chicago, captures the kind of traps, the kind of limitations figured by an imposed name—especially when that name is "Latina" laced. I cite Cisneros's prose at length from the chapter tellingly entitled "My Name":

> In English, my name means hope. In Spanish, it means too many letters. It means sadness, it means waiting . . . *I would like to baptize myself under a new name, a name more like the real me, the one nobody sees.* Esperanza as Lisandra or Maritza or Zeze the X. Yes. Something like Zeze the X will do. (11; emphasis added)

Here, Esperanza dreams of changing her own name—it is not shortened for a marquee by another. Note, in addition, that Esperanza has not diminished her Latina identity; she has, if anything, accentuated its exotic eccentricity as she tries to reimagine herself as "Zeze the X."[26]

Hayworth, too, learned in her lifetime to overcome somewhat the manipulations to which she had been subject early in her career. Sensitive to the significance of names in christening corporations, and taking advantage of recent film successes like *Gilda*, Hayworth began (late in 1946) to renegotiate her contract with Cohn at Columbia, demanding from then on a share of the studio's profits. The name of the corporation she founded was Beckworth, an amalgam of her daughter's name, *Beck*y Welles, with that of Ha*worth* (without the *y* but pronounced the same), Rita's mother Volga's maiden name (Leaming, *If This Was Happiness*, 127).

Co-*escritores*

Cisneros, Derrida, Fanon, Spivak, Castellanos, and Hayworth have shown the degree to which one's everyday life, one's everyday self-perception,

and one's ethnic community may be impacted by the intrigues of something we still naïvely call show business or the "entertainment industry."
Theodor Adorno, following upon the findings of Walter Benjamin, knew
what he was talking about when he called it a "culture industry." In his
meditation on the signature, Derrida, especially, shows the way to link
the efforts of those of us who work in cultural studies with the "objects"
under our observation.

In a bit of gossip the chisme-*queen Liz Smith might have passed over, John Searle was so
annoyed by Derrida's critical response to his writings that he refused Northwestern University permission to reprint his essay "Reiterating the Differences: A Reply to Derrida" (*Glyph *2, 1977) in
their book collecting the pertinent documents of the debate. Searle, the apparent darling of some
editor at the* New York Times Book Review, *where his bitter anti-Derridean darts often appeared,
continued to harass Derrida to the bitter end. Taste this bitter pill issued from Searle's mouth in
2000: Searle: "With Derrida, you can hardly misread him, because he's so obscure. Every time you
say, 'He says so and so,' he always says, 'You misunderstood me.' But if you try to figure out the
correct interpretation, then that's not so easy. I once said this to Michel Foucault, who was more
hostile to Derrida even than I am, and Foucault said that Derrida practiced the method of* obscu-
rantisme terroriste *(terrorism of obscurantism). We were speaking French. And I said, 'What the
hell do you mean by that?' And he said, 'He writes so obscurely you can't tell what he's saying,
that's the obscurantism part, and then when you criticize him, he can always say, "You didn't
understand me; you're an idiot." That's the terrorism part.' And I like that. So I wrote an article
about Derrida. I asked Michel if it was OK if I quoted that passage, and he said yes" (from Feser
and Postrel, "Reality Principles"). I had the pleasure of personally debating Searle at an APA
(American Philosophical Association) Q & A at Berkeley, in March 1998, where I accused "Dr.
Philosophical Tool" to his face of being a stooge of the status quo, to which he sarcastically
replied in the affirmative. I thought his devoted acolytes in the crowded hotel meeting hall were
going to lynch me. Searle, though insufferable, does weave a good tale, and his disclosure of Gaul-
on-Gaul antipathies between Foucault and Derrida are blogworthy.*

For, in a very real sense, any of us who work to reveal the traces of
Cansino's legacy cosign Rita's odyssey—we are, in addition, copartici-
pants, cotravelers, and accomplices.

Derrida had uncovered a similar conspiracy in his tête-à-tête with
Searle/Sarl. "What a complicated signature" (*Limited Inc.*, 31), Derrida
says, as he determines the identities of the "investors" silenced and
masked by the apparent unity of the corporately endorsed signature
"©1977 John R. Searle." Derrida cleverly suggests, however, that this signature includes those individuals Searle thanks for prior consultations on
the merits of his writing in the first footnote of his "Reply to Derrida"—a
footnote that is appended, curiously enough, to the title, the "head" of
his article: these include one "D. Searle" and "H. Dreyfus." Things really

get tricky when Derrida confesses his own close personal and intellectual association with H. Dreyfus—meaning, implicitly at least, that Derrida is a coinvestor of sorts in Searle's (Sarl's) critical piece that allegedly attacks Jacques Derrida. Talk about a "complicated signature"!

In the same way, we (those of us with some investment in all-things-Rita) may be seen to cosign the textual space, the textual artifacts, cinematic or otherwise, bequeathed by her person. I have wagered the consequences and taken the somewhat precious move of illicitly appending her signature as coauthor of this chapter.

Short Subjects

Before I bring this extended, not-so-sordid meditation (several, actually) to a close, I would like to share some brief tidbits à la Gene Siskel (RIP) and Roger Ebert about a few of Rita's films; also included are suggestions for future critical inquiries. It being in the nature of books produced by professor-types to share topics for further inquiry, and fatigue on this project

rapidly settling in, I thought it best to open "Rita-archaeology" to the scholarly and not-so-scholarly masses. Unless otherwise attributed, factual information is culled from sources cited above (Ringgold, Morella, Leaming, Kobal); I bear responsibility for any unattributed interpretations.

A quartet of frames from *Dante's Inferno*.

Dante's Inferno

Harry Lachman, director
20th Century Fox, 1935
Philip Klein and Robert Yost, screenplay

Harry Lachman directed this splendid, orgiastic collage of a film, which marries old footage (mostly sensational nude writhings and tortuous gyrations in a splendidly sensual hell) from the first version of the film (Fox 1924) to a new storyline featuring Spencer Tracy and Claire Trevor.[27] Tracy called it "one of the worst pictures ever made." Rita's father, the aforementioned incestuously bent Eduardo, was the choreographer for the feature, and thus seventeen-year-old Rita Cansino (still *Cansino*) made her attributed screen debut as a dancer on the doomed cruise ship/"inferno" named *Paradise*.[28] Noteworthy are the representations of duplicity, of masking, that wind their way through the film—in retrospect, these augur Cansino's own lifelong problems with her own masks, literal and figural. The most memorable image of the film? Spencer Tracy as Jim

Carter (carny, cum–venture capitalist, cum-swindler), shadowed by a leering, grotesque gargoyle. The juxtaposition of the evil Carter and his statuesque twin is remarkable.

The hell sequences are kind of hot also—tumescent screen aficionados will have a ball voyeuristically touring the body-strewn landscapes from the twenties—a terrain at least as dense as the one Peter Greenaway recently rendered in *Prospero's Books*, a version of *The Tempest*, with fewer penises of course.

The striking Latin American/European distribution poster by 20th Century Fox for *La nave de satán/Dante's Inferno*, 1935.

Rita Cansino, early in her career, in a scene from *Human Cargo*.

Human Cargo

Allan Dwan, director
20th Century Fox, 1936
Doris Malloy and Jefferson Parker, screenplay

Released May 15, 1936, *Human Cargo* is a tale of illegal immigration starring Rita Cansino and set in . . . Canada! Vancouver to be specific. Allan Dwan is on board this time as director of this B movie about the United States and its borders. Rita Cansino plays an illicit border crosser by the name of Carmen Zoro—talk about an *overdetermined* name, what with the popularity of Zorro serials at the time; unfortunately, Cansino does not stay on the screen too long: "Rita dies before the climax, an illegal alien blackmailed by a smuggling ring" (Ringgold, *Films*, 68). I have not been able to track down a copy of this film, but given its storyline, I believe it might be read to some advantage with Orson Welles's bordertown classic *Touch of Evil*.

Gilda

Charles Vidor, director
Columbia Pictures, 1946
Jo Eisinger, screenplay

It all comes together here, a movie if there ever was one that symbolizes Hayworth as statue, as cinematic simulacra—this is the Hayworth vehicle that puts truth to the credo that *mutum est pictura poema*/a picture is a silent poem, as a screening of *Gilda*, bearing in mind all the circuitous wonders of Hayworth's biography, yields a rich allegorical experience. All that Gilda presents is fake (or apparently so) in this masterpiece of film noir: her name, her looks, her hairline, and lastly, in her grand would-be striptease musical number "Put the Blame on Mame," her voice—Hayworth's voice was dubbed by Anita Ellis. Directed by Charles Vidor and produced by Virginia Van Upp, *Gilda* was *the* 1946 postwar megahit—before there was Britney, before there was Madonna, before there was Bardot, before there was Monroe, there was Hayworth. And there was Lupe Vélez—but that's a sad tale to be told below.

Rita is Gilda, Glenn Ford is Johnny Farrell, and George Macready is Ballin Mundson. Set in postwar Buenos Aires, the film traces a homo-/hetero-erotic *ménage à quatre* between Ballin, Johnny, Gilda, and, in a touch that would have made Sigmund Freud bulge, Jacques Lacan fidget, and Jane Gallop smile, a concealed sword hidden in a cane—between Hank Quinlan's citizen cane in *Touch of Evil* and Ballin Mundson's cock-proxying swordcane in *Gilda*, Freudian Welles/Hayworth aficionados have a lot to think about. In *Gilda*, Glenn Ford as Johnny comments on the gender of this remarkable protagonist cane, waxing eloquently: "It's a her . . . because it looks like one thing and right in front of your eyes it becomes another thing." These loaded lines, these rich semantic stores of metaphorical magic, directly gloss/paraphrase "Rita Hayworth's" life trajectory quite nicely, albeit with an ironic twist. Talk about an anti-heteronormative gender-indeterminate phallus!

Rita Hayworth as Gilda in an uncredited publicity still from the movie of the same name.

Some memorable lines of note from the film: Johnny to his boss-man/sav-

A pair of suggestive publicity shots from *Gilda* from Gene Ringgold's camerific retrospective *The Films of Rita Hayworth*. Ringgold's commentary highlights French audiences' belief that *Gilda* was the first mainstream Hollywood film to feature a two-male, *bisexual* ménage à trois (160), which underscores the value of this more-than-a-fanzine volume.

ior Ballin: "I belong to the boss"; Ballin on Gilda: "She was born the night she met me"; Gilda to Johnny: "Good evening, Mr. Farrell, you're looking very beautiful"; Gilda, on the arm of a recent male hunk pickup she's scored to spite her lover Johnny and in the face of that self-same Johnny: "If I had been a ranch . . . they would have named me the Bar None"; Gilda, saucily: "I can never get a zipper to close. Maybe that stands for something, what do you think?"; Ballin Mundson, outing himself clearly, quite strikingly in 1946: "You'd be surprised to hear a woman sing in my house"; and lastly, Ballin and Johnny, in an exchange that gives new meaning to overdetermination:

Ballin Mundson [referring to his knife cane]: It is a most faithful and obedient friend: it is silent when I want it to be silent, but talks when I want to talk.
Johnny Farrell: Is that your idea of a friend?
Ballin Mundson: That is my idea of a friend.
Johnny Farrell: You must lead a gay life.[29]

The Lady from Shanghai

Orson Welles, director
Columbia, 1947
Orson Welles adaptation of Sherwood King novel

Rita Hayworth plays Elsa Bannister in this film directed by Orson Welles and noted briefly above. The most useful scene with regard to our ongoing Tex[t]-Mex odyssey appears at the film's climax, where Elsa, her husband (Everett Sloane as sexually inert yet deliciously lascivious Arthur Bannister), and Orson Welles (as Michael O'Hara) square off in a mirrored room at an amusement park. This gallery of images, reflec-

A quartet of screen grabs from *The Lady from Shanghai*. The movie, directed by Welles, was released June 9, 1948, by Columbia Pictures Corporation and Mercury Productions.

tions, and distortions figurally reinforces the plot of the film, filled as it is with deception, infidelity, and noirish intrigue. The scene concludes with a violent and allegorical shoot-out featuring Arthur, Elsa, and a score of mirrors, smashed and shattered on the floor—Welles as O'Hara lives to speak the movie's denouement. The stunning, visually *diastrophic* conclusion to *The Lady from Shanghai* can be placed above Rosario Castellanos's challenge to women; Castellanos's words play with the images like a conniving *supplement:* "the feat of *becoming what one is* . . . demands . . . above all, the rejection of those false images that false mirrors offer woman in the enclosed gallery where her life takes place" ("Woman and Her Image," 244). Unfortunately, Welles's film would seem to suggest that potentially self-validating moves like these (destroying false mirrors) lead to destruction for strong, singular women who dare to buck the system.

Fin

Conclusion or Follicular Denouement

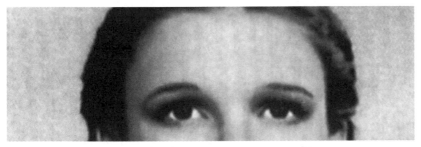

"Can you even dye my eyes to match my gown?"[30]

—Dorothy, *The Wizard of Oz* (1939).

> cause this music
> is a color struck dermatologists dream
> a hand cream
> smoove enough to soften
> this black skin white masquerade
> frantz fanonmena escapade that porcelana lovesongs
> make oppression fade away
> —Paul Beatty, "No Tag Backs"[31]

This review of the life and times of Rita Hayworth reminds us of a lesson Fanon taught with regard to Afro-Caribbean subjects and that I have appropriated here for what I have been calling the Latina body politic. Writing in *Black Skin, White Masks*, Fanon writes of the need "to teach the negro not to be the slave of their archetypes" (34).

Rita's *corpus* teaches us to do much the same thing, and in many ways her offering of wisdom was at the price of her own happiness—the same may be said to a certain extent in the case of Fanon. "I came into the world imbued with the will to find a meaning in things, my spirit filled with the desire to attain to the source of the world, and then I found I was an object in the midst of other objects" (109), Fanon writes, and his words capture the pain, the real pain that ethnic manipulation, ethnic obfuscation, perpetrates upon collectivities and individual bodies, individual selves. The photolytic powers of the seductive Tex[t]-Mex dissolve the psyche at its weakest moment, at the movies: in the dark, in a world of simulated dreams, we let our guard down and let the sexy dancing lights into the space of our Self. There it lingers, malingers, stays, puts down roots, remaking, in the process, what we speak to others of as our self.

Castellanos chronicles the risks of resisting this process as she speaks in a related fashion of women in relation to men: "The victor—who plants his heel on the cervix of the vanquished enemy—feels in each heartbeat a threat . . . in every move, an attempt to revolt" ("Woman and Her Image," 237). The threat of an ethnically indeterminate woman or (worse) an ethnically determined "Mexican" woman was observed to clearly endanger the profit potential of various studios, bosses, and handlers. This perceived threat, this subtle knowledge of and reinforcement of mainstream U.S. attitudes vis-à-vis Latinas/os, led directly to the transformation of the Brooklyn, New York–born Margarita Carmen Dolores Cansino into the tempestuous West Coast simulacra Rita Hayworth.[32]

In her later years, Hayworth, a victim of alcoholism and Alzheimer's disease, became more and more detached from the world around her, though she continued to make occasional, often scandalous and outrageous public appearances. Even these finally stopped as Cansino's waking world became less and less tethered to material, concrete realities.

Hayworth's life ends with the kind of irony humanists and poststructuralists alike love and cherish, with the sculpted simulacra ending her life in an unambiguously fictional space.

Timothy Carlson, writing Rita's obituary for the *Los Angeles Herald Exam*, described this simulated living space to his readership on May 16, 1987, the day after Hayworth died: "In 1981 [Hayworth's daughter] Princess Yasmin Khan was given permanent control of her mother's estate and [she] . . . provided round-the-clock nurses [for her mother]. Yasmin duplicated [Rita's] Manhattan apartment with the furnishings of Hayworth's Hollywood home so she would not realize she had been moved from the city where she had reigned."[33]

Carlson describes here a simulated space with a surprisingly sensual, reassuringly spiritual and altruistic aura. For Hayworth (née Cansino), all is not as it was when it began.

This time, a simulacra was created, not by the studios, but by her own daughter, woman to woman, "Latina" to "Latina," to give her soul some peace, to give Rita's tortured personage a break—some needed, loving distraction before the film on the reel broke off for the last time and the lights went up in the house.

1991 Postscript: Rita's Story Hasn't Ended

A few days before I missed the original deadline for the first incarnation of this chapter, I ran across the following item in the San Diego County edition of the *Los Angeles Times*. The byline was by Robert Epstein under the title: "Latino Actor Writes Open Letter to Hollywood—Is It All in a Name?"[34] Epstein tells the story of one Gary Cervantes, who "paid $1200 for a full-page advertisement in . . . *Daily Variety* to tell casting agents, directors, producers and story editors that the person known as Carlos Cervantes for the past nine years and one hundred roles was no more. It will be Gary Cervantes again. Carlos is no more." There are some memorable lines in the piece, especially resonant in the wake of our Rita revelations. "I was," "Gary" confesses, "a Mexican *Leave It to Beaver*." Epstein finishes the clause for the chameleon/actor, "but there were few roles for Beaver Cleaver Cervantes and when he tried for Latino roles, he was told he didn't look 'Mexican enough.'"

Gary/Carlos ends his ad with the following sign-off: "I am reminded daily by Hollywood that I am Latino, and I am labeled Hispanic out of convenience. But I am an American. [signed] Gary Cervantes."

A snapshot from Gary Cervantes's Internet Movie Database (IMDB) listings.

1995 Postscript to the Postscript

Like anyone these days, I rent motion pictures at the corner video outlet. And there I chanced upon "American" Gary Cervantes's latest motion picture role—Gary, né Carlos, plays the swarthy Latino Rolex-watch thief who obliterates pale Steve Martin's leg via gunshot in Lawrence Kasden's otherwise moving *Grand Canyon* (20th Century Fox, 1991). At least they let him grow his hair out for the role.

2005 Postscript to the Postscript to the Postscript

"Gary"'s career is getting increasingly complex.

Postscript Las Vegas

I am at the heralded and boisterous House of Blues at Mandalay Bay in Las Vegas with Michael Harper, whose friend "Jeff," an LA radio-exec has greased us onto the guest/schmooze list (*¡cerveza gratis!*) for a Cinco de Mayo celebration. There I am introduced by a mutual friend to Brooke, a former Los Angeles Raiderette cheerleader, current Miller Lite Girl, and

B-level soft-porn celebrity. After food and drinks, I am privy to the sad tale of Olga Morales, now "Brooke" of Brooke.com (dead site) and SimplyBrooke.com (also dead)—there remains a trace of a career at castingyou.com/brooke-morales.

Brooke, aka Olga, takes me with her down memory lane and tells of a young teenager Olga Morales growing up in Agoura Hills, California, a bubbly teenager who had fallen hard for a cute Anglo hunk in the neighborhood. Upon hearing the name "Olga," said SoCal hunk broke into laughter.

The *why* of this Anglo troglodyte reaction is left to students of Henri Bergson's *Laughter*, readers of Freud's *Wit and Its Relation to the Unconscious*, and patient researchers of Southern California anti-Mexican sentiments.

O̶l̶g̶a̶ "Brooke" Morales on the sidelines, from her days as a Los Angeles Raiders cheerleader, circa 1992.

The short of it was that this sensitive and beautiful young model, winner of the Miss Hawaiian Tropic Pageant at the age of seventeen, changed her name to Brooke, forever.

Today Brooke goes by the name of Brooke Morales—her beautiful "Olga" decapitated with the precision of an electrologist's pincers. You can see this renamed mannequin traipsing around sets in various states of undress in *Penthouse Love Stories* (1986), *Reform School Girls* (1986), and *Score with Chicks* (1994).

Somewhere in her celluloid Alzheimer's-fed simulacra, Rita Cansino laughs, cries, or screams.

CHAPTER 3
AUTOPSY OF A RAT

Sundry Parables of Warner Brothers Studios, Jewish American Animators, Speedy Gonzales, Freddy López, and Other Chicano/Latino Marionettes Prancing about Our First World Visual Emporium; Parable Cameos by Jacques Derrida; and, a Dirty Joke

Once Upon a Time

We need, right now, a time tunnel, some high-tech, envaginated corridor, to enter the next dimension of our Tex[t]-Mex—something to transport us back to the 1960s, when your gentle author's synapses were being filled with vast arrays of delicious and decadent animated "Mexicans." What's more, we'll need to use this enabling portal to move forward again, something to hurtle us back to 1990 and a signature holiday special.

A photograph of *Time Tunnel* memorabilia buttons that I purchased on eBay in late summer 2005, when this book was in its final preparation for press.

I loved Irwin Allen's Time Tunnel *as a kid growing up—yes, that Irwin Allen, the schlockmeister producer of* Voyage to the Bottom of the Sea, The Towering Inferno, *and* The Poseidon Adventure. *In the 1960s and 1970s, when I was not reading DC Comics or channeling MAD Magazine, I was watching TV all the time with my sister Josie—she's a sound editor, a postproduction ADR (Automated Dialogue Replacement) specialist, in Hollywood of all places! My sister, Tejana, Chicana, and a true agent of the silver screen monsters, the motion picture engines, that vomit the Tex[t]-Mex fertilized ova from screen to television, from the Internet to your local magazine stands. But I forgive her!*

Time Tunnel was one of disaster maven Irwin Allen's television triumphs: the chance to move through time using a supercool tunnel—it presaged my love for the slippery, cloaked corridors of Borges, Pynchon, Varo, and Derrida. So let's pretend. It is crucial that we do—dynamically pretend, play with the glee and rigor of a premad Nietzsche, pretend and remember. . . .

* * *

Mexicans move as naturally and comfortably in the dark as cats or wolves or owls do. . . . Mexicans get drunk and sing like cats beneath the moon.[1]

Richard Rodriguez takes a stab at ethnography in *Days of Obligation: An Argument with My Mexican Father*.

There was something about him, Harry, that amused me. He was such a monster.

Oscar Wilde's vain, sexually adept protagonist anticipates Richard Rodriguez's anthropological acuity in *The Picture of Dorian Gray*.[2]

I am not prejudiced, but I think he is part troll.

A somewhat tolerant elf holds forth from Santa Claus's North Pole enclave in Paul Fusco and Bernie Brillstein's *A Very Retail Christmas*.[3]

Tanquam in speculum/as in a mirror: A screen grab from *Alf* episode 49, wherein Alf gets a ventriloquist's dummy—the marionette gets a dummy! Again, the shade of Borges smiles at this televised revision of his "Circular Ruins" and we have to smile through our tears.

Incision One | Skeletons in the [Refrigerated Coroner's] Closet; or, Rudolph the Red-Nosed Reindeer Is Not the Only One with a Manifestly Odd Genetic Fingerprint

It is Christmas 1990 and U.S. citizens, resident aliens, and immigrant visitors from Peoria to Cotulla, from Ithaca to Oxnard, and from Laredo to Panama City are in the mood for mindless holiday entertainment, some colorful and delectable mélange of the predictable served up in heaping doses.

Enter television. Those not quaffing eggnog, caroling off-key holiday melodies, or covetously seeking mistletoe are likely to be watching TV. The lucky ones are tuned to NBC on December 24, 1990, and are watching a yuletime special called *A Very Retail Christmas*, a clever updating of the Santa Claus story produced by Paul Fusco and Bernard ("Bernie") Brillstein—the cinematography was by David Callaway, with Fusco doing most if not all of the puppet designs.[4]

An augural aside: Fusco and Brillstein are the Hollywood dynamic duo best remembered for an exotic, somewhat popular situation comedy called *Alf*, which played several years in the eighties.

If you have chanced to wash the memory of this program from your overtaxed synapses, it is enough to recall that *Alf* featured a loud-mouthed, furry, outer-space "alien" who invades the life of a typically pale, TV sitcom family—picture a testosterone-enhanced, cynical ET with Brooklyn attitude and you get the picture.[5]

Back to our story. *A Very Retail Christmas* chronicles a corporate struggle, a mercantile war, between Santa Claus, with his merry group of look-alike elves, and a rapacious multinational toy corporation CEO, with his den of "suits," lackeys, and trolls (yes, *trolls!*). Producers Fusco and Brillstein should be commended for producing their Christmas parable, applauded for their adroit revision of Santa—the classic tale of Old Saint Nick reimagined as an ironic parody of the mercenary go-go 1980s.

For this Christmas epic is more a tale of mergers and acquisitions than a chronicle of a cheery fat man's altruism, more like a Dickensian (*Hard Times*) allegory of "filthy lucre" set in the frosty North Pole. A portly, benevolent feudal despot (Santa Claus) squares off against the evil embodiment of late capital (the CEO). Ironically enough, even as we live, breathe, and are sustained by global capital, it is expected that we viewers will nostalgically ally our sensibilities with the besieged, jolly, fat, feudal chieftain, and we thoughtlessly do so.

I know I did.

The CEO is played with William Shatner–like restraint (that is, no restraint) by Ed O'Neill, who played the "funny" misogynist-cum-shoe-salesman named Al Bundy (one part Willy Loman, one part Norman Mailer, one part Larry Flynt) from the Fox Network's late, lamented, vulgar comedy *Married . . . with Children*.

O'Neill is one of the few live actors on the program, as the rest of the players are marionettes (as was Alf): intricately designed, Muppet-like anima-

Unctuous Al Bundy, played by Ed O'Neill, one of the main actors in *A Very Retail Christmas*, seen here in a screen grab from a Swiss fan Web site. This grab, I might add, is from an episode of *Married . . . with Children* entitled "Wabbit Season," episode 508, wherein Bundy apes Bugs Bunny—not unimportant to what will unfold in the present chapter.

trons made of felt, rubber, control wires, and synthetic hair, with a group of skilled puppeteers somewhere above and beneath the scenes moving them about. Here, let us pause. Momentarily allow an image of the cave from Plato's *Republic* (Book VII) to play upon the viewscreen of your consciousness: shadows, fire, puppets, and clueless chained voyeurs—all figure in the arguments that follow.

And as the recollection of that peculiar platonic precursor to motion pictures dances across your synapses, let us span a couple millennia so as to append this caution culled from Gilles Deleuze and Felix Guattari's *On the Line*: "[As with] rhizome[s], puppet strings . . . do not run back to the assumed will of an artist or puppeteer, but to the multiplicity of nerve fibers that form in their turn another puppet following other dimensions connected to the first."[6] Somewhat chastened (*verbum sapienti sat est*), let us put Deleuze and Guattari's enigmatic emendation to one side and return to *A Very Retail Christmas*.

Our aforementioned CEO wants to monopolize the production of toys, profiting handsomely while dictating the entertainment consumption of children. So he cooks up a scheme to get Santa out of the way, palming off his company's line of ultraviolent wares (mostly military-theme war toys) in the process. Fusco and Brillstein's satiric allegorization of corporate development (with no little attention paid to the influence of the military-industrial complex) is to be applauded by progressive critics everywhere—and on NBC no less!

The world's largest arms manufacturer flexes its ironic muscle in this circa 1995 Web advertisement banner.

When not packaging excellent sitcoms (*Seinfeld*, *Frazier*) and insipid news broadcasts (*NBC Nightly News with Tom Brokaw*, which—some would argue—itself featured, until his recent retirement, a state-of-the-art animatron), the "Peacock" Network is nothing more and nothing less than a public relations front for its parent company, General Electric, one of the United States's largest military contractors: "We bring good things to life," indeed!—the irony of their corporate self-presentation is almost too much to stomach.[7]

But let us not chase after another aside, as it is not the corporate/military-industrial allegory that concerns us here in this chapter—or, better put, taking Jane Gallop's words out of her lovely mouth, that particular allegory *aborde* (come[s] to, enter[s] upon, approach[es], accost[s]) the main events of this chapter.[8]

It is another allegory toward which we now move, one plainly visible in what Cuban theorist Severo Sarduy called "the oscillating frontier of the flickering screen."[9] For in order to get rid of Santa, our scheming CEO (one part Adam Smith, one part Hobbes, one part Donald Trump, and one part Leona Helmsley) looks around for a mole to penetrate Santa's North Pole estate—a cagey, spy/saboteur whose mission will be to gum up the works *chez* Santa *central*.

It is all very 1980s; one half expects Ivan Boesky and Ronald Reagan to make cameos.

Santa's North Pole enclave is a hard nut to crack. Taxed by the challenge of identifying a capable infiltrator, our barbarous CEO comes upon a *swarthy* "troll" who is able to mix in unnoticed amongst the lot of cheery, singing elves at Santa's toy shop. The plot turns on a coincidence of *appearance*: the same size and build of his fantasy-tale cousins, our as-yet-unnamed troll *passes* for an elf. This troll, however, is not *pure* troll. He is only "*half*-troll": one part elf, one part troll to be exact. A singularly shaped puppet on the screen, our miscegenated protagonist has features that are quite clearly exaggerated: a half-breed puppet.[10] Of course, this ought not to shock us too much; nothing is ever very subtle in the physiognomy of puppets: Barney is no Olivier.

Our soon-to-be-named elf/troll has a huge nose, an ugly scary scowl,

acting!

a low brow, a scraggly beard, and a funny accent—perhaps "funny" isn't quite the word; "placeable," "identifiable," or "symptomatic" are closer to the sense I want to convey. He is, in short, to paraphrase Wilde's beautiful *bon vivant* Dorian Gray, "[an] amus[ing] monster."[11]

Were this not the late-twentieth-century United States of America but 1930–1940 Central Europe, we would not be surprised to see the likes of Dr. Joseph Goebbels authorizing the use of similar puppets for Third Reich anti-Semitic children's shows.

But we *are* in the United States, not in Nazi Germany. Specifically, we are in California, where *A Very Retail Christmas* was produced and staged.

Many Mexicans are in evidence: some documented, others not.

And by now you must have a sense of where all this is going. The name of this philandering, two-faced, two-skinned (both elf and troll) operative? The imp with the temerity to threaten Santa Claus? The mestizo who would depose our benevolent, bearded, white-haired yuletime benefactor? His name is Freddy López.

Freddy López.

Latino name, Latino physiognomy: unshaved, accented, and duplicitous—Iago is his spiritual godfather, Caliban his great-uncle; Othello is somewhere there, too, given the López puppet's "skin" color. This mixed-blooded creature's shrewd, greasy evilness is palpable; he is nothing more and nothing less than a shadowy *bandido* running amok in the pristine, white, snowy confines of the North Pole.

I argued above in the *Touch of Evil* chapter that in the late twentieth century, Latino and Latina bodies in the U.S. mass media serve as vivid synecdoches for a particular and peculiar sensually charged form of evil potentiality—Freddy López adds his body (courtesy of Fusco and Brillstein) to this growing roster.

"Villains in Rehab," Guillermo Nericcio García.

Happily for all save the diminutive Mr. López, it is not long before the nefarious miscreant's plot is uncovered. In the well-rehearsed logic of the holiday-Christmas-show genre, evil can only survive till the end of the last station break: Dr. Seuss's "Grinch" undergoes a transformation that gives new meaning to the term "bipolar." An ugly Abominable Snowman, once a deformed deer's nemesis, turns a new leaf in the closing reel of *Rudolph the Red-Nosed Reindeer*, and so on.

The archetype of Santa Claus is overdue for semiotic analysis. My own interests lean toward a chronicle wherein we ponder Santa's odd resemblance in classic Western iconography to Moses, God, and (surely the oddest doppelgänger of them all) Karl Marx.

And so it is with *A Very Retail Christmas*, where the ugly, cruel Santa-hating troll with a heavy Spanish accent is rather quickly sniffed out by a coterie of pale, miscegenation-fearing elves. One elf is plainly pained by the encounter with his putative mirror other; confronting this genetic anomaly, he declares with measured disdain: "I am not prejudiced, but I think he is part troll."

I am not prejudiced, but I think he is part troll.
   The phrase is slightly haunting.

Really perturbing and curious.

Slowly, carefully, let us allow the shadow of this Latino-esque mannequin named Freddy López to follow us throughout this chapter as we review the status of animated Latina/o bodies in U.S. mass culture. It will take time for some clear thought, some focused, quiet meditation to think through the implications of Fusco and Brillstein's production. We will need all the critical imagination possible to reconcile the bifurcated, yet somehow also mediated, contours of Freddy López's body, to conclude our autopsy of this particular mestizo puppet, this jarring offspring of the Brothers Grimm and Pancho Villa, of Pinocchio and Topo Gigo, so as to move on, somehow, to the next body patiently waiting in our hermeneutic morgue.[12]

Incision Two | An Amalgamated Inquest; or, How Ethnicity and Gender Share a Common Ancestor

Ethnicity as Genre, Genre as Gender, Gender as Genus, Genus as Genital, Genital as . . .

The great subplot lurking within this chapter is tension filled. How does a comparativist trained somewhat to grapple with the complexities of ethnicity in the Americas rhetorically also convey his suspicions about the dynamics of gender politics? I need first to lay some exegetic instruments on the table.[13]

ethnic adj [ME, fr. LL *ethnicus*, fr. Gk *ethnikos* national, gentile, fr. *ethnos* nation, people] 1: neither Christian nor Jewish: HEATHEN 2: of or relating to races or large groups of people classed according to common traits and customs.

genre n [F, fr. MF, *genre* kind, gender—more at GENDER] 1: KIND, SORT 2a: paintings that depict scenes or events from everyday life . . . 2b: a distinctive type or category of literary composition. RELATED to *genus*.

genus n [L *genus* birth, race, kind—more at KIN *genera* pl] 1: a class, kind, or group marked by common characteristics or by one common characteristic; a category of biological classification ranking between the family and the species, comprising structurally or phylogenetically related species or an isolated species exhibiting unusual differentiation.

gender n [ME *gendre*, fr. MF *genre*, *gendre*, fr. L *gener*, *genus* birth, race, kind, gender—more at KIN] 1: SEX 2a: any of two or more subclasses within a grammatical class of a language (as noun, pronoun, adjective, verb) that are partly arbitrary but also partly based on distinguishable characteristics such as shape, social rank, manner of existence, or sex.

gender vb [ME *gendren*, fr. MF *gendrer*, fr. L *generare*—more at GEN-ERATE] 1. Engender.

genital adj [ME, fr. L *genitalis*, fr. *genitus*, pp. of *gignere* to beget, more at KIN 1: Generative 2: of, relating to, or being a sexual organ.

My none-too-subtle juxtaposition of loaded terms here no doubt tips my hand. I want to read the "ethnic" as a close semantic cousin of "gender"—skeletons coming out of the closet to venture a telling chiasmic pun.

The word "genre" figures as an antagonistic wild card in this Faulkner-like etymological blood allegory, establishing a genetic link between the term "gender" and the term "ethnic" while also moonlighting as a metonymic emblem for literature in particular and textuality in general. I do not have the space here to play at nomography, to author that set of laws that would sanction the methodological intersection of ethnic American theory and gender theory—we do, after all, have some cartoons to screen.

But what I do have the time and space to suggest is that it would take a feat of imagination worthy of Disney to imagine a critical context in which one would not in some way underwrite the other. Let me give you an example.

In my just-related saga of miscegenated, animatronic automaton Freddy López, an ostensibly trifling network television Christmas special leads to a heady matrix incorporating Latino stereotyping and enigmatic whispers concerning pathological anti-Semitism and the dynamics of Nazi ethnic scapegoating. This knotty nexus was revealed with the assistance of an epigraph culled from the works of no less a stand-up savant than Oscar Wilde, and it did not come easily.

It will help some to disclose that my inquiry into stereotypes has been guided by Sander Gilman's compelling work on the figuration of ethnic types—it seems reasonable to agree with Gilman that "where and how a society defines the body reflects how those in society define themselves."[14] Needless to say, a comparative analysis of Jewish stereotypes is not so far afield from those with a decidedly "Latina/o" flavor. Gilman's *Difference and Pathology: Stereotypes of Sexuality, Race, and Madness* also represents a compelling, influential trove of expository findings—the chapters "The Hottentot and the Prostitute: Toward an Iconography of Female Sexuality" and "Black Sexuality and Modern Consciousness" especially figured in the development of the present study.[15]

Not surprisingly, many provocative meditations on representation are themselves filled with scandalously racist representations. For instance, some of the best theorizations of image manipulation in the twentieth century are to be found in the insidious machinations of the Nazi war machine—both Paul Virilio and Klaus Theweleit have mined this contentious vein of history.[16]

Additionally, I believe it perfectly reasonable to read Hitler's, Mengele's, and others' obsession with Jewish physiognomy and anatomy as a subset of mid-twentieth-century German art history—*an aesthetics of difference* must always be read as a subset of a general concern for forms and symmetry, or aesthetics proper.

But our reliable, predictably vile Nazi fiends are not the only culprits.

Consider this: as much as any other theoretical source consulted in the production of this study, including Susan Sontag, Roland Barthes, Rosario Castellanos, and Severo Sarduy, it was Oscar Wilde and, in particular, his novel *The Picture of Dorian Gray* that provided me with the rhetorical/critical means of intervening on the site of Latina/o representation.

Even so, I believe it crucial to broach genial decorum and intellectual generosity to add that Wilde's glance is downright primitive when it comes to Jews in England—our modernist poster child for queer theory is also at once an anti-Semite as well as a wry, charming misogynist.

Some select examples: Dorian: "A hideous Jew, in the most amazing waistcoat I ever beheld in my life, was standing at the entrance, smoking a vile cigar. He had greasy ringlets, and an enormous diamond blazed in the centre of a soiled shirt . . . . There was something about him, Harry, that amused me. He was such a monster."[17]

In 1889, the American publisher J. M. Stoddart came to England looking for short stories for his magazine, *Lippincott's Monthly*. He invited to dinner Arthur Conan Doyle, the proper and respectable doctor who had recently created a detective called Sherlock Holmes, and Oscar Wilde, the flamboyant young "apostle of aestheticism," who was famous as much for his witty conversation and eccentric dress as for his writing. Two wildly different novels resulted from this meeting: the second Sherlock Holmes story, and the sensational story of sin and aesthetic theory, *The Picture of Dorian Gray*.

Although Wilde's lifestyle was not primarily homosexual at the time, his preoccupation with male beauty features heavily in the novel, especially in the intense and worshipful reactions of Basil Hallward and Lord Henry Wotton to the beautiful Dorian Gray.

When *Dorian Gray* was published in the magazine in June 1890, it caused a sensation, and some booksellers refused to stock it. One review complained, "Why go grubbing in muck heaps? . . . It is not made sufficiently clear that the writer does not prefer a course of unnatural iniquity to a life of cleanliness, health, and sanity." Wilde, pointing out that with few exceptions, he does not actually describe Dorian's evil deeds, replied, "Each man sees his own sin in Dorian Gray. What Dorian Gray's sins are no one knows. He who finds them has brought them." Wilde removed the more overtly homo-

Oscar Wilde in 1882.

Wilde presenting his work to a scandalized public; cover of *Lippincott's* magazine; Wilde and Lord Alfred Douglas in 1892.

THE PICTURE OF DORIAN GRAY. By OSCAR WILDE.

A leaf from a young-adult edition of Oscar Wilde's *Picture of Dorian Gray*.

A few chapters later, the same redoubtable manager is described by Wilde's narrator as "beaming from ear to ear with an oily tremulous smile . . . [Dorian Gray] *felt as if he had come to look for Miranda and had been met by Caliban*" (95; emphasis added).[18]

Given that Wilde's Jewish theater owner stands barring a portal that might give access to Dorian's heterosexual desire (Sibyl Vane) in a book by and large sustained by a gay male economics of desire, there seems to be space here to open up a critique of the dynamics of gendered desire that would not drop out issues of race and ethnicity.[19] I have only mustered an egregiously preliminary sketch of this in my juxtaposition of ethnicity, genre, genus, gender, and genitals at the head of this, the second incision. Sadly, compatriot coroner, we must move on. Our exquisite Mexicanesque corpse awaits us.

Incision Three | An Additional Delay in the Postmortem as We Examine More Instruments

Autopsies

autopsy n [Gk. *autopsia* act of seeing with one's own eyes, *aut-* + *opsis* sight, to be going to see] 1: a postmortem [L. *post mortem* after death 1: Occurring after death. Examination].

What, then, are we going to see?

An autopsy is an examination of a dead body. A true *etiological* science, it seeks to determine the origin(s) of death via empirical observation. But etymologically, "autopsy" refers also—as odd and as counterlogical as it may seem—to the act of "seeing with one's own eyes." And we must attend to this peculiar duality, for what if how we see, how we see ourselves with our "own eyes," has been affected by how others have seen "us?" What happens when our eyes consume and our psyche is tattooed by technologically sophisticated and ubiquitous versions of "us" as others have imagined or, more to the point, theatrically suggested we appear? Furthermore, imagine that these representations; these othered, othering visions; these popular because familiar, and familiar because popular images; these familiar and popular as they are profitable and caustic hallucinations spring from the minds and pens of adversaries, individuals, or descendants of individuals with whom we have been or still are at war. Plato's cave, surely, provides the setting, but with Hollywood and the Pentagon as set designers and dressers.

What, in the end, are "we" "going to see?" This would seem the best time for a visual vivisection of select, salient video—in short, it's time for an expository *autopsy*.

While other critical studies have addressed the impact of what Adorno called the "culture industry" on ethnic Americans, few have focused on Latinas/os in the United States. Those that do, with a few notable exceptions (Allen L. Woll, Arthur Pettit, Chon "not the son of Manuel" Noriega, Rosa Linda Fregoso, and Alfred Charles Richard, Jr.), have been of the coffee table variety, aiming primarily at cataloguing the glitz and glamour of Hollywood *estilo latino* (Hadley-García).[20]

I ought to confess that our exegetical enterprise is more than just a wee bit colored by psychoanalysis, especially in the way these jottings aspire to diagnose the impact of stereotypes on the collective psyche of U.S. residents of Latin American descent.[21] If I venture to use "psychoanalytic" as an adjective to define my project, I also ought to point out that it is a Lacan-inflected version of the psychoanalytic dais that I here picture: *analysand, analyst,* and methodology are caught up in a vortex of suspicious intrigue and interaction.[22]

Said disclosure brings me to a second confession with a telling caveat: your Chicano analyst is heavily invested in the subject(s) he has and will soon annotate. That having been said, let me assure you also that the intellectual desires financing this exercise have been aroused by something more, something other than the "rage of Caliban seeing his own face in the glass."[23]

Speaking of glass—here is a plate, or, at any rate, a plate of art; the journal that published the first version of this chapter allowed it to festoon the cover of the issue it appeared in. It is a gloss of all that precedes and follows in its wake.

Back to glasses—this glass is not *my* glass—the "glass" is someone else's, less a *reflecting* mirror than a *projecting* lens, or, perhaps better said, a projection that walks about in the guise of a mirror.

Are we being too careful? I think not: the detective story paradigm within which psychoanalysis flourishes mandates that even the couch is suspect.

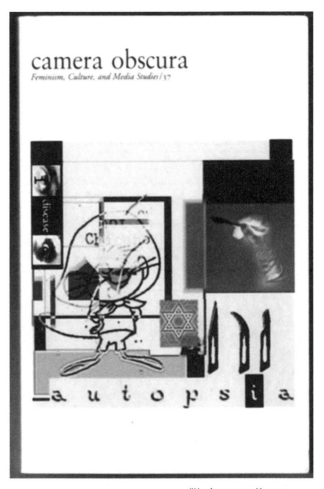

"Mexicanesque Maus or Autopsy of a Rat": the cover I designed for *Camera Obscura* 37 (1998), wherein the first incarnation of this chapter on Speedy appeared.

Stereotypes

Forgive me an indulgence with the dictionary—it seems such a pat move, but then again, etymological speculation seems one of the best ways of displacing accreted layers of murky sludge that make words seem self-evident. I will now excuse myself to the "sedilia," those special comfy chairs high priests in cavernous cathedrals use when not officiating, and give the proceedings over to my friend the dictionary—in this case, a different dictionary, that fecund, etymological trough called the *Oxford English Dictionary*. There, as we can plainly read, a stereotype is "a one-piece printing plate cast in type metal from a mold (matrix) taken of a printing surface." The term had its origin in the domain of publishing, itself an industry charged with the manufacture and dissemination of words and images.

Dissemination, semen—rising from the sedilia and leaning forward, I say: "Does it take such a stretch of the imagination to see publishing as a subset of reproduction, that is, to read stereotypes as being governed by genetic laws of reproduction?"

I return to the chair.

Pursuing etymological inquiry further, the *OED* continues: "Stereo" comes from the Greek "*stereos*": "hard," "solid," "firm," "stiff." Our eyebrows lift as we notice how "stereo" is also linked, via alleged Indo-European primogenitors, to the English verb "to stare." Publishing, engendering, hard, stiff, staring: hmmm. Which brings us to the second half of the word "stereotype": the suffix "-type." "Type" derives from the Greek word "*typos*," which means a "model," a "symbol," or, more to the point, "an archetype." Like a tease, the *OED* then quietly drops that the word is thought to derive from another Greek word, "*typtein*."

Now the inquiry reaches heights of intrigue usually only associated with pulp fiction, for that word "*typtein*," offered as an afterthought or as nonchalant speculation, has the idea of a blow, of a violent impact, of a "mark made by a blow," resonating within its semantic ancestry. In the past, this term described the physical force artisans used to craft raw materials at hand into *artifacts*. The sedilia is no longer needed, as we are now in a position to further our understanding of "stereotypes."

Look closely.

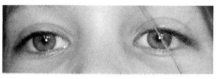

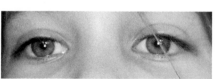

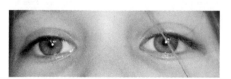

We . . . stare . . . -type.

We *stare*, and then we *type*, that is, we "write" or, better put, overwrite that which has been seen in terms of other scenes that have been received previously. Confronted by individuals or communities different from that which has already been encountered, we resort to our ready treasure trove of stereotypes.

Before I shake your hand, and say ¡*hola!* or hello, others have come before me, paving the way as it were for our introduction—imagine that you and I had never met a Mexican national or a Latino, but creatures like Freddy López and his clan *color* our rendezvous with the dynamics of the palimpsest; the Mexican is suffused by his or her animated Mexicanesque predecessor. As we saw above in the introduction, it is Menelaus greeting Telemachus in reverse, a stain on our blood that enters all spaces we enter before us.

Through this circuitous (cynics might say *dubious*) route, we have rediscovered how the hierarchy of meaning that sustains the term "stereotype" includes *physical* and *figural* violence: blows on metal (*typtein*), blows on paper (typewriting), *blows on flesh* (stereotyping).[24]

So that violence is not only an implicit result of the use of stereotypes—the emotional violence that, say, we associate with individuals who are the butt of a stereotype's *joke*.

No, *violence* is a fundamental component of this noun's genealogy. *Violence is in its blood.*

If you will forgive me the license of reading these accumulated definitions and etymologies like poems, several items come to the fore: *staring*, *printing*, *repetition*, *blows*. In these words and between the lines, we come to see how "stereotype" conceals a muddied, muddled history—a

constellation of nouns and verbs, acts and processes that provide a backdrop for our inquiry into the relative status of Latino and Latina figures in the mass cultural emporium of the United States. Having sullied our hands with the knotty, "rhizome"-like roots of the term, we are at last prepared to think through the lasting control they exert on the popular imagination.[25]

Strikethrough, elide, render, rend—but still the law of the palimpsest rules, hence my take here, "The Typed Subject."

What is more easily distributable, reproducible, and recognizable than a stereotype, and what does more violence to the possibility of dialogue between diverse communities than these grotesque caricatures, carried within the mass cultural collective imaginary, so easy to deploy when one is threatened or surprised? We have uncovered an insidiously short path between "stereotype's" material printing press origins and the vulgar ethnocentric/slur-hurling dimensions of the word in our day-to-day life in the Americas. I will end this incision with a graphic scalpel of my own making—I call it "The Typed Subject."

Whether or not we ever reveal the "real," our animated inquest must move forward—the cause of death must be ascertained, seen with our "own eyes." And we must do so if only to attune ourselves to the dynamics of disinformation in the television age. Things are getting faster, hundreds of channels looming ominously on the horizon—as I have written in another place, "image, image everywhere, and not a thought to think."[26] We need to improve our ability to critically engage with visual ideology, or we will fall victim to its logic.

There is no choice really.

In short, our critical project tags us as *ocular linguists of the syntax of visual despotism*—and I agree with the Italian American writer Robert Viscusi, who holds that "the dialect of dominance has never been, and one suspects, never can be—fully naturalized."[27] One dominating influence on this dialect is the heft (the weight and spatial density) of the symbiotic relationship our organism shares with images we foster.

In another decade, in another context, Michel Foucault chanced upon the logic of this tyranny when he spoke of "the ultimate language of madness [as] that of reason, but the language of reason enveloped in *the prestige of the image*."[28] One villain in all this intrigue is quite clear: motion pictures. Without doubt, film's rapid growth in the first part of the twentieth century changes irrevocably the way one reads the world—in particular, that part of the world called Mexico. And while this development heralded "a technical invention that gave rise to the discovery and the perfection of a new art," as Erwin Panofsky pointedly notes,[29] it also brought about a watershed moment in what might be called the History of Visual Textuality as new storytelling technologies were married to older, more traditional forms of entertainment, and older, more traditional forms of prejudice.

At the same time, these changes increased the ability of various institutions and individuals to shape the attitudes and expectations of millions, those willingly and voyeuristically surveying reality from the comfort of their seats in dark, crowded picture palaces. Velocity-sensitive French cultural cartographer Paul Virilio has seen through this particular ruse. Noting a futurist innovator by the name of Pastrone, Virilio concludes that "the [motion picture] camera's function was less to produce images (as painters and photographers had long been doing) than to manipulate and falsify dimensions."[30]

The postmortem has waited long enough, so let us turn now to the rat who sets the standard for the manipulation and falsification of *mejicanidad* on the planet.

They cannot represent themselves; they must be represented.

—Edward Said's epigraph in *Orientalism* quoting Karl Marx from *The Eighteenth Brumaire of Louie Bonaparte*

"Speedy Gonzales"

This classic Speedy montage (circa 1970) is digitally adapted from Maurice Horn's *World Encyclopedia of Comics*; on the right is the latest (1996) incarnation of Speedy as celebrity front man for the Frito-Lay corporation. Given Frito-Lay's prior history of developing the infamous Frito Bandito ad campaign of the 1970s, it is not surprising to see their recent schmoozing with Warner Brothers and their family of Tex[t]-Mex mannequins. For more on the Frito Bandito, see Chon A. Noriega's *Shot in America*.

Speedy Gonzales: from the fifties and early sixties and on to the present day, this ubiquitous Latino mouse has mesmerized cinema devotees and television viewers the world over. Witty, savvy, and fast, Gonzales (whose business card proclaims him "the fastest mouse in all Mexico"[31]) served as a comic celebrity in legions of Warner Brothers animated adventures with a supporting cast of (by turns silly, by turns pathetic and filthy) furry and feathered friends.

Until quite recently (the Cartoon Network embargoed Speedy shorts in 2001), Speedy's vignettes were still popular on Saturday mornings and weekday afternoons via syndication in both the United States and Mexico.[32] These cartoon masterpieces, directed by Robert McKimson and Isadore "I" "Friz" Freleng, epitomize show business's "acme" in terms of return on investments, having reaped critical acclaim in the form of Academy Award nominations as well as the material rewards that they continue to garner through home video and corporate merchandising opportunities. Where is anyone to put this remarkable creature, this crowning achievement of mainstream U.S. ethnic stereotyping?

As an English-speaking child of Mexican descent living in Laredo, Texas, I laughed convulsively at the devil-may-care exploits of Speedy and his retinue of lazy, shiftless cohorts, who are, in the words of the "gringo *pussygato*" Sylvester, nothing but "miserable little sneakin' crooked cheese thieves" (*Here Today, Gone Tamale*, dir. Friz Freleng, 1959).

In *The Pied Piper of Guadalupe* (dir. Friz Freleng, 1956), Sylvester adds more *predictable* abuse: "That's all you can do is run, run, run; you cowardly little cheese thieves."

"Predictable?"

Predictable in that it did not take a terrible stretch of the imagination, by the mid-1950s, for U.S. moviegoers to conjure the image of a Mexican as a thief—decades-long territorial disputes and wars with our southern *neighbor* helped ensure that this was the case.

The mise-en-scènes in Warner Brothers' wonderfully animated and scored productions are noteworthy: the perennially lazy (save for Speedy: he is an *industrious* thief) Mexican mice live in trash and frequent rowdy, boisterous *cantinas*. Here the assorted swarthy throngs sing the delights of marijuana and alcohol (not that we should, *estilo puritano*, malign said indulgences).

Mired in sullied refuse, intoxicated, and loud when not silently engaging in various petty larcenies, the mice (Mexican rogues, pestential Don Juans) compulsively and serially lust after by turns helpless and delighted *señoritas*. Sometimes they are successful, sometimes they are not—here, Speedy appears quite often as knave exemplar, usually getting his way with "the ladies."

In some animated short features, Speedy is the hero of his Veracruz-like communities, but he can also be the "enemy" when it comes to the issue of sexual desire and coupling—in fact, in *Gonzales Tamales* (dir. Friz Freleng, 1957), it is Speedy's "friends," the mice, who hire Sylvester the Cat to capture the masher/interloper, girlfriend-stealing, would-be Romeo, Señor Rat Gonzales.

Juanny-on-the-spot Speedy intercepts a kiss in Friz Freleng's *Gonzales Tamales*, 1957.

The titles of these short films are noteworthy for the way they tie archetypes and stereotypes (that are to be anticipated if not totally forgiven in animated films) to mainstream American literature: three particular titles here seem to offer most in the way of thematic overlap: *Tabasco Road*, *Tortilla Flaps*, and *Cannery Woe*—clever titular parodies of two novels by John Steinbeck (*Tortilla Flat*, 1935, and *Cannery Row*, 1945) and one by Erskine Caldwell (*Tobacco Road*, 1940).

Here, as with most parodies, there is more to these matters than meets the eye: a careful perusal of Steinbeck's oeuvre reveals more than a trivial problematic with regard to the characterization of Californian Mexicans.

Let's recall what was happening in and around Mexico from 1910 to 1920, as well as the greaser films, the lurid postcards, and the popular obsession with Mexico experienced by the United States at that time. Picture postcards explode, burst out about the same time greaser features are making their way across the country, with the movie series reaching its peak of popularity as conflicts between the United States and Mexico reach a climax of their own.

Across the United States, relatives and friends receive garish, violent, and gaudy "visions" of U.S. servicemen in Mexico (marines at Veracruz and military cavalry along the U.S.-Mexican border).

Mexico at war and the United States at war with Mexico become the reality TV of their age, with throngs of gawking American audiences throwing their eyes and, sadly for some, their bodies into the mix.

The violent melodrama of U.S. soldiers and marines at war with Mexicans staged amid the rustic primitivism of Mexico "itself": the visualized legacy of armed national conflict found in these postal remnants is quite striking. We saw above that some cards feature mutilated, "comically" staged scenes of U.S. Army regulars posed with Mexican corpses.

How does this information reflect upon the exploits of our garrulous Mexican mouse? Can we really track the impact of these military/cultural/technological developments in an innocent animated cartoon?

Well, let us start with this: the Speedy Gonzales one runs across in Warner Brothers cartoons is not derived from a generic vision of a Mexican rural laborer, or *campesino*. If

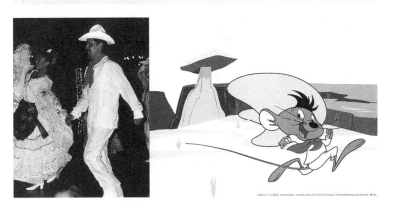

A participant remembers: "A lot of people would go alongside the river and watch the fighting. They would stand and watch like damn fools. They killed a little boy who was standing right close to me. He got hit and started crying, and I knew goddamn well he got hit! Deader than hell, a little boy about six or seven years old, standing there and watching them. And them goddamn people wouldn't get out of the way. . . ." (Courtesy Andreas Brown Collection.)

The traditional garb of *veracruzanos* cross-cut with the fastest mouse in all Mexico.

one looks closely at Speedy and his ilk, one sees that they are garbed in the clothing of Mexicans from the port city of Veracruz.

"*And . . . ?*" some more impudent readers might silently intone with the hint of a *Gilligan's Island* Thurston Howell cadence![33]

Veracruz happens to be a major east coast Mexican city and, as such, has served as a critical port of entry for past and present would-be invaders of Mexico—conquering armies under the tutelage of luminaries from conquistador Hernán Cortés onward have known this all too well. U.S. military regulars *visited* Mexico in this fashion both in 1846 and 1914.

I like the way historian Paul Vanderwood speaks of the most recent of these "visits," lamenting U.S. activities in this regard as an "affair of substantial dishonor." Vanderwood's text goes on to recount that day in

"April 1914 [when] United States sailors seized Veracruz and its revenue-producing customshouse, effectively quarantining the [Mexican leadership] so that internal disorder could eat it away."[34] As I suggested above, these international military interventions coincide with the rise of motion picture technology, the fall of vaudeville, and the opening of cinemas across the United States. As U.S. citizens are being introduced to the wonders of the movies, they do so through the visually memorable spectacle of scoundrel Mexicans—bandits, greasers, revolutionaries; hot-blooded, passionate, fiery women and men.

No surprise, then, that Warner Brothers animators, faced with the challenge of crafting a decidedly Mexican space, for a decidedly Mexican animal hero, call on the collective memory of American adventurism in Mexico. Not for nothing are Speedy and his crew often found hanging out around the docks—as in *Here Today, Gone Tamale* (dir. Friz Freleng, 1959)—lolling about in the trash sporting the garb of Mexican *veracruzanos*. And this coincidence of film, photography, border conflicts, and stereotypes is no accident. What are stereotypes but "bloodstains," the socially conserved oral and textual remnants of communities in conflict?

The promotional image for the "Diamond Post Card Gun," borrowed from the pages of Vanderwood and Samponaro's *Border Fury* (13) and dating to the time of the conflict along the U.S.-Mexican border, tells the tale better than I can.

The postcard camera as gun—we could not make up a better logo for the thesis of *Tex[t]-Mex*, given not only that the history of the representation of "Mexicans" in the cultural space of the United States is filled with acts of violent semantic and semiotic intrigue, but also that this violence continues as ethnocentrism and racism abound owing to the continued proliferation of seeds spitting out of "guns" like that imaged here.

Students of early-twentieth-century U.S. history understand that the image of Mexicans as dirty rogues and rapacious bandits was broadcast round the nation via photographs, newsreels, postcards, and newspapers. That Speedy should tap that contentious vein of moist prejudice is anything but a surprise, as the best, most immediate comedies often derive from collective perceptions that date to earlier moments of conflict. The image Speedy Gonzales broadcasts of rodents of a decidedly Mexican persuasion cries out for critical scrutiny.[35]

Neither Andy Warhol nor René Magritte could have dreamed up such a perfect icon for a kind of violence implicit in the act of taking a picture; the Diamond Post Card Gun is not a bullet-laden agent of *direct* violence, but its womb or matrix of visual reproduction has a palpable, violent agency all its own.

Lest one question the appropriateness of these sustained inquiries regarding the ethnic niceties of a rather silly, albeit nimble, mouse, then one ought to read again the words of Michel Foucault:

> A culture forges, sustains and transmits itself in an adventure with a double face: sometimes brutality, struggle, turmoil; sometimes mediation, nonviolence, silence. Whatever form the adventure may take—the most surprising is not always the noisiest, but the noisiest is not irremediably the most superficial—it is useless to ignore it, and still more useless to sequestrate it.[36]

Speedy Gonzales is neither the most insidious nor the most virulent source of anti-Latina/o racism in the United States, and yet it seems worth the bother to ask questions about his origins, to try to identify (resisting here Deleuze and Guattari's altogether salient admonitions to the contrary in *On the Line*) *the puppeteers fueling the soul of this fast mouse.* But it is not just Gallic pomo theorists who must guide us on our tour.[37]

American popular critics of the media have much to share as well. In their view, Speedy is no Mickey Mouse, Mighty Mouse, Jerry, or even, for that matter, Bugs Bunny. Leonard Maltin, he of *Entertainment Tonight* fame and author/impresario of those invaluable movie guide annuals, speaks of Speedy in his debut film (*Cat-Tails for Two*) as "a caricature of a Mexican peon." Assessing the "Mexican['s]" place in the Warner Brothers animation pantheon, Maltin concludes: "Speedy, like the Roadrunner, is an ever-smiling, ever-confident character who always comes out on top of a situation. His primary asset is his speed . . . but he has little else going for him. He is a one-note personality, and the success of his films depends entirely on strong gags."[38] I must say that Maltin's aesthetic judgment actually fits in nicely with our initial postmortem findings on the logic of the stereotype.

*   *   *

A brief gloss here of several Speedy Gonzales animated short features, along with the given Latina/o stereotype they profit from/reinforce, will suffice to give you a taste of what I am going on about.

Cannery Woe (1961)
Director: Robert McKimson

A peek at the opening credits from Warner Bros.'s *Cannery Woe* (1961), directed by Robert McKimson and written by Ted Pierce.

Cannery Woe introduces viewers to a community of Sylvester the Cat–plagued starving mice who live in a trash dump outside a sleepy seaport. One funny pair of comically lazy mice lives in the tin can pictured here with the label "el steenko sardinas." No, that's not *déjà vu* you are feeling—we stumbled over this outrageous scene earlier in the introduction.[39] I imagine that one might read this representation as a sign of Mexican ingenuity—that these resourceful *veracruzano* mice had gainfully turned rags to riches, tin can into cherished castle.

While one might be moved to imagine this tableau as a sign of Mexican industry (with nimble vermin combo recycling detritus as domicile—an example of Mac-Gyver-like DIY cleverness), more likely than not, the reaction to this representation will be "Mexicans" *in/are/as* trash.

"Chick Inspector" Speedy ogles a dreamy, equally smitten señorita in the denouement of *Cannery Woe*. "Mexican" as synecdoche for roguish, swarthy sexuality meets its acme—pardon me for being dirty-minded, but trace the shape of Speedy in this image for a Rorschach-like erotic experience.

But it is a bit of a stretch, don't you think?

"Mexicans live in shanty structures made of trash" seems the easier read.

Cannery Woe is also interesting for the way it captures the political economic order of small northern Mexican and Southwest American Latino communities, as its storyline features a light-skinned *patrón/político* mayoral candidate who manipulates his darker-skinned impoverished mouse constituents via *pachanga* parties and free cheese.[40] Speedy appears in *Cannery Woe* as a hero, taking cheese from bumbling cat Sylvester so as to aid our aforementioned politician. Speedy's reward from the generous politician for having wrested the cheese from a hapless Sylvester? He is appointed "Chick Inspector." The frame shown here from the close of McKimson's short feature speaks for itself.

We cannot or ought not to overlook the overloaded gender implication of this highly sexualized "reward." Needless to say, when female characters appear at all in Speedy features, it is as the target or prize of male saviors/benefactors. Speedy's view of this fortuitous turn of events in this particular feature is more predictable, his only gloss the succinct yet joyous disclosure that he has received the "best job of all."

So *Cannery Woe* ends with Speedy's acquisition of a lovely, obliging señorita. Lechery, as it was in the early Hollywood greaser movies, is never, ever very far from the minds of Hollywood-forged Latinos, certainly never far from the mind of our philandering Mexican rodent.

Not for nothing does historian Ralph Stevenson speak of Speedy as a "formidable mouse, a rather rakish man about town."[41]

Stereotype reinforced: Mexicans are dirty, never far from trash; "Mexicans" are politically illiterate, impoverished, if clever, thieves out for large volumes of free food and booze in the never-ending search for libidinal recompense.

Tortilla Flaps (1958)
Director: Robert McKimson

(Dialogue: For full impact, read aloud with painfully strong Spanish-language accent.)

Mangy, lazy mouse: You know this Speedy Gonzales? He go steady weeth mah seeeester.

Other mangy, lazy mouse: Speedy Gonzales? . . . He go steady weeth everybody seeeester.

Stereotype reinforced (among others): Mexican males are sexual rogues, thoughtless rakes, likely to penetrate willing and unwilling targets at the drop of a sombrero. I will here ignore the slyly Freudian sibling-lust, incest-taboo-breaching subtext.

Here Today, Gone Tamale (1959)
Director: Friz Freleng

Here Today, Gone Tamale is one of the few animated features in which the Mexican mice actually speak a sort of standard Spanish language; in most of the other films, the furry Latino vermin speak a novel form of Spanglish patois made up mostly of heavily accented English mutations, as in the confession of Speedy's amorous intentions noted above in *Tortilla Flaps*: "He likes mah seestaaahrrr."[42] *Here Today, Gone Tamale* revolves about the tale of a general cheese shortage. Enter a cheese-laden vessel into port—yet another Speedy short that features a Veracruz-like locale. The name of the ship? The SS *Pancho Cucaracha*.

Stereotype reinforced: No heavy duty semiotics needed here: the cucaracha, *or "cockroach," being the domestic predator/scavenger most often associated with Mexicans in U.S. mass culture. Cockroaches are not clean beasts, or at least one does not immediately associate cockroaches with sanitary conditions.*[43]

Sylvester eyes his "Mexican" nemesis in this movie house lobby card for *Here Today, Gone Tamale* (1959), directed by Friz Freleng and written by Michael Maltese.

"Mexicans" and cockroaches—a common "happy" couple in this establishing-exterior shot from *Here Today, Gone Tamale* (1959).

Tabasco Road (1957)
Director: Robert McKimson

In a year that saw Albert Camus win the Nobel Prize for Literature, Jack Kerouac publish *On the Road*, and Theodor Geisel (aka Dr. Seuss) issue the now-legendary opus *The Cat in the Hat*, Warner Brothers' animation crew was also quite busy. One of their progeny, *Tabasco Road*, released July 20, 1957, and another Academy Award nominee, introduces us to a sustained Hollywood studio cine-ethnography documenting the outrageous drinking habits of "Mexicans." One does not have to think long and hard to conjure images of Mexicanesque types in the vicinity of mass quantities of alcohol—tequila companies (U.S. *and* Mexican, I might add) do a handsome job of popularizing and profiting from this vision. In *Tabasco Road*, we meet up with the redoubtable Pablo and his bosom drinking buddy Fernando having a good old time at the El Tío Pepe Cantina. Boozy bandit revelry is the order for the day, and this goal is nicely summed up in the lyrics of one song sung to the melody of "La cucaracha": to end up "muy plenty steenko borracho." Quite shortly into the feature, Speedy appears as a teetotaling "savior" of sorts.

Speedy tries to hold back his cantina-obsessed cohorts in this lobby card for *Tabasco Road* (1957), directed by Robert McKimson and written by Tedd Pierce.

Like some mad fusion of Carry A. Nation, Bill Wilson, and Cantínflas, Speedy Gonzales interrupts the boozy delights of his "Mexican" *borracho* buddies in *Tabasco Road*.

The frame below shows Speedy intervening, cutting off Pablo and Fernando, ostensibly saving them from the inanities of their debauchery.

Stereotype reinforced: Mexicans eschew labor for the more basic allure of serialized intoxication. Fin.

Let this brief gallery of culled images suffice to make our point: the next time you encounter Speedy Gonzales in an animated short, in a TV special, or on a bag of salsa potato chips, and find yourself smiling or laughing, ask yourself what the hell is so funny.

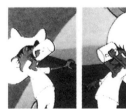 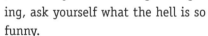 

Oh, and Speedy is funny, or, at least, he *can* be.

And the more I learned about his origins and his creators, piecing together his sordid history, I found myself at one with Judy Garland as Dorothy in Victor Fleming's 1939 version of *The Wizard of Oz*, shaking the hand of that old charlatan Oz and liking him very much in spite of his ersatz omniscience.

Do please know that I am not, or at least not usually, one of those frowning old farts, one of those sanctimonious curmudgeons, who would deny the unwashed masses, or even the ostensibly washed cultural-studies academic masses, the simplest of pleasures.

But such humor must be checked by a curiosity about the dense, transparent cultural syntax that enables this laughter to spread. Speedy is funny because he and his cohorts are familiar; he is familiar because of the history of exchange (cultural, military, linguistic, semiotic) between the United States and Mexico. The logic from which Warner Brothers profits and which it helps to sustain is basic: we have seen Mexicans as simple, lazy thieves before; we see them again, we laugh. Serious business this "funny" stuff.

I must admit that as I was delivering earlier versions of this chapter at lectures across the country, I ran into some, including a fair number of politically active young Chicano university students, who resisted my reading of Speedy as pariah, offering in its place a reading of Speedy as hero or Speedy as subaltern with alacrity or Speedy as Latino social justice advocate, etc. As the argument goes, Speedy is a neo-Zapata or a proto-Zapatista, resisting the gringo domination of sly Sylvester and pathetic Daffy Duck. A "good" Mexican, Speedy is, in this view, a positive role model: fast, clever, erotically able, and so on. In short, he is

A fit of counter-hallucinatory insurgency, as imagined by the author and his Macintosh computer.

nothing more and nothing less than a leader of his people. I offer here a slightly Photoshopified still frame as an emblem of the foregoing revisionist Speedy take.

I wish I had the means to ally myself with this hopeful interpretation of our "Mexican" friend, but I feel it sidesteps the crucial problematic Speedy literally embodies.

Merely doing revisionist readings of Speedy Gonzales cartoons might make the revisioner and her/his audience feel good, but it does nothing to efface the legacy of Mexican representation on U.S. soil—a fertile soil, I might add, from which much prejudice and disdain is harvested.

After all, our role is not to say Speedy Gonzales is "bad" or that our smiling Speedy is all "good"; our goal here is not to merely maledict a somewhat affable animated entity. Rather, I have set myself another task: to understand exactly just how this popular animated star comes to function; moreover, how he comes to function in a way that reinforces politically charged visions/versions of the "Mexican" on "American" soil.

And it is to this task that this postmortem now moves.

Incision Six | More Surrogate "Mexicans," More Surrogate "Jews"

Every portrait that is painted with feeling is a portrait of the artist, not of the sitter. The sitter is merely the accident, the occasion. It is not he who is revealed by the painter; it is rather the painter who, on the coloured canvas, reveals himself. The reason I will not exhibit this picture is that I am afraid that I have shown in it the secret of my own soul.

—Basil Hallward, painter, addresses Henry Wotton
in Wilde's *Picture of Dorian Gray*.[44]

I just draw somebody I know. I think of these [animated figures] as living characters.

—Isadore Freleng, aka I. Freleng, aka Friz Freleng,
on the animator's craft[45]

I have never known how to tell a story. And since I love nothing better than remembering and memory itself . . . I have always felt this inability a sad infirmity. Why am I denied narration? Why have I not received this gift? The gift (doron) of Mnemosyne, Socrates insists, is like the wax in which all that we wish to guard in our memory is engraved in relief so that it may leave a mark.

—Jacques Derrida, *Memoirs for Paul de Man*[46]

"Isadore," "I.," "Friz" Freleng never suffered from Jacques Derrida's declared narratological debility, his stated impotence when it comes to telling a story—yet he and the storied guru of our poststructural moment do share some curious overlaps that it might be beneficial to consider; we will deal with Freleng and his *fictional* "living characters" at length below.

Yet we should not hurry too much here, lest we ignore the mother/father/inventor of deconstruction's salient confession of an inexplicable, congenital condition, a pathology that leaves the afflicted philosopher "not knowing how to tell a story."

We will dawdle here a moment, as said confession regarding narrative and memory relates to our concern with stereotypes. As it were, Derrida's parable (paradoxically, a parable about *not* being able to weave parables), which appears at the head of his lyrical dirge to the late Paul de Man, may be read as a bildungsroman of deconstruction, and by extension, of poststructuralist theory in general.[47]

In this microtale, presented cannily in the guise of a confession of an inability to tell a tale, deconstruction reveals its other self, beneath a mask of sorts—it is nothing more and nothing less than a surrogate or, tellingly, a *prosthesis* for storytelling. Prolific Derrida unable to tell a story?

What then of his umpteen books—what are they? What is he going on about? Deconstruction is not a story? What, then, is it? To tell the tale another way, Derrida scripts a saga wherein deconstruction, the philosophical travails of Jacques Derrida, Esq., emerges as a special species of storytelling charged forever with telling a tale of *prostheses*—of substitutions, of supplementations, and of paradoxes—in short, of *narrating* "why I am denied narration." Deconstruction as Not Story—or, in practical terms, as the branch of storytelling that spends much of its time confessing, that is, narrating, its inability to tell a story. Paradox city. All the foregoing speculations relate directly to our main inquest, my main interest, the autopsy of a rat: for Derrida's confession of narrative impotence is merely a ruse, an entrance to his rereading of Socrates's memory of Mnemosyne, which is itself a dramatic, poignant confession that this memory *of/for*, this memorial *to*, Paul de Man will force the gallant thinker to confront the enormity of his personal and intellectual loss. "Engraved in relief" so that they may "leave a mark," stereotypes (*hard, stiff blows*) reveal their debt to memory.

Five years later, in "Circumfession," the running footnote repartee with/for/against Geoffrey Bennington in *Jacques Derrida*, Derrida will fulfill the promise of this failed story, this would-be-paean-to-de Man-cum-autobiography-of-Jacques by revealing the extent to which his exile to a Jews-only school in Vichy-governed Algeria shaped his obsessions with margins, not to mention his circumcised penis.

Nightmares of circumcision, the cut that marks, the blow that signs your self for all (?) to see are a good segue, a good crosscut (indulge the pun, it is necessary) back to Speedy and Isadore/I./Friz/Yitzak (to find the hermeneutic key to Yitzak, you will have to spelunk some gnarly footnotes shortly—*ojo*).

For what if "the gift of Mnemosyne," the bequest of memory, so like "the wax in which . . . our memory is engraved," is a nightmare? What if one cannot forget a trip to the movies, where marionettes of projected light elucidate the pathetic contours of Mexican-like bodies, which then find entry into the warm, comfy confines of your psyche or your soul?[48]

The cameo appearance here by Jacques Derrida is neither gratuitous nor rhetorically vaudevillian—the expository equivalent of pulling a rabbit out of a hat. Curiously, Derrida shares some remarkable biographical overlaps with Friz Freleng: an interest in the relation of memory to the production of stories; an intellectual/aesthetic interest in names and naming, with a corresponding, not to say determining, personal experience with the same; and, lastly, but not unimportantly, a Judaic biographical trace—not for nothing does Derrida's auto/biographical collaboration with Bennington include Derrida's portrait of himself as "a little black and very Arab Jew."[49] He can't tell a story, but he paints one hell of a picture.

Derrida: arguably, the most influential philosopher of the late twentieth century; Freleng: one of the most influential animation directors for the very same period—how odd and unanticipated that the work of both should so smoothly ally, and how unexpected that the work of one so usefully illuminates the other. Perhaps now we are prepared to receive the memory of Speedy and the memory of a very special version of "Mexico" he embodied and reinforced for those who made him.

The accurate, if not progressive, cover of Yo Ho Video's *Uncensored Cartoons* collection (1989).

Friz Freleng, along with Robert McKimson and others at Warner Brothers, "remembered" Mexico in ways that are not at odds with visions of Mexico popularized during U.S. conflicts with our southern "neighbor" this century. One of Warner Brothers Studios' more prolific, inventive, and successful animated feature directors (along with Chuck Jones and Robert McKimson), Freleng helped give life to Speedy Gonzales. Long before Freleng immortalized "Mexicans," he had cut his teeth on "Africans" and "African Americans"; screen his outrageously offensive takes on the Black Subject in *Clean Pastures* (1937), *Jungle Jitters* (1938), and *Goldilocks and the Jivin' Bears* (1944).[50]

Taking McKimson's character from *Cat-Tails for Two* (1953), Freleng remade Speedy into the toothy velocital fetishist we know today, garnering an Academy Award for a short animated feature with *Speedy Gonzales*, released September 17, 1955.[51] In the following charged passage, we find Freleng talking about how stories and characters were created and developed on the Warner Brothers backlot. Interestingly enough, he is responding directly to a question from historian Walter Brasch, not about Speedy, but about another important animated character in the Warner canon, the rambunctious cowboy named Yosemite Sam.

One last prefatory note before the quotation: Freleng's comments are all the more valuable, since Warner Brothers' animators developed Yosemite Sam using Friz Freleng as their model.

That Freleng should share the following, spurred by the memory of a cartoon figure etched in honor of his own personality and physiognomy, signals our own need to keep our eyes peeled, as the striking cliché has it.

Freleng: "Indirectly, you may be affected by something that may have made you think [a certain way]. *Unconsciously, you may do things that you don't even know why you do it.*"[52] The rather pat, dogmatic accusation that would denounce Warner Brothers as a racist monster of a movie studio, an evil motion picture house disseminating callously bestial versions of "Mexicans" to the global market, must be laid to one side here, as Freleng has stumbled upon a useful truth-effect.

Animators as well as their spectators act, "obeying a law they do not . . . know, but which [they can] recite in [their] dreams"—words earlier attributed to Hitler return here in another context as an approximate paraphrase of a popular animator's confession.

Placed side by side with Freleng's disclosure, these words offer us a better view and clearer access to the enabling ether called ideology—a macro–petri dish of sorts where U.S.-nurtured strains of visually communicated Mexicanesque bacteria thrive.

All this nuance.

Too much, some would argue.

Perhaps I have let the recently deceased Friz Freleng off too easily. For, given the way animation figures in domestic and international marketing campaigns, who better than an animator to reanimate the image of the Mexican in/for an American *socius*?

Let us, then, for at least a minute or two, go after Friz Freleng. For instance, look what we find when we pause and take a sidelong glance at Friz Freleng's own name, or rather, "names." Freleng produced work under at least three related monikers: "Isadore Freleng," "I. Freleng," and "Friz Freleng."

This evolution, ostensibly tangential to our reading of Speedy Gonzales shorts, on closer inspection reveals itself as salient to our concerns. Freleng, a pioneering animation director, began his career at Walt Disney Studios, and moved on to MGM before settling at Warner Brothers. At Warner Brothers, as at Disney, MGM, and other major studios, any kind of non-Anglo naming was viewed with a close eye, especially by the "boys" in distribution and accounting who worried that particular names would hurt box office receipts and the company bottom line.[53]

Freleng soon fell victim to this ethnic-naming conundrum. Walter Brasch tells the story of how the director came to change his on-screen credit line for the Warner studio. Apparently, the studio bosses in the distribution department asked Freleng to change his on-screen credit line, having it read "I." Freleng as opposed to "Isadore" Freleng. Freleng concludes the story in his own words: "Warner Brothers *suggested* [the change]. They didn't order it. They suggested it because down South at that time anything that's Jewish didn't go too well. We couldn't sell the show. [Southern distributors] said that the name is *out*. Warner Brothers said, 'Why struggle with it?'"[54]

Why, indeed?

Freleng's "Jewish" name, the "monstrous" (adapting somewhat Wilde's phraseology cited above) corruption of the name "Isadore" (whose repugnant aroma of East Coast Jewishness might alienate wholesome Southern consumers of good, animated, American fun), had to go—if the bottom line is at stake, why "struggle with it" at all? Consider it a *Semitic sacrifice*, born of *semi[o]tic necessity*.

In various Warner Brothers animated features, Freleng appears both as "I. Freleng" and as "Friz Freleng"—the story of Freleng's rechristening to "Friz" is not as compelling as the shift from "Isadore," but it merits repeating here. Walter Brasch's footnotes again prove invaluable. There we learn of "pioneer cartoon producer Hugh Harman," a friend of Freleng's, who liked a cartoon character by the name of Congressman Frisby and promptly saddled Freleng with the nickname. Freleng picks up the story: "At first[,] I was called Congressman Frisby, then Congressman, and Frisby, then finally Friz."[55] This last name stuck, and Freleng used it ever after in the credits of his productions.

From the sacrifice of a Jewish cognomen on the high altar of movie profits, we now move to the matter of our animated

The riddle of names is endless. A colleague of mine, the Latin American art historian Janet Esser, wrote me after hearing an earlier version of this chapter to inform me of her suspicions that Speedy may well be a "crypto-Jew," supporting her view by the overlap of the mise-en-scène of Speedy Gonzales features and her recollection of Jacob Riis's photography; moreover, she added (in what was, for me, a revelatory declaration), "Isadore was not a Jewish name." Rather, "it was the 'Anglo' name given to Jews named Yitzak who wished or whose families wished to assimilate. . . . Isadore became a 'Jewish' name when enough Jews began to use it." As I am no expert in this regard, I cannot confirm the authenticity of these suggestions, though a quick glance through Robert Singerman's **Jewish and Hebrew Onomastics** *and Benzion C. Kaganoff's* **Dictionary of Jewish Names and Their History** *unearthed nothing to contradict Esser's intriguing and suggestive findings. I did, however, run across a short history of Saint Isidore, from Seville, a seventh-century Spanish cleric/writer whose renowned work* **Etymologiae** *contained all the known world's knowledge and history to that period—the title of his work reassured me that placing my faith in etymologies in this piece was fated from the start. From Yitzak to Isadore to I. to Friz: the evolution in Mr. Freleng's first name constitutes in and of itself a microhistory of Jewish American history. Esser's correspondence came in response to a public lecture of the materials contained in this chapter. A second letter was to prove even more outrageous.*

"Mexican" friend's name. How do we take this information and bring it to bear on the archaeology of Speedy Gonzales? Let us jump to the potentially apocryphal naming of our animated Latino cipher. Animation historian Brasch's views in this regard are again salient here: "Character naming is not a case of spontaneous generation, with names popping in and out at the whim of their creators. It is an evolutionary process with clearly defined historical classifications."[56]

If we buy into the version of events to be found in Jeff Lenburg's *Great Cartoon Directors* and Walter Brasch's *Cartoon Monikers*, Friz Freleng is responsible (along with Bob McKimson) for the birth and the naming of Speedy Gonzales.[57]

Our slide here into the argot of reproduction and patronymics is sanctioned by the circumstances of Speedy's "birth." Additionally, the pace moves to a different beat here, *allegro non tanto*, moderately lively, at the hint of a climax—we cannot have birth without climax.

Climax? I mean this quite literally.

What you may not know is that the famous Speedy Gonzales, our wonderful mascot of clever Mexican banditry, is named after the punch line of a "dirty joke," a joke overheard by director Bob McKimson and retold to a largely Anglo crew of animators on the Warner Brothers backlot; my research suggests that the joke, and variations thereof, was making the rounds of Southern California after 1950, the time when Speedy's name was being tossed around the Warner lot.

I did not find a direct transcript of this originary joke, but Brasch's book does allude to detailed circumstances concerning this peculiar, bawdy tale. As McKimson relates: "A friend of mine told me this joke and the name of the character was 'Speedy Gonzales.' We already had the character developed, but no name. So the next day I told Warren Foster, my storyman, the joke, and we decided that we'd name the Mexican mouse Speedy Gonzales." McKimson emphasizes that although a dirty joke spawned the name, "at no time was the name ever meant to be derogatory. We had no trouble using a Spanish name—as long as it fit the character."[58] The *dirty* joke, you ask? "Speedy Gonzales, the fastest mouse in all Mexico," was named after a lascivious bit about a Mexican man, the aforenamed Speedy, who suffers from a chronic case of premature ejaculation—hence the distinction of the by-no-means-complimentary epithet "Speedy."

Who would have thought it: speedy Speedy Gonzales? In this light, Speedy's familiar outcry "*arriba, arriba*" takes on other tragic, deliciously salacious connotations.

Naïvely, I thought my research was at an end. But there recently surfaced a curious, and no less compelling, counternarrative to contend with—a competing origin myth that can be anecdotally "carbon-dated" to the time when Speedy's character was in genesis on the Warner lots.

Let me explain: I was preparing the final draft of this chapter for *Camera Obscura* in the mid-1990s when I found myself delivering portions of it to a gathering of colleagues for our Master of Arts in Liberal Arts lecture series New Identities.

There, a quiet, unassuming emeritus professor from Recreation Sciences by the name of David Malcolm took me aside and told me the variation of the Speedy joke transcribed below. I was so taken aback and, I must add, delighted that I had him send me a written transcript of the bawdy trifle, which I here share with you—I cite here at length, both the joke and Malcolm's commentary, because of the impact each has on the subject of this study—some parts have been edited for clarity by your author.

> Here is the Speedy G story as I heard it told at a party during 1953–1954 or 1954–1955 by Frank Scott (deceased), then golf coach at (then) San Diego State College: An Anglo husband and wife find themselves forced to share a hotel room with a Mexican fellow by the name of Speedy Gonzales. The worried husband notices his wife and Speedy exchanging suspicious glances. The husband decides there is only one sure way to keep anything from happening between them and that is for him to stick his finger into his wife's vagina and keep it there all night. Sometime during the night the husband has to sneeze and brings his hand to his face as he does so. Immediately afterward, the husband returns his finger to his wife's vagina [the narrator accompanied this with a gesture showing how quickly the husband's hand comes up to his mouth and then returns to safeguard his wife's pudendum]. Suddenly, Speedy Gonzales's voice is then heard saying, "Señor . . . your feeenger . . . eeets up my ahhhssshole" [told, of course, with the exaggerated accent and long vowels].

Professor Malcolm's appended comments are pertinent, so I will include them here as well:

> No doubt "Scotty" prefaced the story with some elaborate explanation for how the three came to be stranded together[,] but I have long since forgotten what it was. I feel certain the above dates are accurate. I came to SDSU (then SDSC) in August 1953. During my first two years, five or six newcomer faculty couples, including the Malcolms and the Scotts[,] frequently met together socially. . . . Scotty was not one with whom I had developed any particular personal friendship[,] and I do not remember ever being with him in a social setting again after I left that group. Amazing the power of negative stereotyping. Although I have never retold the story myself (until now), I still remember it more than forty years later. My sense is that the extreme exaggeration of Speedy's supposed Mexican

accent played a big part in its staying power—at least in my case. I doubt if I would have remembered it at all if Speedy had said "Sir, your finger is up my asshole" in a common middle–American accent.

Malcolm closes his testimony with the following noteworthy assertion: "I wonder about what deep level of my own racism may have been tapped into?"

Needless to say, Malcolm's testimony brought this inquest to a crisis, as I had identified a living historical link between the alleged origins of the mute patient upon my surgical table and the surreal, not to say vulgar, dynamics of the rat's originary patronymic.

In addition, the disagreement between the two genesis myths left me at a loss for words. Did I really have to pick between Speedy the premature ejaculator, and Speedy the wily, homoerotically penetrated agent of a *ménage à trois* miscegenation-phobia scenario? What to do with this unanticipated narrative hallucination, a gift to me from Mnemosyne via her proxy, Professor Malcolm?

I reflected on what I had discovered by returning to the epigraphs at the head of this incision: paintings tell us more about the painters that paint them than about the [S]ubjects they paint. Freleng tells stories; he also "paints," or, more strictly, he animates. Derrida allegedly cannot tell a story, yet he tells them anyway as theories of philosophical stories that are, at once, stories about theories of philosophy—Jorge Luis Borges plied this trade to some success earlier in the twentieth century.[59]

Memory is stereotype, a version of an event "engraved in relief." Speedy is named after the memory of a "dirty" joke: he's either prone to climax or prone to be penetrated as he penetrates, each a result of his driving Latino sexual potentiality. Freleng, who was Jewish, altered his name or, better put, allowed his name to be altered so as to dodge the would-be wrath of anti-Semitic Southern U.S. theatergoers.

The very same artist who is the victim of business decisions fueled by anti-Semitic sensibilities produces animated trinkets that are also, simultaneously, ubiquitous and virulent carriers of anti-Mexican sentiment, obeying unknown laws that are not recited in sleep, but projected, writ large, on the shining silver screen.[60]

Memory.

A stereotype is a prerecorded visual memory byte etched onto the contours of the collective psyche. Strapped for existential input as to the dynamic of Mexican subjects, we turn to stereotypes to provide us with visuo-ethnic "clues" that fill in for empirical data and satisfy the lazy desire of our collective curiosity.

Memory.

Memory itself, as is, and, somehow simultaneously, memory as the apotheosis of memory via narration and, miraculously (or paradoxically), the erasure and displacement of memory via narration—in telling a story we remember that which has been forgotten or put aside, but in telling the story anew we erase or elide the event as it occurred.[61]

It is Plato's cave redux, only we pay to be chained by our jailers at the same time we are pleased by the enchantments we witness.

Shifting metaphors to the realm of the natural sciences, Speedy is what geologists would call a "pseudomorph," that is, an object "having the characteristic outward form of another species" . . . [and/or a] "deceptive or irregular form."

He looks as a "Mexican" would.

He speaks (owing to the nimble vocal finesse of recently deceased Mel Blanc) as a "Mexican" might: who could blame a blameless spectator for reasonably concluding, "So that's what a Mexican, a *clever* Mexican, is like"?

But Gonzales is not *Mexican;* he and his rowdy charges are "Mexicans" as imagined by Americans once at war with Mexico, at war with the specter of the otherness of Mexico. Train it to do otherwise, to be otherwise, as we might, the collective imagination of the Americas will long waste synapses on the acquisition of this nasty rat-cum-mouse—a less pleasant more effective vehicle for the introduction of visual ideological pathogens has yet to be imagined—Aunt Jemima and the Cream O' Wheat porter/bellman come to mind as virulent analogues.[62]

Classic, historic, and ubiquitous representations of African Americans: a "Negro chef dressed in white coat and cap holding a steaming bowl" is the Cream of Wheat corporation's description of its trademark lackey; and Aunt Jemima, in her mid-twentieth-century incarnation—an illustration of the African American Nancy Green.

An undated newspaper clipping by the Associated Press that appeared in the *New York Times* sometime between 1989 and 1991.

A New Look for Aunt Jemima
Aunt Jemima, whose face adorns 40 breakfast products, will be celebrating her 100th birthday with her first make-over in 21 years, Quaker Oats said last week. Her new look, at right, is more suited to the mistress of the house than the cook. Aunt Jemima products represent about $300 million of Quaker's $5.3 billion in sales. The new look will begin appearing in July.

At a glance here, a veritable physiognomical (d)evolution of the Jemima prototype through time presents itself to us, one akin to the permutations of the "Mexican" we have witnessed, that has suffused us, in the pages of this book.

Because of this journey, because of this visual ideological legacy, I feel safe in saying that "Isadore," "I.", "Friz" Freleng and Robert McKimson may be seen as both *nomenclators* and, via neologism, *imagoclators*: beings, almost deities, whose actions lend denomination and visual contour to the creatures they form. Prometheus himself has little on Freleng.

Their animated products are *monsters* (monstrances, demonstrations, etc.) in the strict sense: Speedy as spectacle—via metonymy, Speedy animated short film images come to proxy for the specific national/ethnic community he then comes to emblematize.

Should the dueling taxonomy of geology and linguistics leave you limp or dry, consider, alternatively, how we can think of the furry body of Speedy as an agent of "zoanthropy"—here the taxonomical assist comes from psychology, where said term is used to describe "a kind of monomania in which the patient believes himself transformed into one of the lower animals."[63]

Now that Warner Brothers has been absorbed and reimagined as TimeWarner Inc., it will be curious to watch the future evolution of these characters, to see just how Speedy Gonzales changes in the hands of an ever more duplicitous and complex corporate culture industry. His recent appearance on a bag of spicy salsa chips suggests he will be around for the long haul.

When I first went on the job market in 1988, I used to joke that my mantra was "I am a box of Tide." Eighteen years later, Tex[t]-Mex, perhaps, proves me prescient.

As was stated above, stereotypes may be read as the bloodstains of cultural conflict. Like most bloodstains, they are born from some sort of violence, some form of fracture, some type of antagonism. Like bloodstains, once established, they are almost impossible to get out. They may fade, their color may change, you might be able to even hide them for a while, but they do not usually go away.

Along the U.S.-Mexican border, and culminating in the years between 1910 and 1920, one encounters a portentous set of individuals, circumstances, and events that help establish the stereotype of Latinos in U.S. mass culture. New technology (the motion picture), new industry (the postcard business), and a (re)new(ed) border conflict (General Villa's and General Pershing's forays onto each other's territory) come together to form a series of major and minor spectacles that reach Americans from coast to coast.

The coincidences of novelty, territorial conflict, profit, and pride combine and etch into the collective imagination of the United States images of the Latino that continue to flourish in the bodies of Speedy Gonzales, Freddy López, and even in figures like Manuel Noriega, the notorious Latino strongman now silently festering in some federal facility somewhere, no doubt shorn of his red underwear, harem of prostitutes, icons of Hitler, and volumes of pornography, some found, some planted, on his various estates. Most striking is the way these stock-footage images take the role played by the Muses in poetry—gaining the ear of the creative writer and filling it with predictable nonsense.

Take, for instance, the following example, culled from the pages of Richard Rodriguez's collection of essays *Days of Obligation*.

For those not familiar with the diverse writings of Señor Rodriguez, it might be helpful to note here that said Latino scribe is the sometimes self-loathing, sometimes self-loving, aesthetically centrist (English literature Ph.D.)/politically right of right (sworn enemy of affirmative action and bilingual education) Bay Area Chicano humanist—Aztlán's very own paraphrase of V. S. Naipaul.

Let us listen again to Chicanodom's most heralded native informant, as quoted in one of the opening epigraphs to this autopsy: "Mexicans move as naturally and comfortably in the dark as cats or wolves or owls do. . . . Mexicans get drunk and sing like cats beneath the moon."

Although Speedy Gonzales might take offense at the bestial rendition here of Mexicans as cats, having, no doubt, some species loyalty to his own rodent clan, he would also undoubtedly smile at Rodriguez's lovely version of images that evoke the swarthy contours of the Warner Brothers animation archive.

Of course, Rodriguez is here less native informant than obliging colonial agent—proof of the view that you can never tell how watching cartoons can mess you up. Rodriguez's rant has left your otherwise verbose Mexican American assisting coroner speechless once again. I will leave you here to have a drink and, felinelike, have a go at the moon.

Incision Seven | Alternative Bodies of Ink and Light

I could have spent this entire chapter writing about the psychological damage done to legions of Americans of Latin American descent by stupid, stereotype-laced animated productions that desecrate Latina/o cultural sites, which intervene at the juncture where new apparitions of a Mexican subjectivity might inflect and infect the collective American psyche. These animated creatures, these true monsters, are the personification of the rhetorical figure called the *allonym:* the name of one body taken by another, anticipating and intercepting the figure of Mexico.

These allonymic marionettes act as visually distracting proxies, at times dooming Latino representation in the present to the role of mute spectator or, worse yet, permanent respondent charged with the Sisyphus-like task of always explaining why we are not like Speedy, always asked to explain ourselves with Warner Brothers hallucinations as our backdrop. As when my boisterous senior English Department colleague at the University of Connecticut suggested I moonlight at the taco stand (1988), or as when another playful son of New England merrily suggested I was a wetback (1990)—my encounters with scenarios harvested from Hollywood and shared in the interest of plain old *good fun*.

It was with horror, resignation, and uncharacteristic silence that I witnessed Anglo attendants at my son Lorenzo's day-care center dub him "Speedy" as he danced and sang in Spanish one day back in 1996. Everyone was so happy: the teachers and attendants, my son, then two, bathed in the smiles of his keepers and a tad bewildered by the blank expression on my face, my silence.

* * *

But why linger with all that ancient history when the news afoot is rather sanguine? In the 1990s there arose a somewhat new and popular animated "Mexican," flashed across the nation's television cables and satellite dishes on MTV and Nickelodeon. His name was Ren Høëk, one half of the dynamic duo named Ren and Stimpy. Ren, pictured here on the left, was an anger-management nightmare, an excitable and irritable Chihuahua dog, the brainchild of a somewhat brilliant and neurotic animator by the name of John Kricfalusi.[64]

While not quite as debauched as the Speedy origin intrigue folded into the dirty joke recounted above, this genesis, provided by Kricfalusi's own online presence at Spumco.com, is not without some interest of its own.

The two featured characters started out as separate doodles. One was a psychotic chihuahua and the other was a retarded-looking cat. . . . Kricfalusi would do these funny little drawings to amuse his co-workers. Soon he was doing a creepy Peter Lorre voice and acting out insane scenes with the chihuahua character. At first, these characters had no names. The name for the chihuahua was suggested by Joel Fajnor, an animator who worked at Calico with John. He was visiting Kricfalusi at his apartment in Van Nuys when he burst out laughing as he stared at the mailbox. Kricfalusi asked what he was laughing at and Fajnor pointed to the name on the mail box, "Ren Høëk." John explained that was his apartment manager's name.[65]

The tale ends with Fajnor's suggestion: "Why don't you call your little chihuahua Ren Høëk?"

The "next-generation" animated "Mexican": the always angry and possibly queer Ren Høëk, here knocking booty with his faithful, loving roommate, Stimpson the Cat, aka Stimpy.

Like Speedy, Ren is "Mexican," a *chihuahueño* to be exact. But said *mejicanidad* is not his essence, and therein lies his difference from the annoying rodent Speedy Gonzales. Gonzales's *essence* was a strain of Mexicanicity directly derived from the eyes and cameras of invading U.S. soldiers—most of the gags profit by reinculcating some aspect of U.S. wartime manufactured views (1848, 1914—take your pick) of Mexicans and Mexico. Ren, too, is Mexican, but he lives in what appears to be an Eisenhoweresque-era U.S. suburb. His Mexicanicity is evidenced by his outrageous accent and his pedigree (he is, after all, pure *chihuahueño*), but that does not fix the dimensions of his character.

What defines Ren Høëk is his temper or, more specifically, his on-again, off-again hatred for his housemate Stimpson J. Cat aka "Stimpy." In addition, Ren's bipolar, homoerotic attraction/revulsion for his intellectually challenged cohort provides the plot twists for the majority of their series of animated shorts. Ren has a temper—he loves and he hates Stimpy. That is what is "funny." Even Ren's name is different, more Northern European than "Mexican" or Latino: Høëk. I must add here in all honesty that Kricfalusi reads my take on Ren with more than a grain of salt; to quote the illustrator directly from our limited correspondence: "Hi Bill, Ren is from some nameless ignorant backwards Europeon (funny [*sic*]) nation. [signed] JK."[66]

Contested etiologies aside, Kricfalusi gives us a popular, deliciously odd, and unpredictable "Mexican" anyone can love, or love to hate. In this regard, Mr. Ren Høëk represents an evolutionary step forward from the retrograde theatrics of Speedy Gonzales. And where the sexual politics of Speedy Gonzales are predictable (a Mexican rakish mouse *chasin' after the ladies*), those of Ren Høëk and Stimson J. Cat are unpredictable and, turning to Freud, "polymorphously perverse." The omnipresent suggestion in various episodes of the series is that Ren and Stimpy may be more than *just* roommates. So huge was the rumor to that effect, that Kricfalusi himself finally felt compelled to hold forth in a 1997 article in the *San Francisco Examiner*:

"'Does this mean the rumors are true? Are Ren and Stimpy lovers?'

"'Totally,' said their dad proudly. 'In Ren's case, it's not completely by choice. He'd rather have a beautiful human woman if he could get away

A screen grab and preliminary sketch from *Rubber Nipple Salesmen*, first broadcast in 1992.

with it. Since he can't, Stimpy's easy. Stimpy's madly in love with Ren.'"[67] The images here reproduced give you a taste of their eclectic, erotica-tinged pleasures.

Outside the domain of animated short features, other enchorial, Southwestern Chicano graphic artists are grappling with the ugly legacy of Mexicans and Chicanas/os in film. Writer/Artists like Los Brothers Hernandez (Jaime and Gilbert Hernandez) in *Love and Rockets* are redefining the boundaries of graphic fiction in the late twentieth and early twenty-first centuries.[68]

For example, Jaime's "Flies on the Ceiling"—part of a decades-long graphic narrative/comix project that would make Dickens tired—examines the ongoing story of Chicana writer Isabel "Izzy" Ruebens, who returns to Mexico in an attempt to flee the demons of memory. While in Mexico, the displaced Chicana scribe encounters other demons, some real, some imagined, some both.[69]

The panel sampled here in haunting black and white pictures Izzy's despair in those moments dividing sleep from waking life when the torturous, yet tormenting, yet irresistible allures of memory haunt Ruebens's vulnerable psyche.

Similarly, Gilbert Hernandez's "'A Folk Tale'" shuns the disturbing magical/psychological realism found in brother Jaime's "Flies on the Ceiling" for a no-less-provocative full-blown allegory chronicling the battle of God, Satan, and Death for the soul of Steña (pictured here with Death, sans scythe, in the headgear of a Mexican wrestler).

The allegory ends as it must, with Death winning out over the protests of a demystified God (figured in the garb of an old homeless man) and a comical Satan (whom Hernandez pictures in the costume of a fat superhero).

The largely wordless picture show ends with a none-too-cheery moral: "Death makes no distinctions

(top) Jaime Hernandez's brilliant and damaged heroine Izzy Ruebens. The noir-esque qualities of Hernandez's work are to be noted here: the silent cross, doubled by the shadow of a windowpane, underscores the role of a Catholic miasma, the legacy of theology, in the melancholia of Hernandez's character.

Gilbert Hernandez's comedic, erotic, sadomasochistic reveries from the pages of *Love and Rockets*. Any Chicana/o- or Latina/o-identified subjectivity seeking respite or some sort of ocular hy/eye/giene from the pollution that passes for "entertainment" on TV and the movies—George Lopez included and Salma Hayek excepted (for the moment)—should turn to the pages of *Love and Rockets*.

between young or old, rich or poor, good or bad; he welcomes us all into his heart."

Allow me to give you one more glance at Gilbert Hernandez's work from the middle of *The Blood of Palomar*, a compilation of a series of short graphic stories that originally appeared with the title *Human Dias-trophism*.[70] Hernandez's graphic novella charts the havoc wreaked by a serial killer in the small Central American community of Palomar, but it is also (and not coincidentally) the story of Humberto, a young Latino artist coming to terms with his art at the very moment he witnesses a hideous attempted murder.

The result is an existential, aesthetic, and psychological crisis that leaves the budding artist unable to speak, and, as we see here, unable to move. Hernandez's imposition of a crucifix-like window shadow underscores the theological dimensions of psyche scarring attendant upon this particular artist. The portrait of Humberto, the artist, as a young man provides the perfect counterpoint to the story of serial killer Tomaso in the novel. The efforts of the Hernandez brothers, along with the appearance of anomalies like Ren Høëk, offer hope that the Golden Age of Mexican stereotypes may soon be at an end.

Incision Eight | Postmortem Reverie

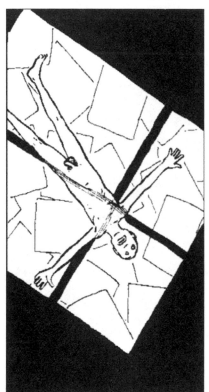

The silly symmetry of Speedy Gonzales's familiarity falls away from us in a careful study of the artistry of Chicano seer Gilbert Hernandez. In this masterful portrait/(self?)-portrait, Hernandez graphs for us the consequences of something he calls "human dias-trophism," the spiritual and physical catastrophe—"dias-trophism" is a geological term that refers to the movement of the earth's plates—of a young would-be artist.

Examining the logic of stereotypes with specific emphasis on those with a decidedly Mexican flavor, we should not imagine for a second that they have been or ever will be completely exorcised.

"Autopsy of a rat": even as I used that optimistic phrase to order this interpretive exercise, I knew only too well that it was our collective unconscious, a conceptual figure designating the psyche of all of us drowned in the fascinating and addicting charms of the First World emporium (an ideological miasma if there ever was one), that was the true body in need of an inquest.

In short, Speedy may well outlive us all. I know also that it will be quite easy to read (and, for some, to reject) the accumulated findings contained within these pages as yet another contribution to a growing number of victims' histories appearing from publishers in the humanities and social sciences. I am quite comfortable with this association: analyses of elided networks of power necessarily mandate a sensitivity to those luckless bodies whose abuse silently (offstage, as it were) sustains the hegemony of the status quo. Sander Gilman writes in *The Jew's Body* that "it is in being visible in 'the body that betrays' that the Jew is most uncomfortable,"[71] and I have taken heart from his lines: our bodies, our faces, our particular—some would say peculiar—*mexicana/o* accent does bring with it certain associations, true or not (is truth ever the point of the story?), that a careful reading of the visual record reveals.

And Speedy is just one emblematic representative of a litany of Latino types. One might say we should all know better than to believe that the images we see have anything to do with the shapes they ostensibly embody, but do we ever really *know* better? Mexico and Mexicans in the American imagination must figure and be interpreted in *other* ways. Rosario Castellanos's ruminations on language evolution are to the point here: "Just as happens with coins, words wear out and lose that sharpness that makes them valuable, words become mistaken, polyphonic. Handled and spit upon, they must be bathed in purity in order to recover their pristine qualities."[72] In this light, it is no stretch to suggest that the word "Mexican" awaits its turn for a long, hot, well-deserved soaking.

Suture Corpse

It is only shallow people who do not judge by appearances. The true mystery of the world is the visible, not the invisible.

—Lord Henry Wotton, *The Picture of Dorian Gray*, Oscar Wilde[73]

I'm just the carbon copy you read when you can't find the original.

—Eve Harrington (Anne Baxter) to Margo Channing's (Bette Davis's) future screen and real-life husband, Bill Sampson (Gary Merrill), in Joseph Mankiewicz's *All About Eve* (1950)

I end these analecta with a confession.

I suffer from a condition I share with most other people I run across in my professional activities as a university professor and my day-to-day activities as a breathing, (sometimes) thinking subject taking up space on the planet.

My confession?

I am both repulsed and fascinated by stereotypes.

They are so much a part of storytelling, so much a part of all things called narrative, that you begin to wonder how you could tell a story at all without somehow making use of these readily available one-dimensional characterizations.

This collage has a history. In the 1990s, I must have done close to one hundred outreach talks to elementary, middle, and high school kids all across Southern California—this adulterated graphic was part of the handout materials for those talks. Rosina Talamantes, a graduate student of mine at San Diego State University, took this drawing and used it to adorn a Joseph Cornell–style box within which she placed her final essay for my theory class; I believe a Ren Høek figurine, since lost, was part of the ensemble as well.

Bloodstains of cultures in conflict (often in *combat*), stereotypes fade, mutate, and evolve, but they never really go away. And they lead to particular pathological conditions, a kind of eye-borne *parakinesia*. But where the classic form of parakinesia brings on clumsy, unnatural body movements caused by the impairment of motor functions, stereotypes attack the inner ontological fibers, leaving behind an awkwardness no less real.

The subtitle of this chapter signals that I have chosen to read Freddy López and Speedy Gonzales as cinematic marionettes, and it is worth the time here to remind ourselves that "marionette" derives from the French name "Marion," itself a diminutive of the name "Marie." The prolix, if amiable, *Webster's Third International Dictionary* suggests this "probably comes from the conception that a puppet resembles an image of the Virgin Mary."[74]

An odd take, wouldn't you agree? But I live for these kinds of etymological apocrypha—these tales philologists tempt us with, which give ironic flavor to our hermeneutic adventures.

Plato (no slouch himself when it comes to parables and puppets), too, might smile at the idea of the "Virgin Mary" serving as the denominating synecdoche for all of puppetry—Christ would probably be less amused, though puppets seem in and of themselves the perfect analogue for the literary genre labeled "parable," a storytelling mode the Nazarene native had down pat.

We need to take something to counteract all we see. We see too much and get used to it. Before we know it, we *are* what we see. It is as if our various and disparate communities suffered something collectively, a condition much akin to what psychological enclaves call echolalia, wherein afflicted individuals pathologically repeat what is said by other people around them.

Via neologism, we can speak now of our virulent *scopto*-echolalia, some mad fusion of a voyeuristic pathology with a Tourette's-like repetition compulsion—a drive to pathologically repeat what we see about us.

All the more, then, must we intervene diligently at the site of our seeing—see again that which we have seen too many times so as to see a way through, and imagine a space where Speedy Gonzales never figures the way he has in the past, the way he figures now in our present.

Lights. Camera. Action.

Let the rat lie open, exposed, with viscera askew, the object of a vivisectionist voyeur's delight.

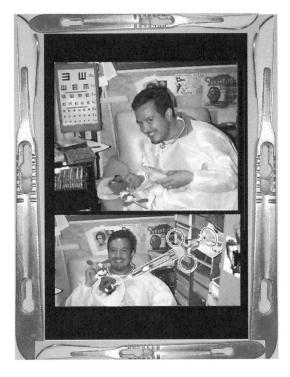

SAN YSIDRO, Calif. — This image, released by the U.S. Border Patrol, shows the legs of a 5-year-old girl inside a party piñata that was discovered on Nov. 2, 2004 during a vehicle search at the San Ysidro, Calif., border station crossing along the U.S.-Mexican border. (04/05/05 AP photo)

Anticipating "XicanOsmosis"
A postscript to Autopsy of a Rat

Along the border, ubiquitous as all get out, as common as sin, is the piña-ta. But here the pirated Powerpuff Girl piñata, a well-crafted Buttercup, to be exact—the cool-cruel feisty one of the oddly conceived, test-tube-forged trio—finds herself "inhabited" by an *other*—an "illegal immi-grant," an "undocumented 'worker,'" a "person of interest," the scourge of Homeland Security wonks and plebes alike: a five-year-old Mexican girl.

The story, replete with mystery and happy ending, is part of the weave of a rebellious, counter-Tex[t]-Mex and warrants retelling:

> Inspectors at border checkpoints have seen it all: people rolled inside carpets, sewn into car seats and stuffed into washing machines, all attempting to be smuggled into the United States.
>
> But inspectors at the Tecate Port of Entry discovered a new twist recently when they encountered a little girl meticulously sealed inside a piñata.
>
> The child was found just before 3 p.m. Nov. 2, when two U.S. citizens attempted to drive a 1990 Acura sedan loaded with several piñatas through the border checkpoint. Suspicious customs inspec-tors decided to take a closer look at their cargo.

"Autopsy of a Rat, Chapter 2," digital media, Guillermo Nericcio García; photography, Jamie Heather Fox-Rice.

(top right) A profile of But-tercup, the belligerent and feistiest member of the *Pow-erpuff Girls* trio.

Like some cool twenty-first-century riff on the Trojan Horse trope, the dangling body of an undocumented Mexican girl, *influenzing* the Mexico-U.S. borderlands, embodies a curious form of what I call "XicanOsmosis" in a chapter below.

"Officers began to take the piñatas out of the back seat, and one seemed to be much heavier than the others," said Vince Bond, a spokesman for U.S. Customs & Border Protection. "This one had a little girl of approximately 4 or 5 years of age inside it."

The girl's mother also was found, curled up inside the car's trunk, and the girl's brother, who is about 9 years old, was found underneath the collapsible back seat.

The large piñata carrying the little girl appeared to be a representation of a "Powerpuff Girls" cartoon character.

The girl was completely sealed inside, Bond said, but she was able to breathe and seemed to be in good physical condition. She, her mother and brother were voluntarily deported to Mexico after they were found.

The car carrying the piñatas bore California plates and was driven by a female U.S. citizen; a man in the passenger seat also is a U.S. citizen. Their names were not available.

Neither will be prosecuted, Bond said, in part because of the sheer volume of immigrant-smuggling cases.[75]

The gods are in a good mood; deus ex machina, they provide our denouement. Staring in awe at the picture here, we confront the odd antithesis of Speedy Gonzales and Freddy López: *not* the animatronic "Mexican" inhabited by non-Mexican animators and puppeteers, but an unequivocally American, decidedly *gringa* animated telepersonality, rendered transient statue (shades of Pygmalion), but whose center, soul, and ego are the warm-blooded body of a cute five-year-old Mexican girl—a twenty-first-century Trojan horse made of paper, glue, and strips of wood carries in its womb a face and body of an American tomorrow.[76]

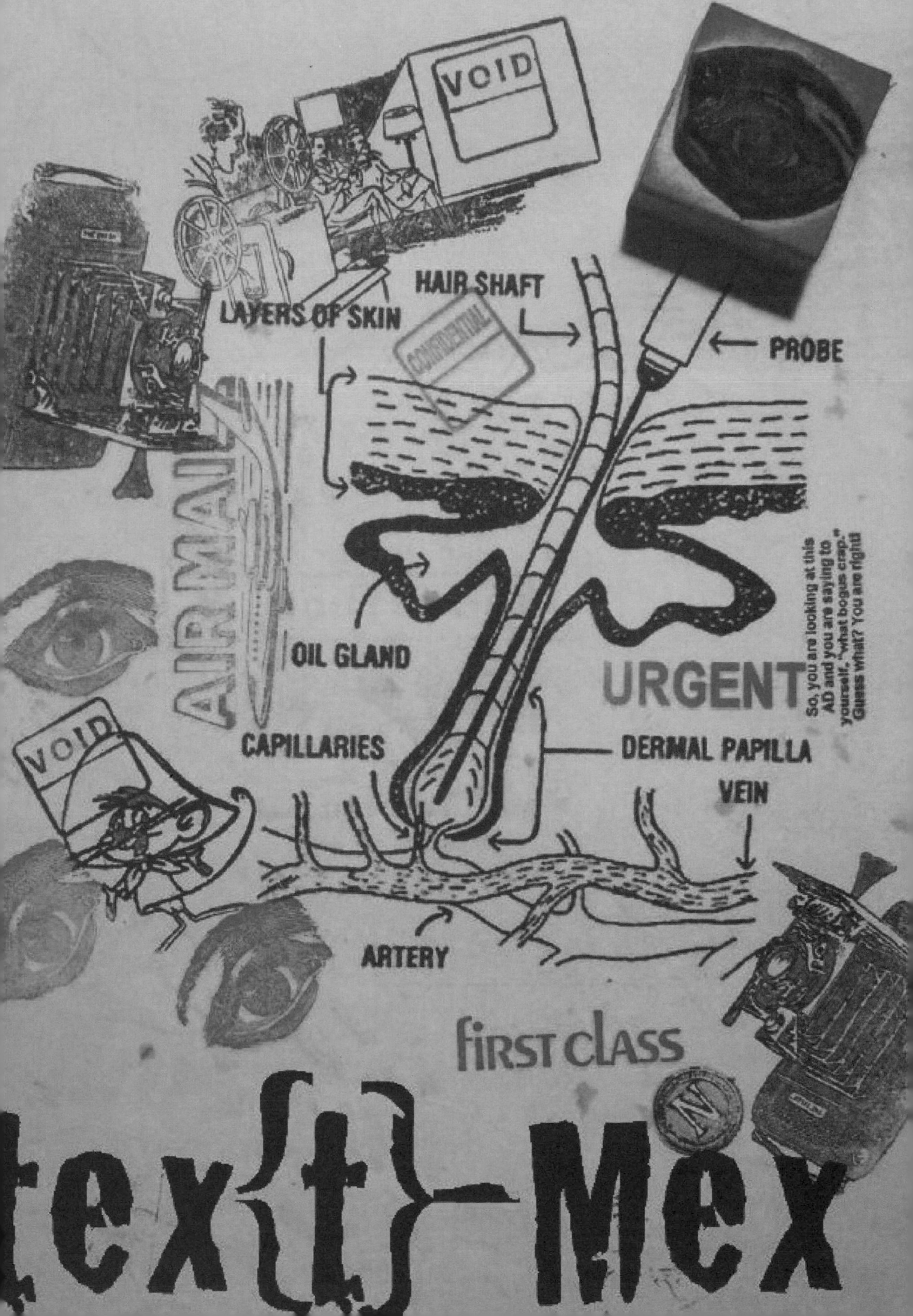

VOID

PROBE

LAYERS OF SKIN

HAIR SHAFT

CONFIDENTIAL

OIL GLAND

URGENT

CAPILLARIES

DERMAL PAPILLA

VEIN

ARTERY

AIRMAIL

VOID

So, you are looking at this AD and you are saying to yourself, "what bogus crap." Guess what? You are right!

first class

tex{t}-Mex

MEXICO Twenty miles southeast of Tijuana
MEXICO Twenty miles southeast of Tijuana
MEXICO Twenty miles southeast of Tijuana
MEXICO Twenty miles southeast of Tijuana

TIJUANA, MEXICO
TIJUANA, MEXICO
TIJUANA, MEXICO
TIJUANA, MEXICO

CINCINNATI, OHIO The suburb of Indian Hill
CINCINNATI, OHIO The suburb of Indian Hill
CINCINNATI, OHIO The suburb of Indian Hill
CINCINNATI, OHIO The suburb of Indian Hill

COLUMBUS, OHIO State Supreme Court
COLUMBUS, OHIO State Supreme Court
COLUMBUS, OHIO State Supreme Court
COLUMBUS, OHIO State Supreme Court

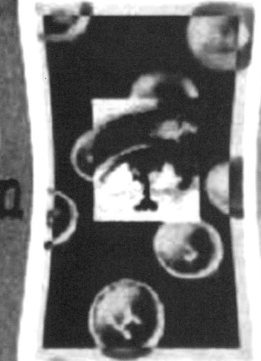

Not mexican

AdAge.com™

Login or Register

Search / QwikFIND [　　　] [Go] ▸ Master Search

[Home]
News
Hispanic Marketing
Interactive News
Media News
Account Action
American
Demographics
Data Center

Career Center
Marketplace

My AdAge
Print Edition
Customer Services
About Us
Media Kit
Privacy Statement

Account Intelligence
AdCritic.com
Agency Preview
Madison+Vine
Point
Encyclopedia

CUSTOM PROGRAMS ▸

Mar. 30, 2005 1:57 p.m.

☐ **Take The Weekly Ad Age Online Poll**
Should the TV upfront switch to a stock market-like business model?

daily | **BREAKING NEWS** | EXCLUSIVELY ONLINE ✺

Online Exclusive: Account Action

 ebaY

EBAY.COM FIRES AD AGENCY GOODBY SILVERSTEIN

San Francisco Shop Handled Auction Company's Ad Work for Six Years

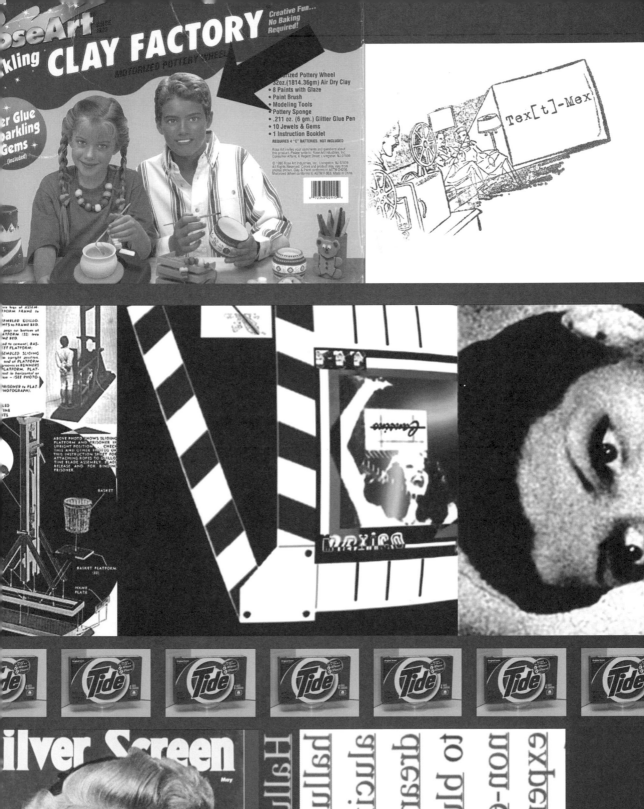

FOX
PRESENTA

LA NAVE DE SATÁN

EN ESPAÑOL

misnumbering error there is no figure 3.28 fix in body of book, yikes!!!!!

if someone came along who CHANGED
the way you THINK about everything
EVERYTHING about the way you think?

WINNER

DERRIDA

if someone came along who CHANGED
he way you THINK about everything
EVERYTHING about the way you think?

WINNER

DERRIDA

Stuart ERWIN
Lupe VELEZ
Jimmie DURANTE

PALOOKA

MOVIE CLASSIC

15c in Canada
10¢

APRIL

HEPBURN'S
GREATEST
RIVAL IS
HEPBURN

GEORGE RAFT
DEFIES
HOLLYWOOD

GAMBLED
MILLION
ON NEW STAR!

THE
STRANGEST
VENGEANCE
EVER
PLANNED!

Universal-International presents

CHARLTON   JANET   ORSON
HESTON · LEIGH · WELLES

"Touch of Evil"

JOSEPH CALLEIA · AKIM TAMIROFF ...·"Guest Stars" MARLENE DIETRICH · ZSA ZSA GABOR

Screenplay by ORSON WELLES · Produced by ALBERT ZUGSMITH · Directed by ORSON WELLES

acting

LIFE

S R LAWRENCE OLIVIER as
HAMLET

MARCH 15, 1948 15 CENTS

pre-kick!

BUTTERCUP

Buttercup is a tough, hotheaded tomboy. Buttercup doesn't have time for plans; she's all action. And don't try getting in her way! She fights hard and has a pile of victims to prove it. Buttercup takes her super strength super seriously. When evil emerges, Buttercup is toned and ready to fight fast and furiously.

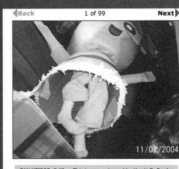

Back · 1 of 99 · Next

11/02/2004

SAN YSIDRO, Calif. -- This image, released by the U.S. Border Patrol, shows the legs of a 5-year-old girl inside a party pinata

AYS OF OBLIGATION

An Argument with

My Mexican Father

BR

ME

DI

RICHARD RODRIGUEZ

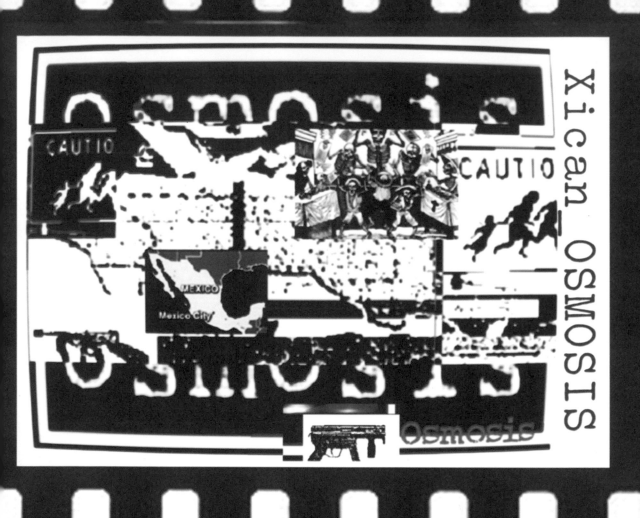

CHAPTER 4
LUPE VÉLEZ REGURGITATED; OR, JESUS'S KLEENEX

Cautionary, Indigestion-Inspiring Ruminations on "Mexicans" in "American" Toilets

Soiled Tile One: The Gospel According to Lupe

From an allegory of a Trojan horse, reimagined with an interior decor straight from the border, we move back again in space and time. Way back.

> *Genesis. Chapter One, Verse One of the*
> *Book of Genesis,* estilo *Tex[t] Mex*

𝔍𝔫 𝔱𝔥𝔢 𝔟𝔢𝔤𝔦𝔫𝔫𝔦𝔫𝔤 𝔴𝔞𝔰 𝔱𝔥𝔢 𝔏𝔞𝔱𝔦𝔫𝔞 𝔟𝔬𝔪𝔟𝔰𝔥𝔢𝔩𝔩 𝔞𝔫𝔡 𝔰𝔥𝔢, 𝔱𝔥𝔦𝔰 𝔱𝔢𝔯𝔪, 𝔬𝔯 𝔱𝔥𝔦𝔰 𝔥𝔬𝔩𝔩𝔶𝔴𝔬𝔬𝔡 𝔱𝔯𝔬𝔭𝔢 𝔞𝔱 𝔞𝔫𝔶 𝔯𝔞𝔱𝔢, 𝔴𝔞𝔰 𝔪𝔞𝔡𝔢 𝔣𝔩𝔢𝔰𝔥: 𝔣𝔩𝔢𝔰𝔥 𝔞𝔫𝔡 𝔟𝔩𝔬𝔬𝔡—𝔣𝔩𝔢𝔰𝔥 𝔞𝔫𝔡 𝔟𝔩𝔬𝔬𝔡 𝔞𝔫𝔡 . . . 𝔳𝔬𝔪𝔦𝔱.

More on this "vomit" below.

Stereotypes, or, better put, metastereotropes like that of the sexy, wanton, Latina spitfire Lupe Vélez, live on in the popular print media and the boardrooms of Hollywood, where actresses and entertainers like JLO (aka Jennifer Lopez, aka Jennie from d'block), Salma Hayek, Penelope Cruz, Cameron Diaz, and Eva Longoria continue to prosper and profit from the patents made by *hot* Latina mademoiselles of another critical moment.

Dolores del Río, Carmen Miranda, and Lupe Vélez writhe across the silver screens of the Americas in the 1930s and the 1940s with such success that alternatives to the vision of the Latina bombshell—hypersexualized, utterly duplicitous, voraciously selfish, and relentlessly dissatisfied—will go on into time ad infinitum.[1]

A publicity glossy of Lupe Vélez by Irving Chidnoff, allegedly signed by the deceased star. In this undated, autographed publicity still, Lupe Vélez performs a photographic gloss on Borges's infamous "Borges and I" poem—who are we looking at? A "Mexican Spitfire"? "Lupe Vélez"? "María Guadalupe Vélez de Villalobos"? or someone else, *something* yet again?

Soiled Tile Two: Disgust

It's enough to make you sick.

Soiled Tile Three: Vomit

We will spill. Together, we will hurl.

Out from the depths will cascade the very things that allow us to be: water, food, nourishment—of course; but image, identity, and ideas as well. The tale of Lupe Vélez offers the anticipated attractions of scandal, gossip, and catastrophe, but it brings as well a cautionary warning regarding the powerful forces of the semiotic as they fuse with that of the existential—*as the waters converge*.

So let us approach the mirror, see the silver screen, seek the self, find *the other*, and let the waters flow. A vixenlike *Oxford English Dictionary*, sensing our need to license our licentious use of "vomit" and "vomitoria" as thematic and rhetorical pipelines, stands ready for her cameo: "vomitorium . . . 1. A passage or opening in an ancient amphitheatre or theatre, leading to or from the seats"; here, the *OED* quotes no less a figure than Tobias Smollett, who adds that a vomitorium is a place "entered by avenues, at the end of which were gates, called *vomitoriae*" (1766, Smollett, Trav. II, 228).

LUPE VELEZ SUICIDE OVER LOVE TRAGEDY

Notes Left by Mexican Actress Explain She Preferred Death to Becoming Unwed Mother

Illustrated on Page 3, Part 1

Lupe Velez, 34, volatile Mexican film actress, whose star for many years blazed brilliantly in Hollywood, ended her own life yesterday by an overdose of sleeping pills, leaving two poignant notes in which she wrote of unrequited love and expectant motherhood.

She was found dead in bed in her home at 732 N. Rodeo Drive, Beverly Hills, lying as if asleep under an eiderdown quilt and clothed in blue satin pajamas.

An undated newspaper clipping documenting the tragic suicide of Lupe Vélez.

This is a telling illustration, for in reading and regurgitating the life of Lupe Vélez together, it is as if the pages of this chapter were like the confines of a masterfully appointed and gloriously designed theater—perhaps my footnotes or asides enact *vomitoriae* of sorts.

What happens next is worthy of Hollywood; the *OED* next hands us, or, better put, *shows* us, what it calls an "erron," or erroneous definition (said erron, of course, is both near and dear to the heart of this chapter, as it is the closest thing the *OED* has that can pass for gossip—"errons" as illegitimate, yet *recorded*, bastard etymologies): "[vomitorium:] 2. Erron. A room in which ancient Romans are alleged to have vomited deliberately during feasts." So the *OED* allows herself to have it *both* ways: vomitorium as theatre portal *and* erron, a Roman space of post-feast purging—a theater and a toilet or, with specific regard to our inquiry into Lupe Vélez, a star site and a spectacle of expulsion, a proscenium *and* a latrine, in the midst of a semiotic and semantic barfing up of a Latina spectacle.

More on the niceties of vomit and subjectivity to follow, because in asking us to recall the life, career, and death of Lupe Vélez, and, in particular the circumstances of her "sic" death—vomiting owing to an overdose—the dynamics of said exit fall under our purview.

Soiled Tiles Four, Five, Six, and, Truly Soiled, Seven: Four Epigraphs Make a Late Cameo: Irigaray, Fanon, Castellanos, Faulkner

Speculum in the Toilet

Theoretically there would be no such thing as woman. She would not exist. The best that can be said is that she does not exist yet. Something of her a-specificity might be found in the betweens that occur in being, or beings. These gaps reopen the question of the "void," and thereby most commonly give rise to vigorous, horrified rejection and a move to plug the hole with speculative "tissues" and "organs." . . . Woman has, and will have, no place and thus no existence. This will be true even in her privation of being, which it is the essential task and ceaseless effort of dialectic and dialectic's indispensable intermediaries to bring or bring back to the fullness of the self's possession of substance.

—Luce Irigaray[2]

Waiting for Me to Appear in the Toilet

I am overdetermined from without. I am the slave not of the "idea" that others have of me but of my own appearance. . . . I cannot go to a film without seeing myself. I wait for me. In the interval just before the film starts, I wait for me. The people in the theater are watching me, examining me, waiting for me. A Negro groom is going to appear. My heart makes my head swim.

—Frantz Fanon[3]

Pregnant in the Toilet

In the maternal cavity, a mysterious event takes place, a kind of miracle that, like all miracles, arouses astonishment: it is witnessed by the attendants and experienced by the protagonist "in fear and trembling." Careful. One sudden move, carelessness, an unsatisfied whim, and the miracle will not happen. Nine unending months of rest, of dependence upon others, precautions, rites, taboos. Pregnancy is a sickness whose outcome is always catastrophic for whomever suffers it.

—Rosario Castellanos[4]

Castrated in the Toilet

. . . they saw that the man was not dead yet, and when they saw what Grimm was doing, one of the men gave a choked cry and stumbled back into the wall and began to vomit. Then Grimm too sprang back, flinging behind him the bloody butcher knife. "Now you'll let white women alone, even in hell," he said. But the man on the floor had not moved. He just lay there, with his eyes open and empty of everything save consciousness, and with something, a shadow, about his mouth. For a long moment he looked up at them with peaceful and unfathomable and unbearable eyes. Then his face, body, all, seemed to collapse, to fall in upon itself, and from out the slashed garments about his hips and loins the pent black blood seemed to rush like a released breath. It seemed to rush out of his pale body like the rush of sparks from a rising rocket; upon that black blast the man seemed to rise soaring into their memories forever and ever. They are not to lose it.

—William Faulkner[5]

Our eyes and ears upon the tiles, anxious with the chore of vomit exegesis, we pause to greet our visitors—Luce Irigaray, Jacques Lacan's canny, cunning nemesis and psychoanalysis's dazzling French femme fatale; Frantz Fanon, Freud's postcolonial doppelgänger, who knew how to probe with style and dramatic flair the psyche of the wretched of the earth; Rosario Castellanos, Mexico's underrated feminist diva, a woman who deserves better recognition for having anticipated, by a decade, the legendary French feminisms of Irigaray, Kristeva, et al.; and, last but not least, William Faulkner—Southern seer—the Old South's gossip, who revealed to his readers so much about the rich American tapestry of racialized hate. Fanon and Castellanos, old hands, ably assisted us with Rita Hayworth earlier; Faulkner and Irigaray, an unlikely duet, are new to our cast.

All four give us so much to mull over and chew on.

Moving slowly, we digest carefully—lest we eat too fast and end up getting sick.

We begin with the last epigraph above: while there may be more famous scenes of vomiting in the history of Western literature (take, for instance, the thirty-third chapter of Gustave Flaubert's singularly lurid *Madame Bovary*, where a trail of black effluvial retch exits Emma's corpse's mouth, figuring the sins of sex and greed enacted by the other mouth, the other *marge*, that perpetrated if not emblematized these sins—*Il fallut soulever un peu la tête, et alors un flot de liquides noirs sortit, comme un vomissement, de sa bouche* [Ch. 33]). . . .

I got carried away; Emma's black flood took me away from Lupe—it is almost as if I owe Vélez an apology. . .

As I was saying, while there may be *more famous* literary feats of throwing up, you would have to read a mountain of books to get close to the scene of racialized puking that Faulkner weaves into *Light in August*, his epic allegorical meditation on the complexities of miscegenation in the American South, epitomized in the remarkable and singular figure of Joe Christmas.[6]

The selection from Faulkner that I eviscerated from the tail end of the novel begins with a witness vomiting and ends with a castration—a castration that looses a biblical flood of black blood that symbolizes both Joe Christmas's miscegenated, dark, magic, sinful, violent sexuality (you can almost "hear" Frantz Fanon's eyes roll as you reread this quotation) as well as the displaced, elided African "darkness" that no volume of white blood can dissipate. Faulkner is useful to us here, as this chapter treats with issues that pertain to reproduction, race, ethnicity, and violence. That I will be referencing said categories with regard to the body of a Latina woman involved in a lifelong affair with motion pictures and the entertainment industry explains why Fanon, Castellanos, and Irigaray appeared above, before Will Faulkner's none-too-subtle cue—when a Latina gets into bed with Hollywood, we are going to need more than one psychoanalyst around to help us wade through this mess.

But I am getting ahead of myself again and should stick to the facts, the plain facts, and nothing but the facts, at least for a little while, to let you get your fill.

Soiled Tile Eight: Pepto Bismol/Crypt Abysmal

This chapter is authored in the spirit of a twenty-first-century Foucault-stained archaeology project—some odd farrago of words, images, history, hearsay, gossip, and philosophy that might accurately characterize the figuration of Mexicans in mass culture here in the United States.

It concerns moments in the career of Lupe Vélez, or, as she was born, María Guadalupe Vélez de Villalobos. Her origins were in San Luis Potosí, Mexico; from there she moved north to California and experienced an ascent to the heights of cinematic fame in Hollywood and, of course, exited this world via her eventual suicide in a "fake hacienda on Rodeo Drive" on December 13, 1944, five months pregnant with the baby of her jilting lover, Harold Raymond.[7] In a scene that anticipates the denouement of Marilyn Monroe, Kurt Cobain, Hunter Thompson, and others later in the last century and into the next, Vélez's staged exit comes to define the dynamics of her career and delimit the discourse of her cinematic legacy. But as much as my chapter concerns itself with a now-forgotten Hollywood tragedy, it is also driven by a curiosity about the material outcome of her success across the United States.

After Vélez, one came to expect a certain type of Latina in film—perhaps more than any other figure save Dolores Del Río and Carmen Miranda, Vélez and her handlers helped concretize an image of Latina "exoticness," sensuality, and silliness that dogs those who have inherited her mantle in film and, most importantly, those Latinas and Latinos not in film, whose lives unfold in the powerful shadow of Hollywood's convincing confabulations.

Soiled Tile Nine: Vomit Exegesis In and Out of Lupe Vélez's Toilet

With Lupe Vélez, we come face-to-face with the elusive and exhilarating allure of celebrity, a category Richard Burt and Jeffrey Wallen remind us "is all about exclusion—what you can't have." Burt and Wallen's take on icons of fame and glamour is to the point: "What is desired is something that is not achievable by degrees, by slowly moving up the ladder, or by transmission, by a passing on of what one knows. What one desires, in celebrity, is what one cannot have. Hollywood celebrity is built on distance, on the unbridgeable gap that defines desire—one desires here precisely what has been reproduced, the image."[8] Tag-team-critics Burt and Wallen speak here to a kind of existential jump cut or crosscut, whereby our fated celebrity evolves *overnight* from *no* one to *some*one. But when that someone is Mexican, and living in the context of the United States, more thought must be sprinkled on our dish.

We need to know more, think about more, take more into account—we must affix to our notion of stereotypes and celebrity a sensitivity to the power of parody in our critical inquests: merely self-righteously outing the damned purveyors of stereotypes will not end their eternal cycle, and acknowledging the unreality of a desire will not, in the end, diminish in any way the very real *pull* of that desire. In this regard, the singular rhetorical flourishes of the dynamic Sianne Ngai are useful, especially when she reminds us in her meditation on animated ethnic types that

> racial stereotypes and clichés, cultural images that are perversely both dead and alive, can be critically interrogated not only by making them more dead (say, by attempting to stop their circulation) but also by reanimating them. Thus while animatedness and its affective cousins (liveliness, vigor, and zest) remain ugly categories of feeling reinforcing the historically tenacious construction of racialized subjects as excessively emotional, bodily subjects, they might also be thought of as categories of feeling that highlight animation's status as a nexus of contradictions and as a technology with the capacity to generate unanticipated social meanings and effects—as when the routine manipulation of racialized bodies on screen results in an unsuspected liveliness undermining animation's traditional role in constituting bodies as raced.[9]

When Ngai ends by stating that "animation calls for new ways of understanding the technologizing of the racialized body as well as the uneasy differential between types and stereotypes" (596), she gives a new way to understand Lupe Vélez's over-the-top antics, a new way to see in her and her celebrity a means to ending a circuit of unmediated consumption and vomiting; a cinematic vomitorium where the traces of filmed subjectivities stay behind, the residua we come to know with familiarity as our unconscious.

But "Stop!" one might cry out. "Vélez was a *person, not an animated cartoon character—save your quotes for Speedy Gonzales.*"

Perhaps.

But when you are dealing with the seductive hallucination of a "Mexican" in the semiotic and cultural history of the Americas, especially in the United States of America, rigorous lines dividing animated puppet (Vélez) from animated puppet (Speedy) are hallucinations themselves.

More important in the foregoing gloss is the way that Ngai, generous thinker that she is, hands us a way of simultaneously fathoming Vélez as a victim, as a perpetrator (glammy perp though she was), and as a hermeneutic prototype—we cultural critics, both those in the know and those in the dark (most of the time), can use the bitter, lurid history of a fallen star to gauge the very real day-to-day dynamics that drive the figuration of Latina bodies today.

Soiled Tile Ten: What are you talking about, show us the pictures already!

Here are some stills from a fantastic 1934 boxing flick directed by Benjamin Stoloff called *Palooka*, starring Jimmy Durante and Lupe Vélez—the movie follows the rise and fall of the titular hero making his way through the surly, gamey world of big-city boxers. These more succinctly summarize Vélez's range than any slew of paragraphs.

> Look at her.
> Look at Lupe.
> Look at her as she winks . . .
> . . . back at you.

The opening credits of *Palooka* set the stage for the "flavor" of "woman" being featured in the production. Lupe Vélez winks at us in the dark in the audience of the theater, and as she does so, we are let in on her secret, we are part of her secret, and perhaps we will be the target of her secret. All that matters is that we are put into play in a way where her celebrity and her Latina-ness are part and parcel of the same dialectical dream of taunt, desire, and seduction.

In these tandem shots, Lupe Vélez winks at her watchful spectator, you and me.

Awash with stereotypes, *Palooka* features African American early Hollywood regulars Louise Beavers and "Snowflake" to wile away the audience's time between shots of Vélez as a hot-blooded, tempestuous, and duplicitous floozy. An industry designed to cook up tasty treats for mass consumption, Hollywood regularly dished out more than we can now stomach.

Feature films, especially 1934 United Artists vehicles (this one directed by Stoloff, with writers Jack Jevne, Arthur Kober, and Gertrude Purcell, and adapted from the comic *Joe Palooka* by Ham Fisher), could be counted on to reaffirm any and all racialized worldviews popular in pre–World War II America.

The Mexican Spitfire has some African American company, for color?—Louise Beavers, cheery domestic, and "Snowflake" grin for the cameras in the opening credits of *Palooka*.

In a dance sequence that may have given birth to an equally curious scene in *Gilda*, mentioned earlier, Lupe Vélez cuts the rug at a fancy club in a scene from *Palooka*.

One of the best scenes in *Palooka* is the dance sequence at the nightclub where Nina Madero dances and attempts to woo Joe Palooka, played by the dopey Stuart Erwin; the scene anticipates Rita Hayworth's magnificent turn as Gilda in 1946.

Note how Lupe as Nina shields her face, semiotically underscoring her facile, self-interested "play" with dope Palooka, who defeated Nina's boyfriend, Al "Mac" McSwatt, played by William "Brother of James" Cagney, so Nina now sets her sights on the new champion. Fickle and ambitious, Nina likes what she gets and gets what she wants.

Enough of *Palooka*.

Let us end this picture show with a flash from a film featuring Vélez that had appeared four years earlier. In 1930, Vélez had played opposite Lew Ayres in *East Is West* for Universal Pictures; I found this unattributed publicity still in a box outside a junk shop in Studio City—I don't know if it is an "original" or not; I don't think so, at any rate. The photo depicts Lupe's voracious and violent Latina diet in a memorable fashion.

Said *taste* would have consequences for Vélez and Latinas in the ensuing generations.

Undated (circa 1930) *East Is West* publicity still (facsimile?).

Lupe Velez (*sic*) gets second billing over schnoz vaudevillian Jimmy Durante in this, the original, lobby card for *Palooka*, 1934.

Soiled Tile Twelve: Listening to Other Critics
Talk while Hidden in the Stalls

Critics hurl at times, as well. And we? We *attend*.

Let's have our first serving from Joanne Hershfield, a sober admonition that contends that "representations of race and gender in Hollywood cinema need to be examined not only within the context of public discourse but also *in relation to pressures* of the market during particular historical moments."[10] And, as I have argued elsewhere, one of the reasons Latina stereotypes propagate is that it is remarkably profitable to do so.

I sometimes wonder if my own fascination with Latina and Latino celebrities is not in some way caught up in a sordid economy wherein I help fuel and drive some peculiar re-reification of these figures.

In any event, let us return to Joanne Hershfield's findings, to the moment in her piece when she humbly offers that her "argument brings to light some problems with existing studies [not identified] that are concerned primarily with the relation between ideology and representation" (153). In a sequence cited above on Orson Welles and Chicano and Latin American advocacy, I referenced the drive in Hollywood during World War II to befriend Latin American nations—this was part of the war effort for a Washington very, very concerned about the prospect of a southern front being developed by Germany in Mexico, Central America, Argentina, and

Two views of Lupe Vélez: from 1929, on the cover of the April issue of *Movie Classics*; and from 1937, a publicity glossy of Vélez at the height of her stardom.

Brazil. In this light, Hershfield's reminder about Ella Shohat and Robert Stam's identification of exotic stereotypes in *Unthinking Eurocentrism* as the "tropes of empire" is very useful. Hershfield's shorthand glosses of Latina stereotypes are also quite good, reminding us how these figures tend to focus on the stars' bodies, with Latin American women most often being linked with "verbal epithets evoking tropical heat, violence, passion, and spies"(153). In another recent study, "The Demands of Authenticity," Brian O'Neill offers us a lot to chew on, noting how for Latinas, "lots of eye-rolling, body movement, double entendres, frantic bursts of Spanish dialogue, and fractured English marked by malapropisms" are the name of the game.[11]

Other critical treatments of Lupe Vélez include that of Alicia I. Rodríguez-Estrada, who reminds us of how, in the eight Mexican Spitfire series movies, "stereotypes abound, including Carmelita's lack of breeding, her social unacceptability, her refusal to put her show business career aside, [and] her lack of desire to have kids." When Rodríguez-Estrada writes of "Vélez's sexual personification . . . mesh[ing] with her ethnicity," she invokes that odd marriage of geography, politics, eugenics, and aesthetics always at work when one traces the history of ethnicity in Hollywood.[12]

The best piece presently available on Vélez is Henry Jenkins's "'You Don't Say That in English!': The Scandal of Lupe Vélez," which, according to Jenkins's Web site, will be appearing in an anthology of female comic performance published by New York University Press. Allow me to quote at length a telling movement from Jenkins's Web reverie:

> The following is one of the many stories Hollywood told about Lupe Vélez. This version appeared in *New Movie* in 1932 and begins when Lupe is 12 years old:
>
>> Even at that tender age, Lupe had sex appeal and no race is as quick to recognize this quality as the Mexican. The house was surrounded by boys of all ages, who whistled in various keys. For Lupe those young swains were simply a means to an end. She had an absorbing curiosity about motion picture stars and she discovered, young as she was, that her kisses were marketable. She would bestow a chaste salute on a masculine cheek in exchange for a picture of a star or a colored ribbon to wind in her dark braids. Thus, men became to her tools to gain the things she wanted, and the house was besieged with them . . .
>
> This remarkable story links together the origins of Lupe's transgressive female sexuality (her willingness to use men as "tools" for her own ends) with the origins of her desire for film stardom. Lupe, the young Mexican girl, desires glamour photographs of Hollywood stars

and is willing to trade her sexual favors to get them, to exchange bronze flesh for glistening celluloid. Underlying this story is a perverse suggestion of child sexuality.[13]

Jenkins's revelation shows how Vélez's overdetermined sexuality evolves with the certainty of DNA—as if Latino spitfireness was an attribute that could be traced at the level of the chromosome. Even less subtle than *New Movie* is the online bio of Vélez that used to be maintained at the Mr. Showbiz Web site and that heralded Vélez as "born to a streetwalker mother." Vélez herself allegedly plied the "oldest profession" in some of the raunchy burlesque houses of Mexico City in her early teens.

Other Velezians teach us much. For example, Brian O'Neill's testy corrective for those of us who would content ourselves with merely self-righteously indicting the "badness" of stereotypes, their evil dynamics, and the like merits rehearing: "I am not interested in simply pointing out the 'errors,' 'distortions,' and 'stereotypes' within these pictures; rather, I suggest that Hollywood Latino/a images . . . reflect two socially powerful discourses: first, those represented *mirror* the imagined national identities of Latin American elites[;] second, the *resilience* of Hollywood's attitudes towards Latin America" (361; emphasis added). I might add something here that the terse O'Neill does not: many of these "attitudes" have everything to do with the contiguity of Southern California and Northern Baja in Mexico.

For those of us spelunking the noxious caves of Hollywood's history with Latinos, O'Neill's findings are quite rich, as when he reminds us how actor Paul Muni devised a special preparation for his Latino roles—like the year 1935 when he played Johnny Ramírez in *Bordertown* and spent two weeks "swimming in tequila" in Mexicali (364); or when he outs Hollywood's prime research resources for Latin American–based action: *National Geographic* magazines and the racist, elite gossip of Latin American governmental attachés working in Southern California embassies (365). His research alerts us to the dynamics of a plotted whitewashing, designed so that "in the foreground of Hollywood's Pan American productions, only light-skinned good neighbors—like . . . Lupe Vélez—could represent the region" (365).

Soiled Tile Thirteen: Anger-y Vomit

Time and again in the pages of this book, I wrestle with facets of stereotypes. How, for instance, am I to approach the career of a woman who helped concretize notions of the female Latina subject for most of the Western world?

Never can I seem to effectively articulate the uncanny, dogged power of stereotypes, those "bloodstains of cultures in conflict," which swim with lyric efficiency through mass culture with an almost libidinal force. Stereotypes imprint themselves upon their purveyors, their projectors, and their witnesses in a way that is hard to characterize without seeming to exaggerate.

By the end of her career, Lupe Vélez is full, so damn full of "her" self, her "spitfire"-ness, her hot-blooded Latin-ness, her expression-istic spiciness. One might argue optimistically that our spitfire is filled with lies, untruths, and distortions, but she is full all the same.

One quick premature conclusion at the head of this paragraph: Lupe Vélez is so full of her self, or, better put, so full of these carnival-mirror others, that *she has to purge, has to vomit it all out of herself* in a self-manufactured spectacle that leads to her death.

Lupe's Deathbed, Beverly Hills

Harold Ramond—the Heel—pays his last respects to Lupe

The infamous page 340: sordid images as they appear in lurid black and white in Kenneth Anger's *Hollywood Babylon*.

And now, we are ready; ready, in the midst of a protode-nouement for our lurid, filthy-tiled exercise, to treat you to Kenneth Anger's written version of Lupe Vélez's suicide, in which the salty rhetoric of gay camp fuels the fires of Latina stereotypes to an almost ethereal level. Anger's tongue-in-cheek obituary, or, should I say, *obitch*uary, aims to cheekily and gleefully chronicle the final moments of Lupe Vélez's Hol-lywood dream-cum-nightmare—a *taste*? He names his Vélez chapter "Chop-Suicide," evoking the name of at least one of Vélez's survivors, "Chop," one of her darling Chihuahuas.

Now Anger's anger or kitschy rage is not reserved for Lati-nas alone, and a reading of his legendary *Hollywood Babylon* (a page from Anger's book appears opposite) will soon disabuse you of any regard you might retain for those pearly denizens of the silver screen. Most, like Anger, speak of Vélez's "regurge-all" denouement as an accident, a mistake born of the unhap-py coupling of barbiturates and a taco. Even the mythology seems painfully covered with a Latin-esque mise-en-scène; all that's missing is the cactus, the tequila, *bandoleras*—you know the props. Enter Kenneth *Anger*, stage right:

> When Juanita the chambermaid had opened the bedroom door at nine, the morning after the suicide, no Lupe was in sight. The bed was empty. The aroma of scented candles, the fragrance of tuberos-es, almost but not quite masked a stench recalling that left by Skid Row derelicts. Juanita traced the vomit trail from the bed, followed the spotty track over to the orchid-tiled bathroom. There she found her mistress, Señorita Vélez, head jammed down in the toilet bowl, drowned. The huge dose of secanol had not been fatal in the expect-ed fashion. It had mixed rech-erously with the Spitfire's Mexi-Spice Last Supper."[14]

Anger's epochal scene enacts in metaphorical glory a regurgitation of epic proportions; again, clinical readers might point out that vomiting is an involuntary act—controlled by the medulla oblongata and not under the direction of the will—of the subject, of the psyche; but let us give credit where credit is due; let us give the director her credit as the final credits roll again and see Lupe Vélez's magnificent suicide, her dramatic regurgitation, her epic upchuck, witness there in all its glory the final eruption, the lucid dismissal, of a raging, contentious bolus of imposed stereotypes that Vélez just could not stomach. Gaze upon the sexy Latina not-mother killing herself and her unborn child; see the living, now dying embodiment of an anti-Mexican mother, a not-*mamacita*, on the stage of her final *toilette* and toilet.

But there is a certain something about Anger's touch here—the paper is slimed with the blood of a certain sword. Anger's typewriter is almost as deranged, almost as twisted, as Jim Osborne's pen.[15] Osborne, American underground cartoonist extraordinaire, inks a particularly abhorrent gloss on Velez's last moments.

Whether Vélez's exit was perfect or a perfect nightmare, what matters here is the staging of it all: Vélez's own attempt to frame her finale and Anger's rhetorical staging. These staged scenes, one lived, the other rhetorical, force us to keep in mind an uncanny reminder: that death brings with it the spectacle of an irreversible divorce, of the body from the soul. Does it take all that much faith to believe that this twin suicide of mother and unwanted child, Hollywood superstar and incipient child star, warrants further inquiry?

Jim Osborne's india-ink rendition of a particularly vivid, awe-full scene from the denouement of Vélez's life.

Celebrities, our gods on earth, provoke a certain set of uncontrollable emotions—the outpouring of affect for the recently departed Princess of Wales was sincere (all the more scary, uncanny, and profound because it was so); alluding to Vélez as a goddess or a god on earth is more than metaphorical—it reminds us of the power that projected, industrially reproduced and distributed bodies have on spying, consuming subjects.

If I linger a tad too long, it is owing to the depth, the ubiquity of this most fixed stereotype—the Latina bombshell; and Lupe Vélez had a lot to do with the manufacture of this trope, and she profited handsomely from it as well. By the time she makes *Palooka* with Jimmy Durante, she has managed, with her handlers, to perfect a loopy, sexy, hot persona that would hold her in good grace with American audiences for decades.

Soiled Tile Fourteen: The Past Is the Future Is the Past

In a 2003 interview, Christine Spines of *Premiere Magazine* asks of Salma Hayek: "In the beginning you were repeatedly cast as characters dripping with primal sexuality. Was that something you promoted in yourself?" Hayek's response is to the point: "That sexual side is a very small part of me. But those characters are more of a reflection of how other people saw me—it's more about who *they* are" (41). The echo here is pronounced; she is very much swimming through a stream, or, better put, swimming against the stream, swimming against the sewer-borne effluvia of a tainted fetid channel of Lupe Vélez's vomit.

Salma Hayek flaunts her evocative "Mexican-ness" in this Internet giveaway for *After the Sunset* (2004), directed by Brett Ratner and written by Paul Zbyszewski.

Penelope Cruz interviews and photographs Salma Hayek—a Latina, Mexi, Spanish mixture of immense importance. This interview and set of photos is the veritable *King Kong vs. Godzilla* of "Mexican" semiotics in the twenty-first century.

You have your doubts? Take a peek at a couple of publicity stills available via the Internet in November 2004 from Hayek's latest vehicle, *After the Sunset*. You can only swim against the stream so long.

It gets even more complicated when a Spanish photographer, Penelope Cruz, who is also an actress, gets in on the art of representing "Mexicans" by photographing and interviewing Hayek—as in the *Interview Magazine* splash from 2004 shown here.

Or when Hayek, promoting her Frida Kahlo film for *Premiere Magazine* in September 2002, opts to allow herself to be posed (shades of Speedy?) awkwardly on an old autopsy gurney as garnish for a curious interview.[16]

Hayek, a latter-day "Mexican Spitfire" without Vélez's manic comic timing, is, however, quite savvy about the next-generation sewer trap she finds herself swimming in, with, and against: "Well, a week and a half ago they [the U.S. Census Bureau] officially declared that Latins were the country's largest minority. And because I spoke up about the lack of Hispanic representation [in Hollywood], now everybody always wants me to go into the drama and become a victim every time they interview me. It's a cliché. It's like you complain about the cliché, and then you get asked these questions so you can be the cliché of the Latina complaining about the cliché."[17]

In a way, the "Mexican" Hayek has it better than the television wunderkind, Chicana/Tejana diva Eva Longoria, she of the presently (Fall 2005) top-rated show in the United States, *Desperate Housewives*. There Longoria plays Gabrielle Solis, "a woman who is rarely seen in anything but delightfully sparse undergarments."[18] In a titillating glossy-magazine spread (see Eva in whoresque thigh-high stockings; thrill to her confessions regarding rabbit vibrators and morning sex!), this twenty-first-century avatar of Latina "progress" confesses to her interviewer, Mr. Jacobs, something more to be expected in the pages of this chapter, something that brings her into line with the Tex[t]-Mex gods and goddesses (martyrs?) in whose footsteps she walks, in whose skin she squirms (and vomits?). Queried as to her attitude toward her face, Eva (like some latter-day Mexican Eve) confesses: "When I was growing up, they called me La Prieta Fea—*the Ugly Dark One*. I'm the darkest one in the family. But I actually think it helped me develop a personality. *I couldn't rely on my looks*."[19] Now, with the magic of cameras and ABC Television, she can and does, and in doing so, helps to reinscribe, by the writing of her body through the portals of our eyes, where it is etched onto the reading retinas of our mind, a next-generation version of the Latina that seems very much in sync with those that have come before and those that are doomed to come to us in the future.

Envying Speedy Gonzales's treatment in the last chapter, Salma Hayek affords herself a turn atop the semiotic autopsy table.

Soiled Tile Fifteen: Homage

Film knows film. And sometimes, the best critical response to a particular medium comes from that medium itself. This is the case with Lupe Vélez, as the most provocative views of her life history have come from the camera of painter Andy Warhol, who, in December 1965, made one of his perplexing independent movies, this one on Vélez, with a piece entitled *Lupe*, starring

Is this the place to add a whisper of doubt regarding the salience of the entire Tex[t]-Mex *project? By this place in the book, you've come to know the argument—silver-screen hallucinations of the Mexican pave the road for "real-world" racist and ethnocentric attitudes and actions against Mexican and Mexican American bodies in the United States. But having grown up in Laredo, Texas, I know only too well what a damn good job we all (as we say) do keeping each other in line with slurs like "indio," "prieto," "india," "prieta," "meko," "meka," "mayate," etc. Most of these select epithets come down to us from conquistadores and their criollo and mestizo descendants, but damn, if we don't do a good job of keeping said verbal coinage current, keeping our currency of racisms in general circulation.*

Edie Sedgwick, from a script by Ronald Tavel. Most recently, Chicana film-maker Rita González has authored a cinematic/sinematic project on Vélez that folds together the life of Vélez and Warhol's odd filmed meditation—all this, through the eyes of a Chicana/o drag queen named La Lupe, pictured here.[20]

A cross-dressing Latino movie lover channels Lupe Vélez in this moving scene from Chicana filmmaker Rita González's *The Assumption of Lupe Vélez* (1999).

González's revelatory short film, entitled *The Assumption of Lupe Vélez* (1999), functions simultaneously as biography, criticism, and fiction in its attempt to disclose a Velezian cosmography that reveals woman, celebrity, fan, and industry. A media artist and independent curator/writer who lives and works in Los Angeles, where she is finishing her Ph.D. at UCLA, González is most interested in the "constructions and elaborations of biography and myth."[21] In the words of her distributor, SubCine, the artist-run and artist-owned Latino film and video organization based in New York City, her filmed reveries "portray the manufactured transformations of everyday people into cultural icons—Margarita Cansino into Rita Hayworth, Michael Jackson into Peter Pan, and Lupe Vélez into Hollywood Babylon celebrity."

The opening frames of *The Assumption* are haunting but, curiously, *not* out of sync with the rolling waves of our Velezian pastiche.

A more extensive treatment of Rita González's outrageous filmed short appears in Rosa Linda Fregoso's "'Fantasy Heritage': Tracking Latina Bloodlines." Fregoso's nifty conclusion is worth underscoring in view of the attempted sacralization of Lupe that soon ensues herein: "Perhaps the meaning of 'Mexican Spitfire,' of the Mexicana who spit fire (as the literal translation [escupe fuego] of her nickname would read), has less to do with sexuality (sexual promiscuity [e.g., Vélez's legendary trysts with Johnny "Tarzan" Weissmuller and Gary Cooper]) or cultural temperament (hot-bloodedness) and more to do with moods and emotions. Perhaps to have been a 'Spitfire' means more: an artistic temperament that is 'touched with fire'" (125). In this view, celebrities, touched by the lights of the cameras that capture them and allow their mechanical reproduction (cue Benjamin here, but also Rosalynd Krauss, Susan Sontag, Roland Barthes, et al.), are deities prone to a kind of serialized adoration/immolation.

Soiled Tile Sixteen: Celebrities and Icons

Let us toy a minute with a notion of twentieth- and twenty-first-century magic—let us play with the idea of reading Hollywood stars as icons with a decidedly rich history. And to understand the sacred function of celebrities in American mass culture, to learn the oddly moving matrix of desire and repetition at the heart of our stars, it behooves us to move to the work of medievalists—those experts in the arcane art of archaeologically meditating upon the dynamics of the sacred and the sign, the magic of the signifier.

Jeffrey Hamburger, writing in his magnificent and beautiful book *The Vision and the Visionary*, spends a chapter, "Vision and the Veronica," documenting the odd medieval history of the Veronica.[22]

The Veronica is the *vera ikon* (*note:* this derives from a false or illicit etymology, as Hamburger notes, yet as with the *OED* and its tales of "erron," I value it all the same)—the real deal. The Veronica is, as the *OED* herself reminds us, "the cloth or kerchief, alleged to have belonged to St. Veronica, with which, according to legend, the face of Christ was wiped on the way to Calvary, and upon which His features were miraculously impressed. This cloth is preserved at St. Peter's, Rome, and is venerated as a relic." The New Testament records how a miracle occurred on the way to the cross: Jesus Christ's image was imprinted on the proffered hanky. Hamburg-er, in loving detail, documents the medieval cults (in particular, novitiates, young nuns) that built themselves around this special relic:

> For [most fifteenth-century viewers] there existed myriad reproductions of the Veron-ica, all different, yet all aspiring to authenticity. In the face of the Roman relic's inaccessibility [do please note—and it's another thing I love about medieval-ists—Hamburger's fondness for puns] . . . genuine replicas—a notion fraught with paradox—enhanced and elaborated the image's claim to reflect and reenact an unmediated dialogue with Christ. (317)

"Lupe Vélez" at her throne in another scene from the vision-ary camera of Rita González.

We should pause here and linger on this image of an "unmediated dia-logue" with an ever-present god. If we were making a film, we would call it a crosscut, as we fold in here the idea of Hollywood films and our imag-ined real-life relationship with movie stars because of the time we spend with them in the dark of a movie house or even in our semidark bedrooms where our synapses fire, or are fired (shades of Plato's cave, that lovely precursor to Hollywood movie palaces) by our eyes' unmediated dialogue with the reproduction of these latter-day celebrity gods.[23]

Later in the same chapter, Hamburger aptly notes that Elaine Scarry, following Jean-Paul Sartre, tells how "'the face of a beloved friend,' if imagined, 'will be, by comparison with an actually present face, "thin," "dry," "two-dimensional," and "inert"'" (318)—a recollection Hamburger relates to the Veronica relic, "whose images lent life to a face that the viewer longed to see, but had in fact never seen" (320).[24] Resisting the call to italicize the next lines from Hamburger, let me instead merely fore-ground their import for a study of the logic of worshiped images—icons or celebrities:

The New Testament's version of an instamatic camera is immortalized in this represen-tation taken from the collec-tion of the Alte Pinakothek, Munich.

The unflinching gaze of the Holy Face invited a reciprocal glance of equal intensity: an exchange that authorized not only the object, but, by extension, empirical experience itself. Images of the Veronica contributed to a process by which vision, once cloaked in subtle distinctions between corporeal and intellectual sight intelligible only to a spiritual elite, became the stand by which all religious experience was authenticated and in which all, in turn, could participate. (320)

Jesus's facial fingerprint, his physiognomic signature, some *sacrosanct* and magical great-grandfather of the 8-by-10 publicity glossy, is both relic and icon—both an alleged physical link to the son of God *and* a representation of the man, the son of god, himself.[25] This is not the least of the reasons that cults of the Veronica prospered throughout medieval Europe.

And so the telling tale of a leading medievalist holds the key to a cinematic legacy in the twentieth century. This comes as no surprise to me at all; it's always the medievalists who sanction a sensitivity to what I call the incestuous progeny, that odd oversexed exchange between image-dominant and word-dominant narrative across the ages.

. . . And now the cat is out of the bag, or the plumber reveals his plunger, or the pipes are really clear, because, dear reader, you can now well imagine where we will soon swim. In the odd, disputed death of Lupe Vélez—whether in the white-washed version where, like Mary after her death, she rises, godlike, into the ethereal heavens flanked by her twin Chihuahuas Chip and Chop; or in the tawdry, camp, queered Kenneth Anger version, where she dies in the reek of a skid-row, vomitorial mise-en-scène—we witness the death of an icon, the erasure of a sacred soul. This is the direct result of a purge, of a sacrifice, of a bizarre ritual (Anger lights my fire) in which our beloved Santa Vélez embodies some fusion of Calvary and Hollywood, where the Vatican and Tinseltown merge, as our marvelous spitfire-cum-martyr ends her time on the planet.

Holy Tile: Flushed; or, Communion Time

Let the sacrament unfold, the silver screen turn on; enter, stage left, Julia Kristeva, high priestess, presiding:

Since food is not an "other" for "me," who am only in their desire, I expel *myself*, I spit *myself* out within the same motion through which "I" claim to establish myself. During that course in which "I" become, I give birth to *myself*. That detail, one that they ferret out, emphasize, evaluate, that trifle that turns me inside out, guts sprawling; it is thus that *they* see that "I" am in the process of becoming an other at the expense of my own death. During that course in which "I" become, I give birth to myself amid the violence of sobs, of vomit.[26]

Kristeva's redolent lines, coupled with Vélez's tragic denouement, put me in the mood for some sort of lyric periphrasis—with Vélez, through Kristeva, we are between purging and devouring, in some odd, peculiar, and pungent fusion of the bulimic with the vampiric. Sacred icons and Latina bombshells move us to these acts, these cosmo-magical supplications.

David Carrasco's "The Sacrifice of Women," his denouement chapter of *City of Sacrifice: The Aztec Empire and the Role of Violence in Civilization*, includes a pertinent meditation on Mexica female sacrifice that illuminates our Velezian toilette—in particular when he notes how "ritual movements of women's bodies through a series of *cosmo-magical* circles . . . transformed them into the hearts of plants and the inspirations for war."[27] In this light, and with no need for obsidian knives, Vélez's suicide and the coverage that attends upon it (including this chapter) enact a ritual of public sacrifice. Earlier in Carrasco's landmark study, the wily rasquache Chicano swami unleashes the term "cosmo-magical," an adaptation of the more traditional term "cosmovision" used by Aztec scholars to denote the Mexica worldview:

> Cosmo-magical . . . emphasize[s] two *dynamic* aspects of the more general cosmovision. First, there is the capacity of rites and places to dramatize, with maximal potential sacredness, the interactive relationships people in the social realm have with the gods and creative forces of the cosmos. . . . In other words, cosmo-magical means that divine energy and force inhabit buildings as well as people, hills as well as temples, graineries as well as pyramids, costumes as well as animal skins and feathers, stones as well as bones, [theaters as well as movie stars, celebrities as well as their spectators (excuse the graft)]—and that all these elements and others participated, and performed in the ritual life of the ceremonial landscape of the Aztecs. Second, cosmo-magical refers to the creative juxtaposition of opposites in which the *destruction* (by knives, fire, water, arrows, [toilets, barbiturates,] etc.) of sacred objects contributes to the *recreation* of the forces of fertility in the underworld, on earth, or in the heavens.[28]

Carrasco's neologism allows us to come in tight for a bracing close-up: Lupe Vélez's toilet/toilette is reborn as a baptismal font and sacrificial altar all at once—the primordial symbol of septic evacuation, the commode, reshapes itself in cinematic/sinematic splendor. That Vélez's *suicide* folded within its matrix the simultaneous *filicide/prolicide* of her unborn child(ren), a staged deconstruction of fertility in the underworld and Hollywood (the same place?), just adds complexity to our psychologically Gordian, cinematographically sordid tableau.

From the cosmo-magical valences of medievalist Latin Americanist Carrasco, we return to our culinary-monikered Euro-medievalist Jeffrey Hamburger, who, in telling the tale of the Veronica, writes of how the whole industry of medieval reproductions of this bizarre handkerchief-cum–signature of god "functioned as an ersatz body, one that the nun, in her role as *sponsa Christi* [bride of Christ], showered with kisses" (323). In rescuing Lupe Vélez's corpse from the infamous and scandalous discourse of tawdry Hollywood gossip, I am in a sense asking all of us to assist in a closeted ritual, a sacred rite, wherein we would conspire together to lift Vélez's body off the floor and move it to another space.

We are cleaning up the mess, shining the tiles, and closing the door on one of the more bizarre chapters in the history of Mexican bodies in the bathroom of American mass culture.

But we are also lifting to *the lips of our watching eyes* the body of Lupe Vélez, worshiping again at the cinematic font, the ceramic fetiche/ fetish, of our venerated departed goddess of the silver screen.

fin

An undated, unidentified publicity still of Lupe Vélez picked up in a Studio City antique shop, August 2005.

SEDUCTIVE HALLUCINATION
GALLERY TWO INTERSTICE
THE SECOND

Being a Second Archive of Visual Pathogens

Hallucinations—like they were ephemeral, like the ghost would pass—would disappear in the light of day, in the morning.

But it is more like in mourning.

Because these seductive sirens have heft, have gravity.

Cartoons have gravity—just look at what is going on in the Middle East (February 2006) with regard to the political gravity of cartoons: contentious illustrations Mohammed (turban as bomb, virgin rewards in heaven for exhausted smiling of suicide bombers), cartoons that may well lead to next-generation holy wars, next-generation crusades.

Time will tell.

Back to the Americas: the substance of the Tex[t]-Mex project, and the purpose of its coming XicanOsmosis antidote, has been the wily retinue of animated, conjured, fabricated, costumed "monsters" that pass for "Mexicans" in the popular imagination of the United States—monsters like the posed corpses from the U.S.-Mexico military skirmishes that find their way onto postcards (the e-mail of their day); like the "half-breed" in Orson Welles's Touch of Evil *that drives its Falstaffian anti-hero, acted out by the film's director, to murder and more; like Speedy Gonzales, child of the imagination of Warner Bros.' genius animators and monstrous acme of the American stereotype industry; like Lupe Vélez, whom we just consumed again, she who was already consumed by the voracious gods of Tinseltown. We are, in all of this: dutiful worshipers and, oddly, merciless rogue gods, gods like Poseidon, pissed off at Odysseus and looking for payback.*

One more gallery and miles to go before we sleep! (Perdóname, R. Frost.)

Exhibit A.1 | Cruising Batman's Nemesis

Inside a Plush, Self-Fashioned, Chicano Panopticon:
An Argument with Richard Rodriguez

> I have to find a place to stay—alone—to separate myself when, pre-
> dictably, the seething world will become intolerable: a place where I
> can find a lone symbolic Mirror.
>
> —John Rechy, *City of Night* (1963)[1]

From shrouds bearing Christ's face we come to tales of shrouded men, some wearing masks, some wearing tights, some just *tight* in a digital collage I call "Batman's Masked Hijo," Guillermo Nericcio García.

If genres were analogous to household furnishings, it would not require a stretch of the imagination to picture the genre of autobiography as a mirror, an oft-gilded, always intriguing mirror.

Readers of Richard Rodriguez's *Days of Obligation*, the second autobiographical essay collection by the accomplished, ubiquitous, Right-leaning, gay, Chicano curmudgeon, will thus not be surprised to find themselves looking over Rodriguez's shoulder, peering into his mirror time and again in what could aptly be called an existential toilette of a book—mirrors, in fact, are the ruling motif of the work.[2] One note here, at the outset: Rodriguez's subtitle is misleading—positing a contentious dialogue, an "argument with my Mexican father." The collection, however, is less *dialogue* than *monologue*: not for nothing does Johnny Carson appear as a minor motif as our Latino traveler moves from hotel to hotel on his many assignments.

Ostensibly a walk between tragedy and comedy, a rumination on Catholicism ("Is it possible California is Catholic, as New England is

Protestant, by virtue of its mnemonic ruins?" [127]), education, and politics, *Days of Obligation* speaks both *of* and *to* contemporary Latinas/os (particularly from California). A savory memoir filled with contradictions and erratic takes, the "book" gathers essays that originally appeared in the pages of *Time*, *Harpers*, and the *New Republic*, among other publications, as well as commentaries that first aired on the BBC. *Days of Obligation* continues where *Hunger of Memory* left off, with sad-eyed, moody "Ricardo" lamenting his indigenous, *mexica* physiognomy while spewing Right-of-Right annotations on the American nation's decay—imagine E. D. Hirsch, Jr., in brownface, and you get the picture.

"No one in my family had a face as dark or as Indian as mine. *My face could not portray the ambition I brought to it*" (1; emphasis added). Rodriguez's pain here is real, his alienation both evident and poignant. But we should not let it blind us to the serious implications of his findings. Angst ("nostalgia is for a time when I felt myself free of nostalgia" [120]), sentimentality, and the personal have always provided soothing sugar topping to mask the bitter taste of the dictatorial—in this regard, Rodriguez shares company with our William Buckley-for-post-Reagan-America, Rush Limbaugh.

The resulting irony of Rodriguez's self-doubt–hate is that he finds himself American spokesperson on Mexican and Chicana/o issues: "a man who spent so many years with his back turned to Mexico. Now I am to introduce Mexico to a European audience" (1–2). From the outset, this gives us some pause: the global telepersonality for all things Chicana/o is ambivalent regarding, of all things, Mexico—our worlds are broadcast via the fractious lens of Rodriguez's soul.

How fractious? Let us move to its origins: "[I was] repelled by Mexico's association with the old . . . In my imagination, Mexico was a bewhiskered hag huddled upon an expanse of rumpled canvas" (209). The intrigue mounts, for Richard knows his view is skewed and yet he cannot shut up—the lure of celebrity, the need for the collective gaze, a telemirror of sorts, moves him onward.

Allow the following scene, striking in many respects, to serve as a reasonable emblem for Rodriguez's album.

Scene I

Rodriguez, in a Beverly Hills boutique, surrounded by three male attendants who dress him. Enter César Romero (fabled Hollywood character actor, the Joker on TV's campy Batman, etc.).

> *Richard Rodriguez:* I looked into the mirror . . . At that moment, the door opened and Cesar Romero walked into the mirror.

"Great-looking coat," he said, tapping my shoulder lightly as he passed. (157)

For Rodriguez, this overload of male gazes overwhelms—César Romero's touch is a coup de grâce of sorts; perhaps also, a means to a *petit mort*. Append to this interlude Rodriguez's disclosure pages from earlier ("The attention L.A. lavishes on a single face is as generous a metaphor as I can find for the love of God" [154]), and one begins to sense how the dynamics of celebrity and religion intersect with ethnic domains.[3] Rodriguez's autoerotic, autodespotic relationship with his bathroom mirror begins to *color* all.

The aim here is not to declare narcissism a pathology—I am, as is any other late-twentieth-century Western subject, lovingly attached to the mirror that greets me each morning. Rather, it is to see how a particular relationship with the self, with what might be called the autospectatorial, dovetails, in this instance, with Right-of-Right political dogmatism in a beneficiary of Affirmative Action. How does the fetish for the self underwrite disdain for the community: here, Chicanos?

"I lower my eyes. I say to Mexico . . . I cannot understand you" (75), Rodriguez writes.

Confirmation soon follows for his surprised and gratified readers; allow me the luxury of citing here, again, a quotation I incorporated above in my Speedy Gonzales chapter: "Mexicans move as naturally and comfortably in the dark as cats or wolves or owls do . . . Mexicans get drunk and sing like cats beneath the moon" (87). In-depth reporting on the essence of all things Mexican.

But perhaps I am too harsh. Let us move on to other matters. After all, what else does the book hold? Our sensitive Richard clues us in to his research habits on location in Mexico; needless to say, comfort is not at issue. Readers are treated to "prosetelevision," a *Lifestyles of the Rich and Mexican American*, with "an American credit-card company" (21) "protecting" Rodriguez, paying bills and booking tours for our self-proclaimed "Mexican American haute bourgeoisie" (70) representative. Needless to say, this material protectorate underwrites Rodriguez's odyssey in more ways than one.

Large sections of Richard's collection regale us with sad tales of personal and traumatic existential inertia.

Take the chapter "In Athens Once—*please.*" Traveling in Tijuana, fearful of infection, Rodriguez will not drink the water, will not eat the legendary bordertown's "unclean enchantments" (92). Later in the same essay, we find Rodriguez working(!) with a priest friend in an underdeveloped Tijuana neighborhood where he is asked to help. Rodriguez's honesty here is refreshing: "What a relief it is, after days of dream-walking, invisible, through an inedible city, to feel myself actually doing something" (97). But it does not last.

Soon after, distributing pastries following a mass, Rodriguez finds himself assaulted by the hungry parishioners: "Now the crowd advances zombielike against the truck . . . Silent faces regard me with incomprehension. An old hag with chicken skin on her arms grabs for my legs" (98)—if we choose to recall the reference noted above, which saw "Mexico" as an "old hag," we begin to understand the degree to which Mexican American Richard Rodriguez has internalized and amplified Southern California's hatred, its visceral fear, of Mexicans.

Sadly and most surprisingly, Rodriguez is just as ambivalent about his sexuality. Earlier in the book, Rodriguez watches as AIDS support group volunteers are recognized, called to the front of Most Holy Redeemer Church. Since he worked with them, one might imagine that Rodriguez might want to stand with others who have selflessly given of themselves. Most volunteers do walk forward, but not our redoubtable Richard: "These learned to love what is corruptible, while I, barren skeptic, reader of St. Augustine, curator of the earthly paradise, inheritor of the empty mirror, I shift my tailbone upon the cold, hard pew" (47). And so our chatty guide reveals again his "unwillingness to embrace life" (43), hoping, one imagines, for expiation via textual disclosure.

Rodriguez has the sense to know that his "soul is the bathroom mirror" (156), yet we, his indulgent readers, are not spared the singular series of thoughts that accrue as a result. Sample the following choice words.

On literary canon revision:
[T]he American university is dismantling the American canon in my name . . . in the name of my father[,] of Chinese grocers and fry cooks and dentists, disregard[ing] the Judeo-Christian foundation of American (*sic*) narrative. (171)

On African Americans and the civil rights movement:
As America became integrated, the black civil-rights movement encouraged *a romantic secession* [!—my emphasis] from the idea of America— Americans competed with one another to claim victimization for themselves. (168)

On academic progress:
Gay studies, women's studies, ethnic studies—the new curriculum ensures that education will be flattering . . . (169)

It gets worse, as I have saved the "best" for last. First, a gloss of

Rodriguez's view of bilingual education as "[a mere] pragmatic concession . . . to a spiritual grievance" (67)—an understanding fed by a somewhat pathological reverence for Irish Catholic nuns, a body of selfless pedagogues, whom Rodriguez names his "linen-draped silos[!]" (221). This musing leads shortly to questionable conclusions: "From the schoolmarm's achievement came the possibility of a shared history and a shared future. To my mind, this achievement of the nineteenth-century classroom was an honorable one, *comparable to the opening of the plains,* the building of bridges. Grammar school teachers forged a nation" (163). In response, I will only add that yes, the "opening of the plains" was a momentous event in the history of the United States of America, but also in the history of genocide in the Americas. Not even Rodriguez's beloved nuns are responsible for this kind of irresponsible assertion. I find myself at one with up-and-coming Chicano cultural studies critic John Paul Gutiérrez, whose words say it better than I ever could:

> [Richard] Rodriguez's words make me weep, but his ideas make me want to wound him with a broken bottle of Chardonnay.4

I say, *drink the wine first!*

This leaves us with Rodriguez expounding on the Chicano movement, wherein an ethnic American beneficiary exposes an embarrassing lack of generosity on a par with similar declarations mouthed by Supreme Court Justice Clarence Thomas (he of the pubic-hair joke/come-on lines): "Mexican American political activists, especially student activists, insisted on a rough similarity between the two societies—black, Chicano—*ignoring any complex factor of history or race that might disqualify the equation*" (65; emphasis added; I wish I could add something more, some textual prophylactic, to guard you from these pathological words). While Rodriguez's declarations might ring true for a couple of Movimiento Chicana/o activists, angry and frustrated in the heat of organizing resistance to a callous, inert system of institutionalized racism against Mexicans, Rodriguez's findings as statements of general "truth" seem plain uninformed at best and insane at worst. It was a sensitivity *to* the complex matrix of history, race, gender, class, and ethnicity, coupled with an understanding of constitutional justice, that sustained Chicano activism in the sixties, and that continues to inspire the best of Chicano activism and scholarship in the present.

As I wrote the first version of this exhibit (in the summer of 1993), Mexican Americans and Labor sympathizers the world over were mourning the death of César Chávez. That context, more than a decade later, still shades my rereading of Rodriguez's lines: "In the late 1960s, when César Chávez made the cover of *Time* as the most famous Mexican American anyone could name, *he was already irrelevant to Mexican-American lives insofar as 90 percent of us lived in cities* and we were more apt to work in construction than as farmworkers" (67; emphasis added). Let us put the name to such nonsense: Stupidity.

I hate to waste the time to address this selfish and ludicrous statement, but I will try. The fact that Martin Luther King worked by and large in the urban metropolitan context did not stop his words and works from impacting on the lives of rural African Americans and Americans all over the country. And while I will not claim for Chávez as large a legacy as that of King, I will say that his work touched the lives of Mexicans, Mexican Americans, Chicanas/os, and Latinas/os all over this country.

And it is not anger that asks me to indict Rodriguez's ignorance, but empathy (okay, perhaps a bit of anger).

In gazing so long in the mirror, he has both rent and *rented* his soul. The result?

César Romero wins out over César Chávez.[5]

At the same time, Rodriguez's status as citable and anthologizable Chicano of choice is instructive. Let us not marvel at Rodriguez's ubiquity in U.S. mass culture—his is the tale that proves the theses of Noam Chomsky, Carol Squiers, and Cornel West, writers who speak quite eloquently to the absence of resistance from a media that assaults us daily via the "generosity" of corporate capital. In this sense, Rodriguez's views as well as his popularity are symptomatic of larger U.S. ideological tendencies.

Before I close, allow me to add—the foregoing will not have made it clear—that this book must be read by Americanists, cultural critics, and autobiographical devotees of all stripes. When he is not masquerading as a Latino Reagan or cross-dressing as an Irish nun, Rodriguez is actually quite sensitive to the play of histories in the Americas. Take his gloss of the keepers of California's missions as "handmaidens of amnesia" (125) or his incisive critique of the PRI (Partido Revolucionario Institucional), the Mexican establishment political party: "The government of hurt pride is not above political drag. In its male public city aspect, Mexico is an archtransvestite, a tragic buffoon. Dogs bark and babies cry when Mother Mexico walks abroad in the light of day" (61). I felt the need to be somewhat positive so as to hold off the doubtlessly appropriate suggestion that my entry in this gallery is overspiced with *argumentum ad hominem*. By the way, *Days of Obligation*, Chapter 6, "The Head of Joaquín Murrieta," is quite fine—it is the one sequence where neither Rodriguez nor his mirror dominates the scene.

Richard Rodriguez's *Days of Obligation* rehearses a Chicano fin de siècle version of Narcissus. Like some mutated offspring of Roy M. Cohn and Jack Webb, our self-loathing/self-loving narrator polices the precincts of the Americas, boasting here, being pensive there. We his readers marvel at his celebrity as well as his duplicity as we await his tragic fall, simulcast, no doubt, to a nationwide audience—it is instructive to note Rodriguez's attraction to Milton's Satan.

A Chicano who loathes Chicanos, a gay man who sets himself apart from gay men, a gifted, well-trained academic who leaves the academy.

Let us envision Rodriguez's next book: on the cover, Rodriguez's face looking into a mirror—pensive and sensitive; looking back at him, a Houyhnhnm, with Richard's eyes, with Richard's soul.

Rodriguez as our Latino Gulliver.

Better, allow Richard Rodriguez to craft his own denouement.

We are surrounded by the mirrored walls of a San Francisco health club. Richard whispers: "Behold the ape become Blakean angel, revolving in an empyrean of mirrors" (40).

Now let the mirrors fall.

Exhibit A.2 | Lalo Alcaraz's Take on Richard Rodriguez

Lalo Alacaraz's gifted pen skewers Batman-fetishist Richard Rodriguez in this scathing 2004 treatment.

Exhibit B | Bang, Bang

Anecdote: Christmas in Laredo, 1991—one year later, I am not watching the repeat of *A Very Retail Christmas*. I   Kmart buying last-minute gifts. But I am also up to no good, as usual—eavesdropping—being the *metiche* that I am, I am listening in on a heated debate.

The participants? A Mexican American father and his eight-year-old son.

"*Cómprame un juguete, Papi*, buy me a toy," cries the boy.

"No," says the father sternly but with love.

"*Paaaaaaaaaaaapppppppiiiiiiiiiiiiiiiiiiiiiiii*," cries the boy.

I know where this is going.

Someone's going to get angry, or someone's going to drop some change.

It goes on.

On and on and then . . .

Papi gives in. He lifts the gun and walks off with his happy boy, shrugging his shoulders, to wait in line at the checkout stand.

I have two of my own now in 2006; I know that battle; I have lost that war.

But back to the time of the story—it's 1991, December 1991.

So I walk over to look at the toy they were warring over, and I am aghast at what I see.

It is a Texas Ranger Daisy Legend series toy.[6]

If you can't read the copy in the illustration to the right, you aren't missing a thing—it's just more of that *mierda* that Américo Paredes outed two or three generations ago in his *corridos* book: Rangers heroes this, Rangers heroes that.

It freaked me out.

All through South Texas, even down to Laredo, the Rangers were criminal rogues who killed Mexican and Mexican American ranchers and stole their lands.

The brave and heroic (*sick*) Texas Rangers, immortalized in a toy gun sold by the Daisy Outdoor Products company.

None of that mattered. It was Christmas.

Days of Santa Claus and Jesus Christ.

Jesus Christ.

Kmart sold its toy, . . . and the kid?

He was happy; he had his gun.

Me, I was going crazy! Only recently Chicanofied—in Ithaca, New York, of all places—I was standing there with Che on my chest, Paredes on my mind; César Chávez was there, too, like some anticipation of a ghost, haunting my consciousness.

"How could they sell that gun!?"

Now I am talking to myself.

And I am watching myself—watching myself talk to myself and picking up the gun.

I am picking up the gun.

"They might as well make Betty Crocker Easy-Bake Auschwitz Ovens and sell them to Jewish American kids in Beverly Hills! How about Treblinka Toy Gas Pellets for little ones in New York City?"

Icons of genocidal elements available as blue-light special gimmes at Kmart.

I bought one of the guns.

Everywhere I go, I tell the story.
Maybe you can help me, and tell it, too.

Exhibit C | Sade and SoCal

[Sadistic] California Dreaming; or,
Pleasure in the Breaking of Mexican Bodies

No kind of sensation is keener and more active than that of pain; its impressions are unmistakable . . . One must do violence to the object of one's desire; when it surrenders, the pleasure is greater.

—The Marquis de Sade, *The 120 Days of Sodom*

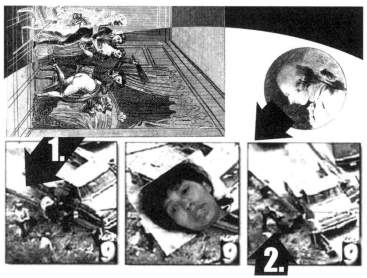

This digital collage, entitled "The Marquis de Sade Aghast as He Rides with Riverside County Sheriffs," contains elements with actual journalistic value; the three frames are facsimile screen grabs from a KCAL helicopter that filmed Riverside County Sheriff Tracy Watson as he (1) menaced Alicia Sotero Vásquez and then (2) pulled her out of her truck by her hair to beat her.

Hit me, hit me.
Strike me, strike me.
Love me, love me.

The peculiar and particular attention paid to Mexican bodies by a predominantly Anglo California law enforcement community reaches heights that we must think past the easy solution of racism to answer.

Following my late-lamented theoretical informant Michel Foucault, and Roland Barthes, who knew so much that he missed the ambulance with his name written on it, I think it's important, if disturbing, to think about the pleasure that comes from such acts as walloping undocumented immigrants on the head and body, pinioning their arms behind their backs as they scream in an incomprehensible tongue.

Pleasure? Yes, pleasure. Sexual pleasure of a decidedly sadistic twist. The exotic, we know, is erotic, and I am beginning to think that the recent history of our Southern California cultural space—Rodney King, the rebellion in LA, the beatings of various Mexicans—has more to do with de Sade than it does with Hitler or Mengele or whomever. That is, that at root, there is an erotic dimension to these beatings.

We might advocate some test beating of a *mojado*, as they are "lovingly" called in Laredo, to test my theory, but my inculcated *viva la raza* politicization saves me from this ugly task. Let's look at a couple of recent incidents to test this Eros-of-violence theory:

As the police baton rises and falls on the body of Ms. Alicia Sotero Vásquez, something must be going through her head, something to explain the sensation, the pain, the fear—all in the midst of sounds that mean nothing. Two Riverside sheriffs are shouting at her and her accomplice, the driver of the truck above, shouting in English. Later, in the hospital, all she can say is: "They beat me worse than an animal. I didn't run, nothing. They took me by the hair. I didn't insult them. I didn't say anything to them."[7] They wouldn't have understood if she had.

As the police baton rises and falls on the body of Ms. Sotero, something must be going through the head of Riverside County Sheriffs Department officer Tracy Watson, something to explain the rage and the glee, the pleasure really, that he takes as he goes about his job.

In the middle of all this, hovering above the scene like a nightingale, like an angel, like a perverted voyeur, the skycam Channel 9 helicopter, our eye in the sky, records all that falls within its lens, all that needs to be seen again and again and again . . .[8]

A blown-up (shades of Michelangelo Antonioni) and augmented screen grab from the KCAL video.

Exhibit D | Spanish ya!

Exhibit D brings to visitors of this second gallery of horrors a taste of what awaits them south of Los Angeles in Orange and San Diego Counties. First, a comic strip by SoCal native Lalo Alcaraz that brought in more than its fair share of letters to the editor addressed to the Right-of-Right chieftains of the *San Diego Union-Tribune*—which, to its credit, at the very least, runs the comic strip daily:

An infamous entry from April Fool's Day, 2005, by Lalo Alcaraz, wherein the rasquache cartoonist *intercepts* Jim Davis's *Garfield*.

Op-ed, *San Diego Union-Tribune*, April 6, 2005.

This highlighted letter to the editor tells its own story—read it and weep. And if Mr. Findley's letter strikes you as surprising or outrageous or just plain Fascist, thrill to the progressive beat that is the *San Diego Union-Tribune*, a paper Mussolini and Franco might get hard-ons just thinking about.

Exhibit E | Mirror, Mirror

Pictures and captions—choices, choices. Maybe "Sophocles meets Ovid" would fit the bill; or maybe that's too obscure. Possibly "Oedipus versus the Metamorphosis" would be the pithier moniker for this priceless image from Hollywood 2005—"Hollywood 2005," which, in its own way, is a child of Hollywood 1930s, Hollywood 1940s, and Hollywood 1950s, Tinseltown, swinging grandparents, genetic instigators of the *transubstantiation* that created Rita Hayworth.

This Associated Press pool photo (I am talking about the one on the right) from the Michael Jackson Child Molestation Trial reveals Michael's

father, Joe Jackson, looming mythologically in the foreground like some distracted but angry Daedalus, petulant over *how his stubborn son Icarus was gonna fry the wings off his ass*. The *picture* of it—MJ cavorting with little boys in Neverland—in Daddy Jackson's mind must scar his synapses, and his own culpability (shades of Ed Cansino, Rita's daddy) perhaps leaves its mark as well. It's an old Hollywood story, really: *a star is born, but the other tale, off camera, is just as familiar: a psyche is going to go to pieces*. Call it *Camera as Gun* (we saw this gun above in the introduction).

Two faces of Michael Jackson. The photo on the left is a BBC file photo of a 1970s-era publicity glossy; the photo on the right is an Associated Press photo that appeared online.

Daddy Jackson's son smiles obliviously behind his father, seemingly blind to the mess his own hands have made. But the other smile is the haunting one, or, more chilling, is the teen-fan poster shot of *hijito* MJ on the left. It is the smile of a child-star *before the operations began*, before the myriad series of interminable surgeries, before the systematic de-Africanizations of his face (and his body?) were set in motion. This tragic photo of the moment strikes the keynote and reenacts our pursuit of Margarita Carmen Dolores

The Catholic Encyclopedia nicely details the intricacies of this mystical transformation—a continuation, in a fashion, of my Catholic sermon on monstrances earlier in the Touch of Evil chapter above. While one may luridly wish to linger on the lines concerning sacred cannibalism, it is the words concerning metamorphosis that more tellingly situate our mediation on Michael Jackson in the service of our reading of Rita Hayworth's body: "We receive merely the Body and merely the Blood of Christ but not Christ in His entirety, the Council of Trent defined the Real Presence to be such as to include with Christ's Body His Soul and Divinity as well. A strictly logical conclusion from the words of promise: 'he that eateth me the same also shall live by me,' this Totality of Presence was also the constant property of tradition, which characterized the partaking of separated parts of the Savior as a sarcophagy (flesh-eating) altogether derogatory to God. We have the two extremes of conversion, namely, bread and wine as the terminus a quo, and the Body and Blood of Christ as the terminus ad quem. Furthermore, the intimate connection between the cessation of one extreme and the appearance of the other seems to be preserved by the fact that both events are the results, not of two independent processes, as, e.g., annihilation and creation, but of one single act, since, according to the purpose of the Almighty, the substance of the bread and wine departs in order to make room for the Body and Blood of Christ" (The Catholic Encyclopedia, Vol. 5 [New York: Robert Appleton Company, 1909]; Online Edition accessed April 8, 2005: http://www.newadvent.org/cathen/05573a.htm). The Bible quote is from John 6:54–56.

On another note, I should record here for history's sake that the Michael Jackson child-molestation trial was the show trial of 2005, with the Scott Peterson murder trial/circus/tragedy running a close second.

Cansino's various metamorphoses into Rita Hayworth in the past.

Exhibit F | Dear Abby; or, Taco Hijinks #1

The harmless splatter of newsprint about Dear Abby is more remarkable for what it doesn't say than for what it reveals. The laughable moniker of "Mr. Taco," after all, is not engineered to send poor Ignacio into therapy. At least, I don't think so.

But what is not said here concerns the comedic sensibility of the woman, Abigail Van Buren, aka Pauline Phillips,

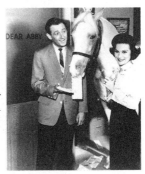

Dear Abby: Here's another one for your funny name collection:

My brother-in-law, "Nacho" — the common nickname for Ignacio — met and introduced himself to a lady in Yosemite. The lady had never heard the name and had trouble remembering it, so Nacho told her to just remember the Mexican snack.

Hours later, when they parted, the lady said, "Glad to have met you, Mr. Taco!"

— Oscar Pompa, Artesia, Calif.

Send letters to Dear Abby in care of Currents, The San Diego Union-Tribune, P.O. Box 191, San Diego, CA 92112.
© Universal Press Syndicate

Sept 28, 1993

and the way said mainstream 'merican worldview comes to permeate and then inculcate the masses. In other words, a setup, for the "joke" that follows . . .

Exhibit G | Taco Hijinks #2

I was an assistant professor ending my second year at the University of Connecticut when this mimeographed (old school!) memo appeared in all the professors' mailboxes in ugly, decrepit Arjona Hall. Touchy Mexican that I am, I threw a fit; Professors J. D. O'Hara and Richard Reynolds were behind the jokes. A year later, two other colleagues, Dick Peterson and Sam Pickering, were talking about going to the UK for the summer— "going across" they put it; I, over-hearing said exchange from the safe-ty of the copy machine, chimed in, "Hey, that's what we say in Laredo, Texas, when we go over to Nuevo Laredo, Tamaulipas, and back; we say we're *going across*."

BEAT.

"What do you know about that, Bill? Didn't you *swim across*?"

Such wits. A regular Dead Poet's Society, this lot.

Ha Ha.

Apologies were profuse, smiles were large, backs were patted—I am *still* getting over that *joke*.

Exhibit H | Frito Bandito

Not to be outdone by Isadore "I." "Friz" Freleng, Tex Avery conspired with the corporate forces of Frito-Lay, Inc., to develop the Mexican Bandit chip spokesperson, the "Frito Bandito" who festooned televisions from the late 1960s to the early seventies. In one noteworthy 1970 television spot, cashing in on the recent moon landing by Apollo 11, the Bandito, with mule, appears on the moon to extort parking-lot fees of Fritos from two rather surprised Anglo astronauts.

The commercial ends with the infamous tag line: "Anyone can be a Frito Bandito, *anyone*," which has a certain Sartrean existentialist feel to it.

On top of that, a Bandito's swarthy signifier would appear by magic on the face of the chip-eating actor.

Mel Blanc, the mouthpiece for Speedy, did the voice of Señor Bandito as well, so the Warner Bros./ethnic American *mezcla*, a tried and true formula for ethnic American mischief in our American twentieth century, is ripe and rich as well.[9]

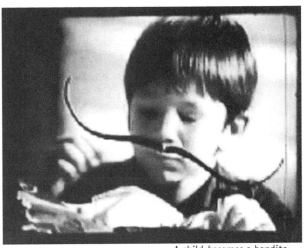

Exhibit I and Exhibit J | Suspicious Mexicans

This final entry in our second small gallery of Seductive Hallucinations comes to us from a guest docent, Miguel-Ángel Soria, of Southern California's Taco Shop Poets, an infamous troupe of chalupa-loving, poesy-hankering young Chicano/Latino writers/performers that includes Tomás Riley, Adrián Arancibia, and Adolfo Guzmán. First let us turn to Exhibits I and J, and then to Soria's commentary.

Exhibit I is from the *Vista*, a student-run newspaper for the campus of the University of San Diego, a Catholic university (think West Coast Notre Dame, but much smaller).

"No crime was reported, *as of yet*"—the criminality figured in the somatic entity of the Latino Bandit is such that it opens itself, as the student journalists did, to a capacity for crime that extends into the future ~~perfect~~ (*sic*). Science fiction overwrites journalism in a parable that recalls the excesses of the early-twentieth-century eugenics craze in the United States and Europe.

A child *becomes* a bandito before our very eyes—here we are witness to an uncanny metamorphosis, of the child, to be sure, but also of the virulence of the "bandit" Mexican in American pop culture. The symbolic nastiness of banditry evolves into something like a "pure" symbolism. The mustache figures a kind of "Mexican" exoticness, but without the criminality/sexuality we expect.

Now, let us turn to Exhibit J, another extract from a newspaper story about an event at the University of San Diego that occurred on March 9, 1992, and that appeared in the paper on March 19, 1992—also from a Photostat, provided by Soria, of the USD *Vista* newspaper.

Let us turn now to our guest docent and his memory of these heady days on a sleepy, largely gringo campus:

> One day I decided to bring my 1958 Chevy Yeoman station wagon to campus. It was a step below the more popular Chevy Nomad, but to me it was a cloud of baby blue satori.

Holy Pancho Villa!—Mexican bandits' ubiquity used to hawk chips! Frito-Lay's "Frito Bandito" from an animation cell.

The car had no stereo so I always brought my boom box to play my tunes. At night I would spend hours combating my insomnia by producing my mix tapes. In each tape I wanted to include all the range of emotions I could think of—Bach and Cepillín and end it with The Dead Kennedys. Juan, my friend, would always advocate for a tinge of banda music to be added to the mix. We continued to study. The daily processional march of blonde sorority girls bringing their shopping spoils from Nordstroms streamed past us. Here, life was a Nike commercial directed by Bertolt Brecht and only we knew about it. The girls would walk by as quickly as possible. They would try not to look at my baby blue wagon and would rarely acknowledge us, the cholo and the Xicano punk rocker spewing the words of Plato and Gramsci. On the third day of studying in our new spot, a lazy Sunday, we saw a school patrol car stop on the street facing the parking lot. The patrol car stopped there for about a half an hour and then left. Ten minutes later another patrol car came into the parking lot, drove past us, and left. We continued to study against the backdrop of compost-drunk impatiens, daisies and pom pom cushion flowers that framed the university parking lot.

The next week, our school newspaper, *The Vista*, had a blurb on its crimewatch section: "Two suspicious Hispanic males were seen in the phase B parking lot. No crime was reported, as of yet." The date given was the same date that Juan and I were in the parking lot and the same day that we had the patrol car drive-bys. Not even Cepillín could cheer us up. The mock crime misaligned the campus for us even more. Now, the mission architecture was an echo chamber to the anti-immigrant environment of California. Chaos theory searches for order where all we see is disorder. We applied this theory to our situation. We organized a protest against the

The headlines from the March 19, 1992, edition of *The Vista*. Courtesy Miguel-Ángel Sória.

A crimewatch bulletin from the February 27, 1992, edition of *The Vista*. Courtesy Miguel-Ángel Sória.

Feb 27, 1992   Vista

Crimewatch

Compiled by Sandi Herold

Sunday, Feb. 16 - Two suspicious Hispanic males were seen in the phase B parking lot. No crime was reported, as of yet.

Monday, Feb. 17 - Three floor mat rugs were stolen from Maher Hall. Losses total $101.60.

Monday, Feb. 17 - A collision took place in the lower Olin parking lot. Minimal damage incurred.

Wednesday, Feb. 19 - There was a collision on Field House Rd. Minimal damage incurred.

Wednesday, Feb. 19 - A window was broken on the East side of Founder's Chapel. Possibly, the window was kicked. No suspects at this time.

Thursday, Feb. 20 - A table was stolen from Olin Hall. The value is unknown at this time.

Friday, Feb. 21 - The left rear window of a Ford Escort was broken. Nothing is missing, and the cost of the damage is indeterminable.

Friday, Feb. 21 - The lock on the door of a grey Honda was punched in. Nothing reported missing at this time.

Saturday, Feb. 22 - The irrigation shed was broken into. Nothing reported missing as of yet.

Saturday, Feb. 22 - Five tapes and 15 T-shirts were stolen from a black VW Jetta. It was parked in the Field House lot at the time of the theft. The damage totals $149.00.

Saturday, Feb. 22 - A black backpack was stolen. The loss totalled $100. The backpack contained a wallet, credit cards, personal items, and $30.00 in cash.

Saturday, Feb. 22 - The driver of a red VW refused a ticket for running a stop sign. She said she didn't agree with the accusation, but was cited for the violation, anyway.

Crimewatch has included both the crimes that have occured on campus and the injuries that have happened throughout the week for the last couple of issues. For the remainder of the semster Crimewatch will only include the crimes. If there are instances that occur that are not reported, please contact The Vista with the information.

newspaper and the school for its treatment of Raza and people of color in general. The school denied the charges and denied that the blurb was making a reference to us. Apparently, the same parking lot had had two pairs of "Hispanics" on the same date and time. Our dopplegängers had escaped their alternative realities and entered our skewed set of circumstances. I guess Juan and I missed seeing them since we were so focused on the patrol cars that drove by us. Despite the school sending two administrators, both people of color, to try and stop the rally, we marched through USD. Like any other march, we did our usual requisite chants of "El Pueblo Unido Jamás Será Vencido" and a few "De Colores" to add contrast to the mix. I was somewhat disappointed when the marchers failed to back me up on my rendition of "God Save the Queen" by the Exploited. Maybe I should have opted for the Sex Pistols version of the song. Fela Kuti, Manu Chau, Elvis Costello, Chopin, The Misfits, Solución Mortal, Seven Seconds, Charlie

Mingus and of course, Los Tucanes de Tijuana. The mix tapes are gone and in its place is my mp3 player on shuffle mode. It is now 2005. No crime has been reported or committed as of yet.

Our guest docent's recall of the events surrounding non-crimes, either by him and his friend or by their hallucinatory doppelgängers, leaves this Tex[t]-Mextified victim running from ghosts, hiding from specters, dueling with phantoms. In a second, it is 1993, and I am playing pool at Club Kensington on Adams Avenue in San Diego. I am playing with Jack Webb (not *Dragnet*'s superego proxy; *of all the names*!), who is the city-beat editor for the *San Diego Union-Tribune*. As we play, I observe a crew of Hell's Angels–style Anglo bikers exiting the saloon right by our table.

"Look out, he'll cheat," a thuggish, mammoth rogue pronounces to Webb. "He's a Mesican."

Instinctively, I whirl around looking for the scary bandit thug. So stupid; I could have used one of Richard Rodriguez's mirrors. I was the "cheat[in'] . . . Mesican." I was the dangerous, swarthy threat—to the bar, to the game, and to Webb.

It's best we leave this gallery and get some fresh air, and prepare for the healing waters of XicanOsmosis.

CHAPTER 5

XICANOSMOSIS

Frida Kahlo and Mexico in the Eyes of Gilbert Hernandez

This book will end in hope.[1]

With hope.

Washed with it, bathed *in* it. We had no choice, what with our toilette, last chapter, our bath with Lupe Vélez's phantom.

We already began to see the evanescence of this somewhat uncharacteristic optimism at the end of the Speedy Gonzales chapter, where I prematurely gave myself over to hope in the scribbled shapes of Ren and Stimpy and the radical vision of our finest Chicano seers, Jaime and Gilbert Hernandez. There, the rationale was clear: the only way to redress the ills of a Tex[t]-Mex semiotic legacy would be to respond in kind.

If we have been victims of photolysis (photolyzed subject-effects, as it were), if we have been broken down with images, then it is through the random and measured, the chaotic and strategic, broadcast of *other* and *othering images* that some progress might come into being.

It's already beginning to happen; it happened, in fact, in poetry, before it really got going with those of us who practice the occult art of cultural studies. For instance, read Tino Villanueva's *Scene from the Movie Giant*, the poet's provocative and evocative memoir/critique, and you'll know what I mean.

But where Villanueva can rifle out ramming riffs of elegiac rage, rant withering streams of prickly poesy, we must rely on images.

Why do you think there are so many pictures in this damn book?—only the generosity of the University of Texas Press has made this possible; and they don't have the budget that Warner Brothers has. These, then, are words and

Tino Villanueva, Scene from the Movie "Giant" *(Willimantic, Connecticut: Curbstone Books, 1993). Watching a cruel racist diner owner, "Sarge," throw Mexicans out of a Texas diner in George Stevens's* Giant *(1956), Villanueva writhes like a wild beast trapped, a teenage Chicano trapped in the dark of a West Texas movie palace—the howl out of his psyche becomes a lyric epic in his poetry: "Put the film /In reverse (I think). Tear out those frames /From time-motion and color; run the words / backwards" (26). Villanueva's experiences, and the verses that emerge decades later in response, may be seen to frame the contours of the present study.*

images in the spirit of another Tex[t]-Mex, inscribed here by the Chicano/Tejano Tex-Mex fingers of a child of Laredo.

XicanOsmosis

osmosis \a:-'smo—s*s, a:z-'mo—\; osmotic \a:-'sma:t-ik\ n. [nl, short for *endosmosis:* alt. of obs. *endosmose*, fr. Fr. *end-* + Gk *osmos* act, impulse of pushing, fr. *othein* to push; akin to Skt *vadhati* he strikes] 1. the tendency of a fluid to pass through a semi-permeable membrane, as the wall of a living cell . . . 2. the diffusion of fluids through a membrane or porous partition.

—*Webster's Revised Unabridged Dictionary*, 1913

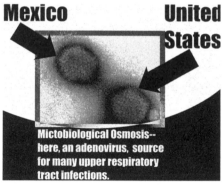

(left) "Aztlán Osmosis,"
Guillermo Nericcio García.

"XicanOsmosis #1," Guillermo
Nericcio García.

Passing through ostentatiously . . .
Had I a curtain . . .
bound looseness . . .
the coarse cells of my heart . . .
subtle sting

—Frida Kahlo[2]

The words jump off the page. Like osmosis, something flows between the black marks on the paper in and through the sievelike apparatus of the eye: "living cells"; "diffusion . . . through a semi-permeable membrane"; "porous partition." These loaded phrases, culled from the metaphorically rich confines of the biological sciences, are not without some value in speaking to processes of artistic and cultural exchange between Mexican and Mexican American artists—and they have some utility as well for the student of culture curious about ocularly borne, transnational semiotic maneuverings, the boisterous miscegenation of "high" and "low" culture.

For instance, let us think about how the eye of Mexican photographer Manuel Álvarez Bravo, capturing images throughout the twentieth century, impacted upon—"infected," really—the artistic glance of a Chicano photographer, Adam Sergio Rodríguez.

The cells are contiguous as a Mexican and a Chicano photographer share symbolic "fluids" with each other. Mexico and the United States, adjacent cultural structures, share histories, finances, and semiotic spheres—the velocity of their transnational semiotic intercourse is dizzying, as if the two cultural spaces were mirrors, facing each other, reflect-

ing each other in a *mise en abyme* filled with attraction and repulsion.

Álvarez Bravo's lucid photographic allegory, *Parábola óptica*, reveals the irony of a medium, photography, often associated with truth, whose fundamental dynamics are so indebted to archetypes of "nontruth," such as framing, inversion, and refraction. In order to represent the truth or some photographic facsimile thereof, the camera, in essence, must and does lie. So it is that Álvarez Bravo's photograph "tells" the tale of a visual domain filled with traps, and Álvarez Bravo, sage Mexican seer, updates and revises Blaise Pascal: *the lens has its* reason *that* reason *will not know.*

Two generations later, Adam Sergio Rodríguez hands us a portrait that traverses a similarly ironic terrain, here inflected with what we can think of as a *signature* leftist politicized Chicano wit. In *Fe ciega*, or "Blind Faith," the photographer's subject places his blind allegiance, his ideologi-

(left) A reproduction of *Parábola óptica* (1931), a photograph by Mexican seer Manuel Álvarez Bravo.

Fe ciega (1995), Adam Sergio Rodriguez.

cal faith, in an American nation that is all too often blind, in essence, to his own radically brown subjectivity. The flag around the model's eyes is at once blindfold *and* bandage, barring sight, of course, but also masking the wound(s) of a twentieth- and now twenty-first-century Chicano being: *dolores del ojo*, *por supuesto*, but *dolores del ser*, as well.

Channeling all this transnational seeping, all this pan-border reproduction, we turn now to two of the more formidable contributors to this aesthetics of the verge.[3] This oozing, sharing, giving, barring, semipermeable aesthetic-cultural space is best evidenced in the works of a Mexican American comic book writer and illustrator from Southern California by the name of Gilbert Hernandez, whom we introduced above during our Speedy necropsy.

Hernandez's wizard inks treat "readers" to a visual fugue, a scandalous and delicious unholy marriage of *X*s: X-rated Xisme and XicanOsmosis; X-rated, in that Hernandez's characters are godless and hilarious "wetbacks" of that metaphorical Rio Grande between decency and outrage, flouting treasured mores and customs with a decidedly post-Movimiento freedom overloaded with polymorphously perverse women and men; Xisme or Xismosos, in that his rapid-fire, gossipy, and quasi-allegorical narratives out all that is loved and cherished within our various Latino enclaves—Hernandez is as likely to reveal camouflaged right-wing racism as he is cherished sacred cows such as Latino Catholicism; and, lastly, Hernandez reveals himself as an avatar of XicanOsmosis, because his forebearers in illustration and literature and film are as likely to come from the United States, Mexico, or Europe as anywhere else— Luis Buñuel, Carlos Fuentes, Pablo Neruda, Frida Kahlo, Diego Rivera, Chester Gould, Dan de Carlo, and Picasso all tattoo the illustrating psyche of Gilbert Hernandez.

In the *cuentos* set in the small, mythical Central American community of Palomar as well as those tales set in Los Angeles and, for that matter, in outer space, Hernandez explores the symbiotic relationship between points Unitedstatesian (*estadounidense*) and points Latin American. One part comic book, one part surreal cinema, one part modernist painting, one part existential philosophy, Hernandez's stories recast tried-and-true archetypes of Chicanos and Latinos, demystifying both the stereotypes of Latinos and comic books themselves in the process. In Hernandez's work, one runs across a comparative and paradigmatic approximation of a unified field theory in quantum mechanics—here, one is literally able to simultaneously articulate the utterly daunting complexities of national boundaries (between the United States, Mexico, and the rest of Latin America), aesthetic boundaries (the novel, oil painting, and comic books), and academic field designations (literary criticism, art history, museology, popular culture).

How appropriate that the biological sciences should provide, for those of us who study arts and culture, a ready model to describe processes to be found in the border that divides and, equally as importantly, defines the cultural dynamics between the United States and Mexico. "Appropriate" in that "biological" concerns and constructs such as "ethnicity," "genotype," and "phenotype"—those *markers* of "human" difference—come to the fore at the U.S.-Mexico border: a place where denizens on both sides of Checkpoint Charlie must confront, celebrate, and loathe each other's difference on a regular basis.

It is in the midst of this border, between its roaring, warring contradictions and collusions, that the most sophisticated representations of XicanOsmotic artifacts, Tex[t]-Mexes sans quotations marks and sans clever hedgings are to be found—a Tex[t]-Mex that cannot be easily homogenized, a Tex[t]-Mex that infects the cultural legacies of at least two nations along and past their contiguous borders. As in the work of the cultural troupe Culture Clash, the plays of Angeleno Oliver Mayer, the music of Los Lobos, the performance art/stand-up antics of Michelle Serros, the events staged by Marisela Norte, or the parodic vaudeville of El Vez, we find in the work of Gilbert Hernandez a syncretic canvas that irremediably fuses Mexico and the United States, Mexicans, Chicanas/os, and even, sometimes, plain-vanilla gringo 'mericans.

The visual arts, then, provide us with an index of *XicanOsmotic* conflict and exchange, and the cellular process of osmosis gives us the means to map these varied movements: it is a remarkable permeable flow. In this reciprocal flux of bodies, ideas, canvases, photographic plates, and, of late, digitized images flowing freely between World Wide Web sites in Mexico and the southwestern United States, one witnesses the synergy, the mestizo dynamics of art history in (particularly) northern Mexico and the U.S. Southwest.

Why linger upon the process of XicanOsmosis in a piece concerned with contemporary popular artifacts forged by Latina/o hands?

Mainly for a change of pace. Earlier scholarly and cultural studies at the end of the twentieth century lingered upon the lands and people bordering northern Mexico and the southwestern United States as subjected sites. They were always tainted by the very real war that forever altered the geographic, not to mention the geopolitical, contours of the Americas—1848 looms as large for a study of the Southwest as 1776 does for one of the United States and England or 1492 does for one of Italy and the whole of Western Europe and the so-called New World.

We have been there, done that: the border as wound, the border as site of conflict, the border as hyphen, or even, following Derrida, as "hymen"—all useful conceptual apparatuses for describing processes, literatures, arts, and communities *at*, *on*, and *in* the border. Osmosis, though, emphasizes another, no-less-important characteristic of, especially, arts and artifacts produced by Mexican and Chicana/o artists and writers—that is, the sometimes slow, sometimes fast process of secretion, absorption, and evaporation across the border dividing the United States and Mexico; and, most important, it is a term that foregrounds a flow that moves in two directions, back and forth.

To speak to the complexity of this osmosis is difficult. To trace how one artist, or a school of artists for that matter, saturates the vision of others working across the U.S.-Mexican border is an exercise in a rigorous form of cultural, not to mention semiotic, archaeology. Consider: Frida Kahlo suffusing the psyche of Gilbert Hernandez (more on this below), or Diego Rivera flooding the vision of José Antonio Burciaga.

Diego Rivera, Águila con el *Atlachimoli* (aguaquemada), símbolo de la religión náhuatl, 1929-1935. Escalera del Palacio Nacional.

A detail from one of Diego Rivera's murals in the stairway of the Mexican National Palace, Mexico City. From the pages of *Escritos de Carlos Mérida sobre arte: El muralismo*, ed. Xavier Guzmán, Alicia Sánchez, et al. (Mexico City: Serie Investigación y Documentación de las Artes, 1987).

Sample here, for instance, a detail from Guanajuato native Diego Rivera's *Águila con el Atlachimoli, símbolo de la religión náhuatl* in juxtaposition with a section from *Last Dinner of Chicano Heroes*, a Stanford University residence hall mural designed by José Antonio Burciaga (one of the original Culture Clash troupe members and a true *mensch*) and executed collaboratively with students and artists from California and Mexico.

It is worth quoting at length from our recently deceased Renaissance man Burciaga on the semiotic politics of placement informing his *Dinner* mural so as to witness firsthand the play of mestizo histories and their relation to the arts in the Americas—an attitude toward public art and the mural worthy of an aesthetic "coined" by Diego Rivera and others:

La Virgen de Guadalupe, patroness of Mexico, received enough votes to sit at the table, but out of respect will occupy a loftier place. In a history mobbed with machos, there was a sincere effort to vote not only for women like painter Frida Kahlo and poet Sor Juana Inés de la Cruz but also for mothers and grandmothers.

Not all of the heroes had to be Chicano—that is, of Mexican roots; the Argentine-born Cuban hero Che Guevara made the list. The martyred Che, a strong symbol during the Chicano movement of the late '60s, will occupy the central position. At his side will be the Mexican revolutionary Emiliano Zapata.

Dr. Martin Luther King Jr. was another non-Chicano who made the seating. President John F. Kennedy also got some votes, but not enough to sit at the table. He will be in the background, along with General Zaragoza and others who did not make the final list.[4]

And, of course, it is not just within the realms of art that odd, unpredictable, and enriching *XicanOsmotic* exchanges occur. Consider in this regard how the prose fiction of William Faulkner, translated into Spanish, impacts upon the developing aesthetic sensibilities of Gabriel García Márquez and his circle of friends, only to then return to the United States once again as the Colombian Nobel Prize winner's fiction inspires the muse of Toni Morrison, only to have Morrison's powerful narratives foster literary progeny from the creative imagination of Marisela Norte (Chicana poet) and the Taco Shop Poets (poets, performance artists, and musicians).

Across and back again, visual and literary seeds flow through the semipermeable fixity of the border—here, the *migra*, or aesthetic border patrol, stops no vehicles (or,

"...and to all those who died, scrubbed floors, wept and fought for us."

A detail from the José Antonio Burciaga mural at Casa Zapata, Stanford University.

perhaps, only an occasional one). These artists have a lasting impact on canvases on both sides of the border and, in some instances, the silver screen—recall here the vision of Coahuila to be found in the cinematic products of directors Alfonso Arau (*Como agua para chocolate*, 1992) and Robert Rodriguez (*El mariachi*, 1992).

Panel 1: Mexico and Frida Kahlo in the Eyes of Gilbert Hernandez

Curiously enough, it is with the artistic vision of Americans of Mexican descent that one witnesses the coming together of legacies and conventions of representation that most often stay firmly anchored within their own isolated estuaries. An examination of the art, photography, and film by Americans of Mexican descent and by Chicanas/os (not always the same thing, as we know) highlights the significant degree of preparation that awaits those wishing to study arts created between and within Mexico and the United States—it also, and not incidentally, provides a necessary tonic.

For instance, in speaking to the rich graphic tendencies of late-twentieth-century Chicana/o art, one must be as sensitive of sixteenth-century Spanish altar design tendencies, and the adaptations these underwent in their introduction to the indigenous peoples of Mesoamerica via Cortés and Spanish Inquisition–era clerics, as one must be of the impact Andy Warhol's Factory had on the First World art market in the United

States in the late sixties; as knowledgeable of the role *retablos* and *lotería* play in Northern Mexican cultural communities as of the (some might say) similar role Elvis Presley played in the Atomic-era, Ike and post-Ike suburban culture of the United States. Consider, for instance, the semiotic etiology of the CLNet screen shot seized from the Chicano/Latino World Wide Web site at the University of California, Los Angeles, back in 1994—it is still there at the time of this writing, fall 2005.[5]

The visual dynamics of this particular image are dense and diverse; moreover, they span more than four centuries and at least two continents. A sophisticated marriage of pictograph and ideogram in its own right, a Mexica graphic narrative couples with the Graphic user interface of the World Wide Web; brought through the eye, prefiltered through an always already camera-inflected (or is it *infected*?) sense of spectacle, yielding what is, in essence, a late-twentieth-century mestizo Web page. With apologies to mathematicians everywhere, I offer a semiotically tinged version of what this equation might look like.

The homepage for CLNet at the University of California, Los Angeles.

The text version goes like this: [Mexica glyph] + [a computer] + [the eye/I] + [camera] = World Wide Web. This awkward illustration does not appear here for purely melodramatic purposes—though I am aware of the potential for that kind of interpretation, and have, in the past, been guilty of such flourishes. The maladroit logic of this fabricated equation gestures at the kind of rhetorical, semantic, and semiotic fusion (juggle that, exegete!) that will be necessary on the part of the critical community to chart the following query: What happens when the multivalent cultural legacies of the Americas, North, South, and Central, are interrogated at the same time as one cross-examines advances in visuo-information technology, while also attending to the various and sundry autobiographical and biographical niceties of the artists producing these works?[6]

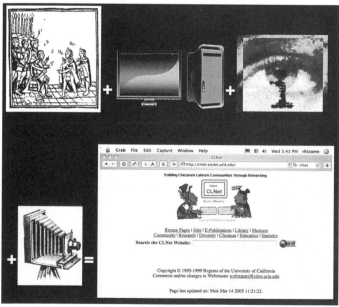

"Aztlán Web Equation #2," Guillermo Nericcio García.

graphical and biographical niceties of the artists producing these works?[6]

To be Chicana/o and, more importantly for the purposes of this chapter, to be a Chicana/o artist, is to live in the mix of more than two worlds, a rich fractious legacy where the courts of Spain; the mute, dark chambers of England; the dynamic cultural imperialism of the United States; and the fractious, revolutionary history of Mexico merge. But said merger is not without its profits.

Panel 2

Let us now quickly dash from the abstract to the specific and to the work of Southern California native Gilbert Hernandez. We will narrow our focus even further, electing to examine how the work of Mexican arts diva/deity Frida Kahlo impacts upon Hernandez's work. From the start, we might note that Hernandez is somewhat at a disadvantage, plying his trade in comic books, a genre most often associated with the banal exploits of *leotarded*, steroidally enhanced musclemen (Superman, Spiderman, et al.); ditzy, hormonally gifted teenagers (Archie, Betty, and Veronica); and outrageous dysfunctional animals (Uncle Scrooge, Mickey Mouse). As such, his and his brother Jaime Hernandez's Dickens-like, fifteen-year, serial graphic fiction project *Love and Rockets* has only recently begun to receive the attention it deserves, both from the community of literary critics and from art historians in the United States and abroad. Still, the Latino community as well as the Raza intelligentsia has been a bit slow to note Los Bros. Hernandez's literary output. Jaime Hernandez is candid about this Raza indifference in a 1993 interview: "Disappointedly, we've had little response from the [Chicana/o] community. The response we've had is that very few Hispanics read our comic books, that we know of. There's no backlash either, because our comic book isn't that important so they don't bother about it."[7] Frida Kahlo, of course, is another story. Few other artists of the late twentieth century have drawn the critical and popular acclaim this eccentric, gifted luminary of the Americas has received.

For an example of the flow of Mexican art onto and into the works of Mexican American artisans, there exists no better microcosm of the process of exchange than "Frida" (1988), the graphic biography of Kahlo authored and illustrated by Gilbert Hernandez. Kahlo, that most autobiographical of painters (only Van Gogh and Rembrandt come to mind as her competitors when it comes to the self-portrait), returns to us translated in a drawn biography by Hernandez, a Chicano born in Oxnard, California. "Frida" is Hernandez's homage to the dazzling Kahlo.[8] Using Hayden Herrera's Kahlo biography, *Frida*, as a skeleton of sorts, Hernandez renders Frida in words and, more importantly, in pictures.

And this is where illustrator Hernandez and biographer Herrera part company, for it is the autobiographical insights gleaned from Kahlo's paintings, more than Herrera's prose, that guide Hernandez's drawing hand as he writes the life of the late Mexican painter. If this is a novelty (a visualized biography of one visual artist by another), one wonders why? How better to render the life of a painter than in pictures?

Hernandez's homage begins with a loaded frontispiece—the image is Buñuel-like in its subtlety, or, better put, its lack thereof—Frida, in an adaptation of one of her many self-portraits, gazes out to us her spectators, surrounded by a constellation of symbolic keynotes (clockwise from the top right): an allusion to Picasso's *Guernica*, which periodizes Kahlo in a world art context; a drawing of a bomb wrapped with a ribbon, a stylized ideogram of André Breton's now-famous quote about the Mexican painter (note also how drugs linger just to the right of the neatly wrapped bomb, signaling Kahlo's use/abuse of the same in the course of her many illnesses); and a semierect devil with a pitchfork. Moving to the bottom left quadrant of the opening panel, Hernandez adds a bottle of booze, a rendition of Chester Gould's Dick Tracy nemesis, Flat Top (which, like the Picasso allusion, periodizes Kahlo while also signaling Hernandez's autobiography, or auto-ergography, his own debt to a tradition of comic art in the United States). To close, the fron-

The frontispiece initial panel from Gilbert Hernandez's "Frida."

tispiece also discloses a chimera Diego Rivera (frog and man), a Soviet hammer and sickle (glossing Kahlo's committed Socialist politics), and last but not least, one of Mexican graphic artist José Guadalupe Posada's *calaveras* (skulls)—Posada's works an inspiration for Kahlo and Hernandez alike.

Diligently working through the sources and inspiration for this portrait of Frida by Gilbert Hernandez, one immediately sees the impact of Mexican, European, and American artists on the work of a Mexican American visual artist. Chester Gould, André Breton, Frida Kahlo: the rich, diverse tapestry fueling Hernandez, driving him to draw through the dizzying and myriad anxiety of influences, reminds art historians and cultural critics of how far we have to go in our efforts to interpret and, through our acts of curation, to monumentalize the legacy of our Americas.

What I like about Hernandez's "Frida" is the way it problematizes the divide between the autobiographical and the biographical while also efficiently and succinctly retelling the life of a prominent twentieth-century artist. In painting, the self-portrait is the counterpart of autobiography in nonfiction prose—and certainly no little amount of ink has been spilled connecting the trajectory of Kahlo's development as a painter with the contours of her life history.

But in painting Kahlo's story, Hernandez takes counsel as much from Frida's oeuvre as from her published biographies, as much from his own experiences and development within the eclectic domain of comic book publishing as from Kahlo's self-portraits. Dick Tracy's "daddy," Chester Gould, has everything to do with Hernandez and almost nothing, save for chronology, to do with Kahlo: simultaneously, biographical and autobiographical categories are fused as Hernandez retells the story of Kahlo's life even as he signals autobiographically his debt to Frida Kahlo.[9] Adapting here a *smidgen* of a semiotic tactic culled from the pages of bookmaking machine Jacques Derrida, it might be ventured that Gilbert Hernandez conjures the space of a collaborative semiotic *hallucination*, wherein he and Frida reside and frolic simultaneously: "What we are talking about here is hallucination in painting. Does painting have to *let a discourse be applied to it that was elaborated elsewhere*, a discourse on hallucination? Or else must painting be the decisive test of that discourse, and its condition?"[10] Allusive and elusive, Derrida deftly reveals (he always was a showman) a means to a seductive hallucination that would *not* always be reinculcating a space of Latina/o representation that destroys, maims, and disables. Displacing, however temporarily, the pages of Kahlo's various biographers, Hernandez's illustrated biography creates a dizzying playground where *both* illustrators' lives *and* works *speak* or *show themselves* together.[11]

A devotee of expressionist and surrealist tactics, Gilbert Hernandez here literalizes Diego and Frida's symbiotic ties that were both sexual and aesthetic. Courtesy Fantagraphic Books.

Panel 3

One of the most celebrated aspects of Frida Kahlo's life was her contentious, erotic, and outrageous relationship with her lover, husband, collaborator, and friend, the aforementioned and aforecaptioned Diego Rivera.

In an image from "Frida" (36), Hernandez pictures the curious, bellicose, yet symbiotic relationship Frida shared with Rivera. Positioning both artists before unseen canvases, Hernandez literalizes the symbolic strands binding chaotic bodies and souls: Hernandez's pen posits a relationship from which any separation (save for the final one of death) is tentative and temporary. And this is but the surface. Figuratively, the shapes and pictorial elements Hernandez includes present a mise-en-scène evocative of Kahlo and Rivera's symbolic universe (skulls, shadows, canvases, a discarded lover lurking in the background)—a universe dominated by the artists themselves, frowning in the foreground.

Advancing to our next panel ("Frida," 36), suppose that now you wish to render that day (August 22, 1940) when Ramón Mercader murdered Leon Trotsky—a man with whom Kahlo shared time, ideas, and her body.

Kahlo was shaken terribly by the dastardly act, enduring twelve hours of police questioning. Hernandez's version of the event tells us this and more, communicating the violence of the assassination while also

depicting Kahlo's link (via facial tattoo) to Marx and, perhaps more specifically, the Soviet Union. Hernandez's dark lines (note how political symbolism sloppily dovetails with a blood-stained hint of romance) provide a ready point of entry for a reconsideration of Kahlo's craft, of her own autobiographical storytelling.

Our next sampled panel finds Frida Kahlo (circa 1946) during that late period of her life when her health was rapidly deteriorating, "first bedridden . . . then enclosed in a steel corset for eight months" ("Frida," 37). Hernandez's rendition of this painful scene ("Frida," 37) artfully renders Kahlo's divided, decapitated body, simultaneously revealing the split self of an increasingly tortured artist. But even as he renders this scene, Hernandez also belies his kitschy, Southern California, Hollywood sensibility, as the template for this moving portrait of Frida comes from director Joseph Green's schlockfest/drive-in B movie *The Brain That Wouldn't Die* (1962); a detail from the poster for this cold-war classic reveals one of Hernandez's sources.

The most plaintive, pathetic figure in Hernandez's panel is the sketchy,

confused protagonist, gawking at Frida through the window. This stickman (a proxy for you and me?), startled yet attentive, peers upon a fascinating, surreal scene: note that the table upon which Frida's head sits is a stylized altar of sorts, with Frida's head as chalice, flanked not by candles but by empty bottles of booze.

A chilling mise-en-scène from Gilbert Hernandez's "Frida" bio-pic. Note how historical events and psychological traumas fuse in Hernandez's high-contrast inks. Note as well the literal and metaphorical use of blood—Kahlo often used blood in her self-portraits and other paintings to underscore tropes of traumatic "connections." Blood, no stranger to osmosis nor to XicanOsmosis, emerges as featured player in the tropes gallery of ethnic American figuration.

Dada meets *The Brain That Wouldn't Die* meets Mexico. Worthy of Buñuel, his attested muse, Hernandez here produces his most eloquent, moving, and disturbing portrait of Frida Kahlo: decapitated, intoxicated, wounded, and, most importantly, a spectacle! The stick figure peering through the window proxies our own witnessing subjectivities. Courtesy Fantagraphic Books.

(right) Detail from Frida Kahlo's self-portrait *The Little Deer* (1946).

Moving briskly on this tour, with me as your obedient prose docent, let us now jump between two illustrations, one a detail of a painting by Frida Kahlo, *The Little Deer* (1946); the other, an evocative riff played off the original, used by biographer Hernandez in "Frida" to bring off his narrative denouement.

Note the movement from *autobiographical* self-portrait by Kahlo to the *biographical* portrait by Hernandez; a facial expression of angst in the first panel emerges remade as peaceful sleep in the second as Kahlo's documentation of an increasingly torturous life is recast by Hernandez as the no-less-violent-yet-somehow-also-hopeful scene of Frida's death. Note, too, how Hernandez has removed the deer's right leg to signal Kahlo's July 27, 1953, amputation, still on the horizon when *The Little Deer* was completed in 1946. Hernandez's comic-book biography again tells the remarkable life of Frida Kahlo, but he also accomplishes much more. This consummate Chicano narrative wizard delivers what the French used to call an *haute nouveauté* (a superior, high novelty).

Of course it is not just Mexican artists that impact on Mexican American artistry. In *Blood of Palomar*, Gilbert writes and draws the story of a serial killer run amuck in Palomar, the fictional Central American community (imagine Faulkner's Yoknapatawpha south of the Rio Grande in García Márquez's Macondo).[12] But just as important in the novella (which appeared serially over a two-year period) is the coming-of-age story of Humberto, the literal portrait of the artist as a young man. Humberto's artistic talent is the featured subplot of this singular detective story/psychological novel, underscoring in an odd way the novella's concern with documenting the impact of murder on a small, insular, which is not to say provincial, community.

These two panels document the impact of Pablo Picasso, George Grosz, Wassily Kandinsky, and modern primitivism on Gilbert Hernandez's india-inked lines. Picasso's hand in this stew is also quite interesting and noteworthy. Born Pablo Ruiz Picasso in 1881 in Málaga, Andalucía, Spain, the heralded Spanish artist had an art-teacher father, who was the precocious scribbler's first art instructor. In the *Blood of Palomar*, it is Heraclio, Humberto's friend, who plays master to the young talent, bringing him books by Mary Cassatt, Paul Klee, and Picasso to educate his young charge. Readers, screeners, seers all, we are confronted with a decidedly delicious semio-/*geo*-/*logicultural* ménage à trois: Oxnard, California (where Hernandez was born); Mexico (Kahlo's crib, though her father's German lineage ought to be thrown into

Gilbert Hernandez's transformation of Frida Kahlo's *The Little Deer*—note especially the amputated hind leg, which alters Kahlo's original painting but obeys the chronology of Kahlo's surgeries. Courtesy Fantagraphic Books.

Rex Carlton's *The Brain That Wouldn't Die* is one of the original cinematic sources for Hernandez's mestizo imagination. We begin to understand how Hernandez's pen marries the visual archive of Hollywood black-and-white schlock films to the sensual contours of twentieth-century Mexican oil paintings—XicanOsmosis at its finest.

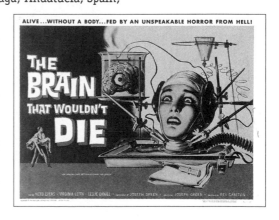

Gilbert Hernandez's Picasso-influenced portrait of Luba, one of his most enduring, strong, and provocative characters from his graphic novels series. The image on the left appeared originally as the full-color back cover of the novel *Blood of Palomar*. On the right, a teacher, Heraclio (quite often a fictional doppelgänger for Hernandez), marvels at young Humberto's artistic range in a key panel from the same novel. Courtesy Fantagraphic Books.

the mix); and Spain, Mexico's motherland, origin of Mexico's mother tongue, that European behemoth responsible for remapping the globe in the fifteenth and sixteenth centuries. Look carefully at the three panels below.

I have sandwiched Gilbert Hernandez's drawing (in *Blood of Palomar*, it is an over-the-shoulder glance at a page from the sketchbook of his budding artist/protagonist Humberto) between Kahlo's singular *Broken Column* and Picasso's ubiquitous *Don Quixote and Sancho Panza* to play up the intrigue between these three panels, one an oil painting, the second an ink-on-paper drawing, and the third a lithograph. This triptych evidences the depth of these circuitous allusions: the fractured, elided pudenda of a half-man, half-woman serial killer, Humberto's portrait of Tomaso in the center panel is informed by the syntax of fractured subjectivity Hernandez had learned from a careful perusal of Kahlo's *Broken Column*, in which Kahlo's broken, bifurcated nude form figures her torn psyche/matrix. Similarly, it was to Picasso's experimental pen strokes that Hernandez turned to represent the incipient talent of Humberto in his story. In Gilbert Hernandez's imagination and in the strokes of his pen, the lush, sensual angst of Frida Kahlo is reimagined through the playful lens of Pablo Picasso's paintbrush, with the leering gaze of Miguel de Cer-

Left to right: Frida Kahlo, *The Broken Column* (1944), Museo Dolores Olmedo Patiño; Gilbert Hernandez, two panels from *Blood of Palomar* (1987); Pablo Ruiz Picasso, *Don Quixote and Sancho Panza* (1955): Kahlo, Hernandez, and Picasso, a decidedly curious and utterly Chicano ménage à trois and a XicanOsmotic artifact of the first order.

vantes—an artist himself, who was rather adept at wrestling with and manifesting the peculiarities intrinsic to the concept of representation—hovering just above this unlikely trio.

Afterword

The borders dividing and defining Mexico and the United States, as well as those no-less-real borders dividing High Culture and Popular Culture, cannot stop the surging of ink, the dance and coupling of photons as they bounce off canvases and comic-book pages into the willing and willful eyes of their readers and viewers. *La migra*'s starched green uniforms, those natty, nifty, and reactionary costumes, made-in-México[13] wardrobe progeny of the spume of Mussolini's fashion Fascists, cannot bar the cacophony of the semiotic intercourse between Mexico and the United States.

Exergue

In an interview with Gary Groth and Robert Fiore, Gilbert Hernandez recalls the origins of his love of comics: "Our mom collected comics in the 1940s, and it's the old story, her mother—our grandmother—threw them out, so she didn't have any left and she'd always tell us about the old comics."[14]

A writer of a different age and the distinct cultural space of Texas, I walked a different path: It is the hot summer of 1966 in Laredo, Texas, and a four-year-old boy and his seven-year-old sister are playing on the bed of their father's mother. Our grandmother's name is Ana Nericcio née Juárez, and among the curious ceramic animals, old photographs, and dainty artifacts, we find a treasure chest of new and old comic books: Archie and Jughead, Betty and Veronica, Hot Stuff, Casper, Richie Rich; an odd Superman, Little Dot, and Big Lotta; occasionally a Sad Sack falls our way. Here my big sister Josie and I play and laugh and break things—Ana's precious little ceramic dog whose head I broke and Ana patiently repaired; I never remember her getting mad. Here I learn to read; here I learn to read

The centerpiece of this final snapshot is taken from the identification card of Ana Nericcio Juárez, circa 1925. Grandma Ana inculcated me into the world of word and image studies through the comic books she hid under the mattress of her bed there at 619 Mier Street in Laredo, Texas. There, under her loving, watchful eye, and with the assistance of my sister Josie, who is the spitting image of Ana now, I became a reader.

another way—like José Arcadio Buendía with Melquíades, like Shelley's voyeur Wretch within his hidden cave. In the dark, safe confines of my father's mother's house, I am forever initiated into the sensual and colorful, semiotic and semantic mishmash of word and image.

Gilbert Hernandez's evocative canvases send me back to this now-lost Utopia of outrageous plots, garish colors, and yellowing cheap paper—it is a world as well of chocolate milk and hamburgers and the singularly selfless love of a beloved grandmother and my always-special sister. The latter taught me to read, and the former provided the fuel to feed that everlasting spark. The elegiac majesty of this reverie runs through my past and present, a pleasure- and pathos-filled borderzone of chaos, a fitting denouement for the twisted legacies, the singular odyssey, of this writer's own XicanOsmosis.

CONCLUSION

(with apologies to Friedrich Nietzsche)
"Have I Been Understood?
XicanOsmosis versus the Tex[t]-Mex"

Would the projectionist stop the last Reel of the machine?
          —Tino Villanueva, *Scene from the Movie "Giant,"* 1993

a part of the truth remains,
a piece or a grain of truth
breathes at the heart
of the delusion,
of the illusion,
of the hallucination,
of the hauntedness

          —Jacques Derrida, *Archive Fever,* 1998[1]

Social note: I have tried to escape in the Prytania [Movie Palace] on
more than one occasion, pulled by the attractions of some Techni-
colored horrors, filmed abortions that were offences against any cri-
teria of taste and decency, reels and reels of perversion and blasphe-
my that stunned my disbelieving eyes, that shocked my virginal
mind, and sealed my valve.
          —"Darryl, Your Working Boy," a pseudonym for
                    the inimitable Ignatius Reilly, from
          John Kennedy Toole, *A Confederacy of Dunces*[2]

No contemplation is possible. The images fragment perception into
successive sequences, into stimuli toward which there can be only
instantaneous response, yes or no—the limit of abbreviated reaction. Film no longer allows you to question. It questions you, and
directly.
          —Jean Baudrillard, "The Orders of Simulacra"[3]

Coup de Grâce

The Chicana/o Tex[t]-Mex is not just the stupefied legacy of a subjected race crying to "daddy" about the wrongs done it.

It is always-already-also the seductive tale of a coup, the corruptive tale of a lurid reconquista, writ large by clever Latinas and Latinos, rasquache Chicanas and Chicanos, Mexicans—sans quotation marks—who would never only live to have their legacies written by the crippled withered hand of the other.

* * *

It is going to be 2006 and I feel like a character in that amazing tale by Jorge Luis Borges, "Tlön, Uqbar, Orbis Tertius," where the uncanny ways of a man-made fictional world begin to creep in upon and change and eventually replace what we call the "real."

An eerie innovation in ocular prostheses reminds us of the creepy intermix of the world of animation and "reality."

But in my nightmare, the incursion is by zombielike animated mannequins, seductive hallucinations.

Marx's words from Das Kapital *provide the score: "sensuous things that are at the same time suprasensible or social" caress my synapses and lace my psyche (lacerate more than lace).*[4]

What caused this? I opened a recent copy of Wired *magazine and look what I see.*

It's a story by Brian Ashcraft on trends fueling the day-to-day life of Japanese girls—in particular, a current rage for ophthalmic prostheses that make you look like a Japanese anime character.[5] *Chronicling an inverted tale—here the mannequin is the model of the woman—we are consumed by the spectacle of Asian girls enchanted with the look of ersatz eyes . . .*

In my nightmare, Speedy Gonzales hands me his hat and calmly wraps his red bandana around my neck.

And I like it. And I am wearing those scary anime contact lenses . . .

* * *

When we are in the dark, in the movies, it is as if the hand of god proffers to us via the silver screen (and now, in the twenty-first century, the plasma screen, a shining fabric with iridescent, tumescent threads), the face of god, or, at the very least, his proxy gods and goddesses.

And he hands us devils and bandits as well.

Both photograph and living flesh, facsimile and relic, these uncanny phenomena reach out like ghosts and touch our souls with photon tongues that reach their place through the open doorways, the inviting velvet lips of our eyes.

That whole stupid argument about the real and the fake, reality and representation, verity and facsimile, unveils itself as a waste of time.

"Mexican"

Mexican

"Latina/o"

Latina/o

"Text"

Tex[t]

All and one, one and all, they reach out to us in a seductive cacophony, a cacophonous seduction, and we?

We, in the dark, pulsing ersatz night of the theater, we drink it all in;

these flashing waters *become our life.*

* * *

Wake up.

Author's Note

This book was written over the last sixteen years in Ithaca, New York; Austin, Texas; Storrs, Connecticut; Willimantic, Connecticut; San Diego, California; London, England, UK; and, last but not least, Laredo, Texas—

on a Mac, of course!

December 1989–August 2006

c/s[6] William Anthony Nericcio y Guillermo Nericcio García

Backstory

1. I have appropriated Michel Foucault here on the "subject-effect" from *Remarks on Marx*, and have also appended Gayatri Spivak's useful deflection of the concept of "subject position" from "Who Claims Alterity," 269–292.

2. Needless to say, I have been guided in these speculations by the work of Frantz Fanon, Edward Said, Edmundo Desnoes, Gayatri Spivak, Carlos Fuentes, Ramon Saldívar, *and* the dynamic ethnic-studies duo of Frederick and Arturo Aldama. María Josefina Saldaña-Portillo, aka "Josie," a fellow Laredo-born *academista*, also taught me a thing or two in this regard.

3. The image here reproduced is a digitized cell "sampled" from Director Robert McKimson's *Cannery Woe* (1960) in *Golden Jubilee 24 Karat Collection: Speedy Gonzales' Fast Funnies*. The allusion to a "political unconscious" refers, of course, to another eighties warhorse, Fredric Jameson, and his *Political Unconscious*.

4. Virilio, *War and Cinema*, 54.

5. See Said's little-known reflection upon Tarzan, Johnny Weissmuller, Edgar Rice Burroughs, Africa, and Hollywood entitled "Jungle Calling," 61–65, 112. The pathbreaking academic study in this area was Bogle's *Toms, Coons, Mulattos, Mammies, and Bucks*; two later, provocative and dynamic

collections in this same vein are Golden's *Black Male* and Cassuto's *Inhuman Race*.

6. Lynda Williams, in her essay "Skin Flicks on the Racial Border," luridly and lucidly explores this topic, concluding provocatively that in *Mandingo*, "interracial lust became a new commodity" (299). Her closing rhetorical movement, wherein she holds that "aesthetic ideals are deeply imbricated in the sexual desirability" of what she calls, in quotes, the "'black subject'" (303), resonates in a cool way with my take on Hitler above and especially with regard to "Mexicans" as synecdoches for a specific form of violent sexual potentiality in the *Touch of Evil* chapter below.

7. Saper, *Comedy*, 86–87; emphasis added.

8. Keller, "Image of the Chicano," 45. Since Keller's work appeared, other works, such as Noriega's *Chicanos and Film* and Rosa Linda Fregoso's *Bronze Screen*, have continued research in this regard. Next-generation work continues apace as well: Wood's "Blind Men and Fallen Women" is a good example.

9. Some of the best work *against film* has come *from* avant-garde and politically progressive *filmmakers*. Sample, for example, the work of DeeDee Halleck (*The Gringo in Mañanaland*, 1995) and that of the remarkable Jesse Lerner (*Cowboys, Indians, Divas, and Poets: A Re-vision of Mexican*

Mythologies, 2002); more work is to be found in the Rockefeller and MacArthur film/video/multimedia media compilation series volumes *Frames of Reference: Reflections on Media* (2000).

10. Padilla, "Recovery," 294.

11. Said, *Orientalism*, 6.

12. I am not just being catty as I speak wistfully of Octavio Paz's "once-lucid" body of cultural commentary. I treated with his chameleon-like evolution at length in "¿Nobel Paz?" 165–194.

13. The late, great Professor Arthur G. Pettit writes about this and other related matters in *Images of the Mexican American in Fiction and Film*. Also useful, though more general, is "Images North and South of the Border" by the late Robert G. Mead, Jr. His denouement is moving and frightening—thirty-two years after penning these words, the situation remains the same if not worse: "The foregoing mosaic of images, true and false in varying degrees, shows us that both north and south of the border we need to know much more about each other" (327). Mead was a supportive force in my first years as a professor at the University of Connecticut; I am in his debt for his counsel. One last piece to check out in this vein is Fussell's "Type-casting."

14. Baudrillard, "Precession of Simulacra," 48.

15. Ibid.

16. Derrida's unsettling and provocative elaboration on the *pharmakon* appears in "Plato's Pharmacy," 61–84. A lucid two-page gloss of this term by Peggy Kamuf appears in her anthology *A Derrida Reader*, 112–113.

17. Said, *Orientalism*, 6.

18. Hadley-García, *Hispanic Hollywood*, 36–37. A careful study of the impact of these early films is Steven W. Bender's powerful and compelling *Greasers and Gringos*. A panoramic

gloss from Bender's book merits a cameo here: "Prompted in the 1930s by the threat of losing distribution of Hollywood films to crucial Mexican and Latin American markets, Hollywood's self-policing body at the time, the Production Code Administration, helped eliminate the most virulent anti-Latina/o references from Hollywood films, including references to greasers. By the time these economic pressures had relaxed in the 1950s and this self-censorship board's influence had waned, the term *greaser* and its close cousin *greaseball* had gradually given way in Hollywood and American society to other derogatory references to Latinas/os, although Hollywood resurrected the greaser from time to time, beginning with the 1961 western *One Eyed Jacks*" (xiv). The best study of these films themselves is to be found in Charles Ramírez Berg's *Latino Images in Film*, part of the Texas Film and Media Studies Series published by the University of Texas Press, the same folks responsible for the present object nestled between your hands.

19. Vanderwood and Samponaro's picture book, *Border Fury*, chronicles the rise of postcard technology, which blossomed alongside the Mexico-U.S. conflict.

20. Vanderwood and Samponaro, *Border Fury*, 174.

21. For more regarding the rise and fall of vaudeville, check out Andrew L. Erdman's *Blue Vaudeville* and editor Robert M. Lewis's *From Traveling Show to Vaudeville*.

There is some evidence in the public record that Mexicans figured grotesquely in the nineteenth-century American imagination as well. These "pre-historic" Tex[t]-Mexicans were featured in traveling circuses as "Aztec Children," "Aztec Girls, From Old Mexico," "Pip and Flip, Twins from Yucatan."

Pictured here admiring each other lovingly are the "Aztec Children," actually "Indian Children from Central America" (Mannix, 89). Sideshow grotesqueries like these provide a lurid sort of pre-history for the Tex[t]-Mex phenomena glossed in these pages.

22. Villa's relations with Hollywood during the Mexican Revolution are interesting in and of themselves. See Margarita de Orellana's "The Circular Look." An extended version of this study appeared more recently as *Filming Pancho*.

23. If it is as Homi Bhabha (*Nation and Narration*) and Tres Pyle (see below) have lucidly argued, that "Nation and Narration" always already share a common genetic lineage, then now, somehow, we *must* add the domain of *technology* to the mix. Motion pictures are as much responsible for mass cultural shifts as jet engines, atomic reactors, mirrored discotheque light balls, and the Internet. So technology changes our relationship to what we see and in the process changes the way we see. I might also add that I am one with Donna J. Haraway, who is of the view that "technologies of visualization recall the important cultural practice of hunting with the camera the deeply predatory nature of a photographic consciousness" ("A Cyborg Manifesto," 169). Oliver Wendell Holmes, Severo Sarduy, and Stuart Ewen have also pursued the development of photography as it relates to the metaphor of hunting. [Forrest "Tres" Pyle's working title for his doctoral thesis at the University of Texas at Austin in 1984 was also "Nation and Narration," and I want to give the former Longhorn, now a professor of English, his props; I am indebted to Pyle for having influenced my work in a Marxist literary criticism seminar early in 1984.]

24. *Sit venia verbo* | pardon the expression.

25. Freud, *Interpretation of Dreams*, 183.

26. On these issues, you won't waste any time rereading all or part of Homi Bhabha's "The Other Question," 18–36.

27. Homer, *Odyssey*, 4:46.

Seductive Gallery One

1. Source: http://dictionary.oed.com. libproxy.sdsu.edu/cgi/entry/50119731 ?single=1&query type=word&query-word=interstice&first=1&max to show=10 (February 24, 2006).

2. The ARTFL Project, Webster's Dictionary, 1913 edition, http://machaut. uchicago.edu/cgi-bin/WEBSTER.sh? WORD=hallucination (October 10, 2005).

3. Starke, *Starke Parade*, 142. Southern California resistance to the ubiquitous lazy Mexican trope is relentless and delicious! Sample here a prime exchange from Gustavo Arellano's infamous "Ask a Mexican" column from the *OC Weekly*:

Whatever happened to the "lazy Mexican"? Now all I hear is that they're taking our jobs.
—*Ronnie Racist*

Dear Gabacho,
Isn't that the stupidest paradox? Really: How can someone simultaneously be a yeoman and a layabout unless he's Shaquille O'Neal? But accusing ethnics of being both is America's most cherished immigrant insult. Every group felt its contradictory sting: Chinese (opium smokers or railroad coolies), Irish (drunks or ward bosses), Scandinavians (oafs or Vikings), Italians (slum dwellers or Mafiosi), Jews (rag-picking parasites or international bankers) and now Mexicans. The insult's popularity draws its venom from our Puritan forefathers, who considered life outside of labor sin: it's a miracle the phrase on Auschwitz's gate, Arbeit Macht Frei (Work Brings Freedom), isn't inscribed on the Capitol Dome. What's strange, though, is how modern-day gabachos forgot the Protestant work ethic long ago;

meanwhile, immigrants continue to pick up Max Weber's flame without forgetting to enjoy life. Bested in both works and pleasure, gabachos seethe, grow fat, and elect evangelicals—and don't get me started about faith without works and its relationship to American sloth. ("Ask a Mexican," Thursday, March 16, 2006 [http://www.ocweekly.com/columns/ask-a-mexican/ask-a-mexican/24704/])

4. German Propaganda Archive, http://www.calvin.edu/academic/cas/gpa/goeb12.htm (October 12, 2005); translated from "Der treue Helfer," 229–235.

5. Danbury Mint: A World of Fine Collectibles. http://www.danburymint.com/heirloom/product1.asp?code=52 (March 23, 2006).

6. Postscript: As this book was going to press, and through the extraordinary research intervention of one of the editors of the book, I was, to my happiness, reunited with my beloved María, who can be had for the handsome sum of $75 and $9 shipping and handling. Said fee being somewhat out of the range of this cultural studies professor, it is to be hoped that one of the readers of this humble volume sees fit to "gift" María to me in the near future.

Chapter One

1. Said, Foreword, iii–x.

2. Welles, *Touch of Evil*, film dialogue.

3. Sarduy, *Written on a Body*, 12.

4. A special thank-you to Mark Schwartz (primary research assistant) and to Laura Rossi (film consultant and research assistant), of the University of Connecticut, for their priceless contributions to the original version of this project.

5. This statement dates to the year 1990 and so, happily, is *not* so true as

it once was. The contributions of writers like Rosa Linda Fregoso and Chon Noriega, among others, have changed our critical terrain; still, I want to maintain that the artsy realm of film studies and the social science–heavy domain of Chicana/o studies still don't always mesh. The reasons for this are legion and pertain to domains historical, institutional, "practical," geographic, and political.

6. Would that we were still paid by the word, like Charles Dickens—the various and sundry epithets for Latinos alone would front one's next pleasure junket to Las Vegas or TJ (Tijuana).

7. Heath, "Film and System, Part I," 7–77; "Film and System, Part II," 91–113.

8. Shalit, remarkably! reveals his gifts as a Derridean.

9. Heston's own mumbled version of Spanish throughout the film is also worthy of further scrutiny, if not outright laughter.

10. Given our guild's tendency to give itself over to the prolific manufacture of neologisms, I am wary of introducing new jargon, though I recognize the value of such a rhetorical move. Jose Piedra's essay "The Game of Critical Arrival" addresses the plusses and minuses of critics' semantic gamesmanship. Piedra writes: "Critical emporiums abuse labeling as a vehicle for the 'official' screening of their members. For a large segment of humanity, membership in the field of criticism becomes an 'official' colonial test no less grueling than literacy and literariness. . . . Is criticism then an unavoidable form of colonial apprenticeship?" (35).

11. Pettit, "Images"; Keller, *Chicano Cinema*, listed under "Image of the Chicano"; Comito, *Touch of Evil*.

12. Leaming, *Orson Welles*, 538.

13. Truffaut, as cited from Alexandre Astruc's review of Truffaut's *Les Mauvaises Rencontres*, anthologized in

The Films in My Life, 291; also cited in Comito's *Touch of Evil*, 229.

14. The first published version of this chapter appeared in an abbreviated form in Chon Noriega's *Chicanos and Film*; owing to space constraints, editor Noriega had to chop out some of my cagier shtick. So, *caveat lector*: While I have updated my bibliography here and there, I have not attempted to exhaustively research all that has been written on Welles since at least 1999. A couple of exceptions: a remarkable essay, "Touch of Shakespeare," by Scott L. Newstok, appeared in 2005—Newstok's fusion of film theory with Shakespearean studies and the border is bracing; also well crafted and lucid is Donald E. Pease's "Borderline Justice/States of Emergency." Lastly, exegetic bon mots of great use are to be found in Michael Dear and Gustavo LeClerc's "Tijuana Desenmascarada," and in the chapter on *Touch of Evil*, "The Borderlands of *Touch of Evil*" (115–136), in Oliver and Trigo's *Noir Anxiety*.

15. Bazin, *Orson Welles*; Collet, *"Touch of Evil"*; Leaming, *Orson Welles*; and Brady, *Citizen Welles*.

16. There are now at least three finished versions of *Touch of Evil*: the 93-minute version distributed in the United States by Universal and in the United Kingdom by Rank, and the restored 108-minute version distributed by MCA on film and on video. This essay is a reading of this second, "restored version," edited by Virgil W. Vogel with Welles, and reedited by Ernest Nims, with additional sequences directed by Harry Keller. Since the first version of this chapter appeared in *Chicanos and Film*, a 105-minute version, "true to the vision of Welles," appeared on DVD, June 8, 2004, from Universal.

17. Said, "Representing the Colonized," 214.

18. Naremore, *Magic World*; Stubbs, "Evolution"; Heath, "Film and System, Parts I and II."

19. Naremore, *Magic World*, 178; Johnson, "Orson Welles," 247.

20. McBride, *Orson Welles*, 137.

21. Ibid., 135.

22. Comito, *Touch of Evil*, 11.

23. Stubbs, "Evolution," 193; emphasis added.

24. Ibid., 183.

25. Ibid., 186.

26. Naremore, *Magic World*, 198.

27. More on this concept, lifted from the nimble mind of Jane Gallop, is discussed below in my chapter on Speedy Gonzales.

28. Heath, "Film and System," 49.

29. See Leaming, *Orson Welles*, 123–130. A treasure trove of materials from this and other productions is warehoused by the United States Library of Congress (LOC). See the Federal Theatre Project Collection at the Library of Congress, *The New Deal Stage*, http://memory.loc.gov/ammem/fedtp/fthome.html (12 May 2005). All the figures pictured here from Welles's work on *Macbeth* are from the archive of the Library of Congress and appear in this collection under the "fair use" provision of the copyright laws: "The Library of Congress is not aware of any copyright in the materials in this collection. Generally speaking, works created by U.S. Government employees are not eligible for copyright protection in the United States. Privacy and publicity rights may apply." For more on LOC and copyright, see their own instructions available on the Internet at http://memory.loc.gov/ammem/fedtp/ftres.html (October 19, 2005).

30. Bazin, *Orson Welles*, 124; emphasis added.

31. Stubbs, "Evolution," 184.

32. Paredes, *With His Pistol in His Hand*, 16; emphasis added.

33. Especially noteworthy is Paredes's ability to see cultural history as a panorama, one that enfolds the hatreds and stereotypes of Old Europe

and their mutation in the DNA of their "children" in the Americas.

34. Alleged nomadic peoples from India, Gypsies in Europe "enjoy" a similarly dismal cultural status as "Mexicans" in the cultural space of America. Two worthy recent treatises on the Gypsy include Mark Netzloff's "'Counterfeit Egyptians' and Imagined Borders" and Judith Okely's "Deterritorialised and Spatially Unbounded Cultures within Other Regimes." Okely's piece is a fine review/article on Patrick Williams's *Gypsy World*.

35. Both Mauricio Mazón's *Zoot-Suit Riots* and the more recent volume by Eduardo Obregón Pagán, *Murder at the Sleepy Lagoon*, provide provocative insight into this signature event from twentieth-century U.S. history.

36. *The Sleepy Lagoon Case*, 17–18.

37. Said, Foreword, vii.

38. Rosaldo, *Culture and Truth*, 152.

39. Anzaldúa, *Borderlands/la frontera*, 3.

40. Rosaldo, *Culture and Truth*, 149.

41. Said, "Representing the Colonized," 225.

42. Lamb, "Convenient Villain," 75.

43. Keller, "Image of the Chicano," 45.

44. Joyce, *Ulysses*, 321. The *OED*'s take on this Irish word is endnoteworthy. Its pages tell of a term "pishogue," variously spelled "pishog, pisherogue, pishrogue," and "pishtrogue," which themselves derive from the Gaelic "píseog, písreog," meaning "witchcraft." "Pishogue" refers to a form of "sorcery" and "witchcraft"; additionally, it bespeaks "a spell incantation, [or] charm" and is a euphemism for "a fairy [or] a witch" (http://dictionary.oed.com. libproxy.sdsu.edu/cgi/entry/50180111 ?single=1&query type=word&query-word=pishogue). In the mouth of Joyce's monstrous Cyclops-proxy, the Citizen, "pishogue" is the term that

allows him to speak the contamination that Leopold Bloom embodies for him. Bloom is monstrous, some odd mishmash of Irishman and Jew, some sad cuckolded mix of man and woman. The mestizo dynamics of Welles's film can, in this light, be seen as some latter-day exercise in cinematic "pishroguery."

45. An unattributed author leaves the following background information on Welles's *Don Quijote de Orson Welles* on the Internet Movie Database: "Orson Welles's *Don Quijote* was released in 1992 by El Silencio Producciones and distributed by Jacinto Santos Parrás—it was finished by Jesús Franco and Patxi Irigoyen; Orson Welles died in 1985)." I was able to track down the source for this aside here: http://www.lib.byu.edu/ news/2005_10.html (November 2, 2005).

According to Spanish film critic Juan Cobos, who had watched an early rough cut of the movie while Welles was still filming material for it, this new version cut and reshaped by Jesús Franco doesn't resemble Welles's vision at all. The film doesn't include all known footage of Don Quixote. There is footage being privately held in at least two collections in Europe. In an unfinished documentary on Welles entitled *Filming the Trial*, Welles said that if *Don Quixote* had ever been finished, he would have called it *When Are You Going to Finish Don Quixote?*

Welles is not the only filmmaker who wrestled with finishing filmed fictions of "Mexicans." Read Jesse Katz's "The Curse of Zapata; He would be fodder for a great movie. The twentieth-century's purest revolutionary. If only Hollywood could get over the fact he was Mexican: filmmaker Gregory Nava plans movie on life of Emiliano Zapata" for a disturbing and riveting tale of Hollywood-borne woes.

Chapter Two

1. Jelinek, *Piano Teacher*, 23.

2. Derrida, *Of Grammatology*, 109–117.

3. Fanon, *Black Skin, White Masks*; Castellanos, "Woman and Her Image" (this work originally appeared in Spanish in *Mujer que sabe latín*; it has been translated with an assortment of other projects in *A Rosario Castellanos Reader*), 236–244; Derrida, *Limited Inc.*; Spivak, "Who Claims Alterity," 269–292; Cisneros, *The House on Mango Street*.

4. Baudrillard, "Precession," 22, 48. Even as we thank Baudrillard for his instructive guidance, we pause a minute to assess his words' impact on the notion of simulated "Mexican" hallucinations. They help. Truth with a capital *T* finds itself exiled, relieving us of restoring the essential Mexican self, sans quotation marks.

5. Taussig, *Nervous System*, 7.

6. Dyer, "Resistance through Charisma," 93; emphasis added.

7. I have grappled in print more extensively with the impact of technology on discursive and semiotic media in "Artif[r]acture." Yes, yet another annoying neologism. I dreamed up the term "artif[r]acture" in order to speak of an object under investigation that was simultaneously *art, artifact, fracture*, and *fractured fact*; the term has specific value for a study of Chicana/o graphic narrative, sequential art, and photography.

8. As quoted in a moving reminiscence by John Lahr, son of Burt "The Cowardly Lion" Lahr, in "The Voodoo of Glamour," 113.

9. *Estadounidenses* = "Unitedstatesians." I have discussed the problem of the term "American" in more detail in "Autobiographies at *la frontera*," 165–187, and, again, in the first version of my chapter one from this book, which appeared as "Of Mestizos and Half-Breeds," 47–58.

10. The Pillsbury Doughboys pictured here are part of a limited edition collector's set; they are, in a way, the holy grail of Doughboys. Let me explain: the image featured here is from the Internet back in 2002 when I first found it. After years of looking for traces of it to document it here in my bibliography, I cannot find hide nor hair of this unique collectible. Ebay.com, http://ebay.com (October 2, 2002).

11. More, much more, on this below in my "Autopsy of a Rat" chapter.

12. Leaming, *If This Was Happiness*, 8; emphasis added.

13. Ibid., 17.

14. Ciccone, "Vogue," *Songs Inspired by the Film "Dick Tracy."*

15. Castellanos, "Woman and Her Image," 242.

16. As a corrective for having witnessed Warner Oland ape an "Asian" in this book, please read Tina Chen's fascinating and pharmaceutical (do you have a bad case of stereotypes indigestion?) *Double Agency*.

17. Kobal, *Rita Hayworth*, 76.

18. Ringgold, *Films of Rita Hayworth*, 171.

19. Those of you reading these lines wistfully faithful in the notion of Progress (a fundamentalist religion without peer), cheerily hopeful of a better Hollywood since the fabled days of yore, or at least since the days of Welles, Cohn, and "Hayworth," might want to cast your eyes at Tim Korte's words cited here from an Associated Press wire story, March 18, 2006, entitled "Spielberg Production Sued Over Haircut." Korte's microepic chronicles a "Mescalero Apache family in southern New Mexico" that "has sued the producers of Steven Spielberg's television miniseries, 'Into the West,' claiming a set stylist cut an 8-year-old girl's hair without regard for tribal customs. . . . The lawsuit says Ponce's daugh-

ter, Christina, responded through her parents last March to an open casting call for work on the TNT network miniseries, 'Into the West,' for a three-day shoot near Carrizozo, N.M. *The stylist cut the girl's hair, the lawsuit claims, 'to make her look more "Indian" and like a male Indian child because the movie casting call failed to produce sufficient young male extras of Indian heritage'"* (emphasis added). At least Rita wasn't trying to pass as a Mescalero Apache—Cohn might have tried to graft a penis on her!

20. Orson Welles worked a depiction of this misogynist, defacing fantasy into the reels of *Touch of Evil*; recall here the scene where Risto Grandi, played by Lalo Ríos, attacks nimble detective Miguel Vargas with a container of acid. The mis-splashed vitriol goes wide of Vargas and hits the wall of a building, defacing a tarty showgirl poster of "Zita" (played with cleavage-flaunting dizziness by Joi Lansing). Zita has already been blown up in the first reel of Welles's film; she is the paramour of industrialist Rudy Linnekar who thinks she hears a "ticking sound" at the beginning of the film.

21. Borges, "Borges and I," 278.

22. With her penchant for self-portrait, Frida Kahlo represents a similar if distinct case; I wrestle with this below in my chapter on Kahlo and Chicano sequential artist Gilbert Hernandez.

23. Morella and Epstein, *Rita*, 21.

24. I do not have space here to pursue a discussion of Spanish attitudes with regard to ethnic bodies named Moor, North African, Jewish, and the like, though the topic relates directly to the foregoing discussion. Needless to say, Leaming's statement is ripe for forensic inquiry. Some works that do address these issues, both recent and dated, include Syed Ameer Ali's *A Short History of the Saracens*; Lee Anne Durham Seminario's *History of the Blacks, the Jews, and the Moors in Spain*; and E. William Monter's *Frontiers of Heresy*. Also of use is *Cultural Encounters*, edited by Mary Elizabeth Perry and Anne J. Cruz. The Gypsyfied image of Rita that appears here is featured in Ringgold, *Films of Rita Hayworth*, 58.

25. These could include, for example, the World Church of the Creator; Aryan Nation; skinheads from Klanti (aka Santi), California; the lunatic, ludicrous, and dangerous "Minutemen" presently (2006) scouring the deserts of Arizona, "protecting" the border from Osama bin Wetback and hunting, harassing, and torturing any Mexican undocumented workers.

26. Renato Rosaldo pursues a comparable line of argument in *Culture and Truth*, 161–167.

27. *Dante's Inferno*, http://imdb.com/title/tt0026262/ (December 16, 2004).

28. Cansino had already appeared in U.S. short features and Mexican films, including *La Fiesta* (1926) as a character named Anna Case; a dancing short with her father, Eduardo; and *Cruz Diablo* from 1934 as "de Fuentes," directed by the aforementioned Fernando de Fuentes. *Rita Hayworth*, http://www.gale.com/free_resources/chh/bio/hayworth_r.htm, date accessed: April 6, 2005; Rita Hayworth, http://www.imdb.com/name/nm0000028/, date accessed: April 6, 2005.

29. *Gilda*, http://imdb.com/title/tt0038559, date accessed April 6, 2004.

30. Judy Garland as Dorothy in Victor Fleming's *The Wizard of Oz* (1939).

31. Beatty, *Joker, Joker, Deuce*, 28

32. Given my efforts in this chapter, it seems prudent to add that Hayworth was not always already a victim; indeed, she profited personally if only temporarily from these transactions. She also had a hell of a life.

33. Carlson, "'Love Goddess' Rita Hayworth Dead at 68," n.p.

34. Epstein, "Rita Hayworth Obituary," F4, F9.

Chapter Three

Chapter acknowledgment: I am indebted to Professors Harry Polkinhorn (Literature) and Peter Atterton (Philosophy) for their comments and suggestions regarding the revision of this work.

1. Rodriguez, *Days of Obligation*, 87.

2. Wilde, *"Picture of Dorian Gray,"* 64, 228.

3. Fusco and Brillstein, *A Very Retail Christmas*, first broadcast on December 24, 1990. For a contemporary review of this not-classic, see John J. O'Connor's "Review/Television; Santa Is Challenged in 'Retail Christmas.'"

4. Fusco and Brillstein, *A Very Retail Christmas*, 1990; http://www.imdb.com/title/tt0281344/combined (December 11, 2003). After years of searching for this holy grail of TV-land, I have yet to seize a copy of the beast; let me appeal here, in the shadows of the endnotes, for someone to find, dub, and mail me a copy of this TV classic.

5. Not to be overlooked here is the luscious, bitter irony of the term "alien" appearing in a book addressing both the "Mexican" Speedy Gonzales and racism in U.S. mass culture; both in April 1997, when the first version of this chapter appeared as an essay in *Camera Obscura*, and presently, in the year 2006, the U.S. Southwest is "enjoying" a highly charged political moment when "illegal alien" immigrant bashing is all the rage. Like miniskirts and recessions, it just keeps coming back.

6. Deleuze and Guattari, *On the Line*, 14.

7. Since I first authored these pages, the *inimitable* Tom Brokaw, now retired, has proved himself to be, rather, utterly *imitable*. Now gracing the news desk for the Peacock channel is one Brian Williams, if anything, even more of an affectless droid than the canine-ic lapdog Brokaw.

8. See Gallop's rambunctious sequence on *aborde/à-côté* (accost/alongside) in her gloss of Stephen Heath interpreting Jacques Lacan diagnosing Sigmund Freud in "Encore, Encore," 43–55.

9. Sarduy, *Written on a Body*, 48. Do please note that I have opted to cite the innovative, gay, Cuban critical theorist Severo Sarduy, in lieu of once de rigueur Ishmaelite Paul de Man, on the issue of Allegory—where once a de Manian cameo might be considered necessary, he is, in 2006, in need of a comeback. A none-too-subtle allegory of theoretical alliance (yours truly's) no doubt lurks there—see it?—in the shadows.

10. Recall the niceties of "half-breeds" detailed above in my chapter on Welles's *Touch of Evil*.

11. Wilde, *"Picture of Dorian Gray,"* 64.

12. A probing theoretical inquiry into the cultural significance of marionettes is Harold B. Segel's *Pinocchio's Progeny*.

13. Unless otherwise noted, dictionary entries in this chapter derive from the Hypertext Webster link on the World Wide Web. The hypertext Webster interface was written by "bsy@cs.ucsd.edu." Speculation suggests his database derives from *Webster's Third International Dictionary of the English Language Unabridged*, ed. Noah Porter (Springfield, MA: G. and C. Merriam Company, 1913). But "bsy" is more cagey about his sources: "I don't know what version of the Webster's

dictionary . . . servers provide, since I do not run the Webster's servers myself . . . I also don't know which edition of whose dictionary these servers use, nor whether these servers are providing copyrighted data." BSY, "Hypertext Webster Interface," 1997, http://c.gp.cs.cmu.edu:5103/prog/webster; http://www. cs.ucsd.edu/users/bsy/webster.FAQ.

14. Gilman, *Jew's Body*, 170.

15. Gilman, *Difference and Pathology*, 76–108, 109–127.

16. Virilio, *War and Cinema*; Theweleit, *Male Fantasies*.

17. Wilde, "*Picture of Dorian Gray*," 64.

18. The most salient rejoinder from the Americas on Caliban is the moving theoretical tract by Roberto Fernández Retamar, *Calibán: Apuntes sobre la cultura en nuestra América*, which appeared as "Caliban: Notes Toward a Discussion of Culture in Our America."

19. For a related, contrary take on Oscar Wilde's novel, see Nunokawa's "Homosexual Desire and the Effacement of the Self in 'The Picture of Dorian Gray,'" 311. For a more general history of Jewish figuration in literature, see Abba's *Images in Transition*. Also useful is Cheyette's *Constructions of "the Jew" in English Literature and Society*, as well as his edited collection, *Between "Race" and Culture*. On a related note, Friedman's *Hollywood's Image of the Jew* is not so far afield from the general concerns of this chapter.

20. I am being a bit harsh here with George Hadley-García's *Hispanic Hollywood*; the volume remains an invaluable archival resource. The exceptions noted here include Woll's *Latin Image in American Film*; Pettit's *Images of the Mexican American in Fiction and Film*; Noriega's *Chicanos and Film* and *Shot in America*; Fregoso's *Bronze Screen*; and three volumes by Alfred Charles Richard, Jr., *Contemporary Hollywood's Negative Hispanic Image*, *The Hispanic Image on the Silver Screen*, and *Censorship and Hollywood's Hispanic Image*.

21. For the impact of Latina/o stereotypes on Latin Americans living in Latin America, the excellent and groundbreaking work of Armand Mattelart and Ariel Dorfman is crucial. In particular, see the once scandalous and underrated *How to Read Donald Duck*.

22. Having name-dropped Lacan, I ought to come clean and signal my preference for the Lacan one encounters in the critical work of Jane Gallop over that to be found in books signed by the illustrious cock-of-the-walk psychoanalyst himself.

23. Wilde, "*Picture of Dorian Gray*," 17. A poignant and incisive rejoinder of sorts to Wilde and all would-be Caliban bashers/loathers is to be found in Edmundo Desnoes's semiotic memoir "Cuba Made Me So," 384–403.

24. I have reflected previously upon these issues—a few enigmatic dispatches are crudely hidden within the footnotes of "Autobiographies at *la frontera*," 165–187. William M. Ivins's lauded *Prints and Visual Communication* is, of course, the priceless and fundamental correlative for all these seriously playful speculations.

25. Watch Deleuze and Guattari chop down a tree so as to get to the "root" of it all in "Rhizome," one of two essays in *On the Line*.

26. Nericcio, "Artif[r]acture," 102.

27. Viscusi, "Coining," 9.

28. Foucault, *Madness and Civilization*, 95; emphasis added.

29. Panofsky, "Style and Medium in the Motion Pictures," 215.

30. Virilio, *War and Cinema*, 16.

31. More on the irony of this slogan below.

32. See Tom Kuntz's "The Nation; Adiós, Speedy. Not So Fast" (April 7, 2002, Sunday *New York Times*; Week in Review Desk Late Edition - Final, Section 4, Page 3, Column 4) for more on

this peculiar embargo; though Fox News reported two months later that the Gonzales sanction had been lifted—viz Michael Y. Park's "Speedy Reaches the Finish Line Friday, June 21, 2002" (http://www.foxnews.com/story/0,2933,55675,00.html)—circa 2006, as this book awaits its birth, Speedy is hard to catch on network and cable stations in the United States.

33. Jim Backus, the voice of Mr. Magoo and the costar of *Gilligan's Island*, was a genius.

34. Vanderwood, *Disorder and Progress*, 178. For other takes on the U.S. presence in Veracruz, see Robert E. Quirk's *An Affair of Honor*. For a different account from the Mexican perspective, see Andrea Martínez's *La intervención norteamericana, Veracruz, 1914* and Maria Luisa Melo de Remes's *Veracruz mártir*. For the always-curious historiography of the U.S. military, see Jack Sweetman's *Landing at Veracruz, 1914*. Most odd and informing perhaps are Edith O'Shaughnessy's (1870–1939) reminiscences entitled *A Diplomat's Wife in Mexico* and translated as *Huerta y la Revolución vistos por la esposa de un diplomático en México*. For more general and lavishly illustrated albums documenting U.S. shenanigans south of the border, see George Black's energetic *Good Neighbor* and the pulp-fiction-style-noir seediness of Eric Hobsbawm's luridly forged *Bandits* from Dell Paperbacks' Pageant of History series.

35. Speedy lives on today in substandard, poorly animated shorts, where he is chased not by cats like Sylvester, but, more often, by Daffy Duck. In addition, the Warner animation team uses a technique called "limited animation," a cheaper, faster method of animation whose flimsiness strikes viewers at a glance. Storytellers disturb established antagonists like cat and mouse at their own hazard—from an animator's point of view, TimeWarner Inc.'s animation division is overdue for a makeover.

36. Foucault, "Contemporary Music and the Public," 322.

37. In another place, another time, Foucault is recorded to have said that we must nurture our *curiosity*, develop a "readiness to find what surrounds us strange and odd," at the same time sharing "a certain determination to throw off familiar ways of thought and to look at the same things in a different way"("Masked Philosopher," 328). I feel the need to justify the degree to which my work derives from the talented, historicist-accented voice of Michel Foucault. It may be a phase, but as a Chicano cultural critic, I have always sensed a coconspirator in Foucault, who asks his readers to move past the politics of "the same." In an increasingly homogenized cultural milieu, where sneaker ads proxy the avant-garde, Foucault reassures those of us who have made the "ideological state apparatus" (chapeau Althusser) of the university a career that our only task is to constructively challenge the cultural status quo. To ask the next question and make it good—"good" without the policing taint of self-righteousness: "Criticism that hands down sentences sends me to sleep; I'd like a criticism of scintillating leaps of imagination. It would not be sovereign or dressed in red. It would bear the lightning of possible storms" ("The Masked Philosopher," 326).

38. Maltin, *Of Mice and Magic*, 266–267.

39. It's actually not that bad; the most egregious animated scene of note comes from the end of the twentieth century in a film I confess I love to death—*A Bug's Life* (1998), directed by John Lasseter for Pixar and distributed by Disney; there the enemies of the heroic ants tank up on filth in a Mexican cantina to the tunes of "La cucaracha" before descending to attack, maim, and kill their miniscule adversaries. Pixar and Disney had

mined this rich vein before when promoting a video-game version of *Toy Story 2*:

> Toy Story 2 Game Angers Hispanics
> LOS ANGELES—The Mexican henchman in the Toy Story 2 video game was supposed to be a funny bad guy in one of the holiday's hottest selling titles.
>   But, *Variety* reports, to many in Los Angeles' Hispanic community, the villain—with sombrero and bands of bullets—was a blatant stereotype.
>   On Friday, The Walt Disney Co. said it would remove the character after angry protesters demonstrated at the Santa Monica headquarters of the game's publisher, Activision Inc. "Unfortunately, there was a mistake made in its creation," said Disney spokeswoman Claudia Peters. "The character does not appear in the movie."
>   "What they are doing is profiting from degrading people. We want an immediate recall," said Oscar de la Torre, a counselor at Santa Monica High School. (*Toronto Sun*, December 13, 1999)

40. To return for a second to our assertions regarding domains Jewish and Mexican above, you will recall how I wrestled with reconciling the theoretical richness of Wilde's *Picture of Dorian Gray* with scenes wherein anti-Semitic epithets abounded. How ironic in *Cannery Woe* that our fat mouse/*político* can be heard to exclaim at one point in exasperation, "*Oi Gevalt!*"

41. Stevenson, *The Animated Film*, 60.

42. I have tried to render somewhat phonetically the phrasing of genius voicesmith Mel Blanc.

43. A literary purge for this view is Oscar Zeta Acosta's *Revolt of the Cockroach People*.

44. Wilde, "*Picture of Dorian Gray*," 23.

45. Brasch, *Cartoon Monickers*, 144.

46. Derrida, *Memoirs for Paul de Man*, 3.

47. Paul de Man's name here calls forth as much his lucid and evocative description of allegory (which is how my autopsy should be properly read at one level) as his autobiographical connection to a history of European anti-Semitism alluded to earlier in my glosses of Oscar Wilde's fiction. See, of course, de Man's *Allegories of Reading*, 234.

48. A recent literary gloss of this scenario is to be found in Tino Villanueva's *Scene from the Movie "Giant."*

49. Derrida, "Circumfession," 58n. The book *Jacques Derrida* is marvelous for a number of reasons, not the least of which is the spectacle of Derrida's auto-erotic obsession with circumcision, his mother, and writing—not since the fabulous Dr. Daniel Paul Schreber put pen to paper has such a playground for Freudian speculation arrived on the critical scene.

50. The Freleng-authored and penned cartoons are available in a series of non-TV-aired animated *classics* available on Yo Ho Video's *Uncensored Cartoons*, 1989.

51. All release-date and director information derives from Will Friedwald and Jerry Beck's invaluable reference guide *The Warner Brother Cartoons*.

52. Brasch, *Cartoon Monickers*, 31; emphasis added.

53. David Kunzle provides a fascinating exposé on the labor politics/dynamics of Disney's animation division in his "Introduction to the English Edition (1991)," *How to Read Donald Duck*. Related issues surface in my retelling of Margarita Cansino's transformation into Rita Hayworth in "When Electrolysis Proxies for the Existential," Chapter 2 above.

54. Brasch, *Cartoon Monickers*, 145.

55. Ibid., 162.

56. Ibid., x.

57. Lenburg, *The Great Cartoon Directors*; Brasch, *Cartoon Monickers*.

58. Brasch, *Cartoon Monickers*, 144.

59. Nor, for that matter, can Derrida paint; read his confessions of artistic incompetence in *Memoirs of the Blind*.

60. Also to be carefully consulted in this area is Michael Rogin's 1996 masterpiece, *Blackface, White Noise*.

61. I have published some thoughts about memory and the U.S.-Mexican border lands in "Remembering: What Is Truth on the Border"/"*Recuerdos: Cuál es la verdad en/de la frontera*."

62. See Manring's *Slave in a Box: The Strange Career of Aunt Jemima* for more in this vein.

63. The etymology of "zoanthropy," from the Greek *zo*, "animal" (as in "zoo"), plus *anthropos*, "man" (as in "anthropology"), *represents* a semantic/linguistic mestiza fugue/fusion with attendant curiosities of its own— a term for the monstrous whose origins are themselves the result of a monstrous comingling, a special miscegenation that weds the bestial with the human. Source: Online Medical Dictionary, copyright © 1997–1998 Academic Medical Publishing and CancerWEB, date accessed April 12, 2005.

I am indebted to Vladimir Nabokov's *Pale Fire* for bringing my eye to the dictionary Zs in pursuit of "Zemblan," wherefore I chanced upon "zoanthropy," and, fruit for a book to come: "zenana," "part of a house reserved for women"—perhaps the book on Rosario Castellanos that has yet to come from my increasingly stubborn and sluggish pen.

64. The bright-eyed, bushy-tailed rhetoric of this section is partially muted by the fact that post-1992 episodes of *Ren and Stimpy* are being overseen by the corporate "suits" at Nickelodeon. Kricfalusi was fired owing to "creative differences" with his producers. Since that date, the show has never been the same.

65. Kricfalusi, "FAQ: R&S On a Napkin."

66. Author e-mail correspondence from spumcoinc@aol.com, January 19, 1995.

67. Walters, *John Kricfalusi*. http://www.angelfire.com/wi/Ren-Stimpy2000/SFKircIntv.html (October 21, 2005).

68. A longer discussion of Gilbert Hernandez's work appears in Nericcio, "Artif[r]acture," 79–109.

69. Jaime Hernandez, "Flies on the Ceiling," 1–15; and Gilbert Hernandez, "'A Folktale' by Loup Garou," 89–96.

70. Gilbert Hernandez, *The Blood of Palomar*; the volume appeared in the U.K. as *Human Diastrophism*.

71. Gilman, *Jew's Body*, 193.

72. Castellanos, "Language as an Instrument of Domination," 252. See also Frantz Fanon's related view of language and/as racism in *Black Skin, White Masks*.

73. Wilde, "*Picture of Dorian Gray*," 39.

74. *Webster's Third International Dictionary* (New York: G&C Merriam Company, 1961), 237.

75. Berestein, "Girl in Piñata Found during Border Check."

76. If not "gringa," then, at the very least, gringa + "Chemical X," the magic substance Buttercup's "father," Professor Utonium, used to make her and, tellingly, their enemy, the mad scientist/monkey, Mojo Jojo.

Chapter Four

1. Scholarship of late has exploded with regard to these singular Latino icons; if you get the chance, you won't waste any time if you peruse Joanne Hershfield's *Invention of Dolores Del Rio*—her take on movie stars as "signs of other signs" is intriguing to say the least. Also quite good is Victoria Sturtevant's "Lupe Vélez and the Ambivalent Pleasures of Ethnic Mas-

querade." The world of Velezian exegesis is in full go-go mode these days, with no less than the likes of Rosa Linda Fregoso contending that Lupe Vélez is "the Chicana Queen of the Bs . . . one of the most accomplished and popular screwball comedians of the time" ("'Fantasy Heritage,'" 116). I should add here in the warm confines of the endnotes that this piece appears in this collection owing to the invitation of the one and only Joy James of Brown University—its first incarnation was as "Lupe Velez, Cinema, and the Toilet: Tales of the Mexican Spitfire in an American Vomitorium," part of the "Conference on Imagination, Imaging, and Memory: Racial, Gender, and Political Violence" sponsored by Brown's Department of Africana Studies (March, 2003).

2. Irigaray, ""How to Conceive (of) a Girl," 166.

3. Fanon, "The Fact of Blackness," 116, 140.

4. Castellanos, "Woman and Her Image," 241.

5. Faulkner, *Light in August*, 464–465.

6. A must-read in this vein, pardon the pun, is Joseph R. Urgo's "Menstrual Blood and 'Nigger' Blood," 391–402.

7. Yet to be translated is the best biography on Lupe Vélez: Gabriel Ramírez's *Lupe Vélez*.

8. Burt and Wallen, "Knowing Better," 87.

9. Ngai, "'A Foul Lump,'" 596.

10. Hershfield, "Delores Del Rio, Uncomfortably Real," 153; emphasis added.

11. O'Neill, "Demands of Authenticity," 377.

12. Rodríguez-Estrada, "Dolores del Rio and Lupe Vélez," 484, 486.

13. Jenkins, "'You Can't Say That in English!': The Scandal of Lupe Velez."

14. Anger, *Hollywood Babylon*, 238.

15. Osborne, "Hollywood Tragedy," 76–82.

16. Cruz, "Salma Hayek,"

http://www.findarticles.com/p/articles/mi_m1285/is_3_33/ai_99165056.

17. Ibid.

18. Jacobs, "The Complete Guide to Women," 99.

19. Ibid.; emphasis added.

20. González, *The Assumption of Lupe Vélez*. The screen grab from *The Assumption of Lupe Vélez* is ©1999 Rita González and appears here with the permission of the artist.

21. SubCine, "Biography of Rita González."

22. Hamburger, *The Vision and the Visionary*, 317–382.

23. The illustration for the *vera ikon*, or Veronica, pictured here is reproduced from the Web Gallery of Art, Virtual Museum, "St. Veronica with the Holy Kerchief," c. 1420, Tempera on oak, 78 x 48 cm, Alte Pinakothek, Munich, http://www.wga.hu/frames-e.html?/html/m/master/veronica (October 5, 2005).

24. Hamburger, *Vision and the Visionary*, 320. Hamburger's last name tellingly colludes with "toilets" in this chapter in some odd, cyphered, Freudian allegory on anality and orality—the spirit of Tlaçolteotl, the Aztec goddess of fertility and fecality, of lust and toilette rituals, may be seen to lurk here and there as well. For more on this, see Simeon's *Diccionario de la lengua nahuatl*, 575, and Gerling's "Tlaçolteotl Is Dead."

25. Etymology: "Sacrosanct" comes from Latin *sacrosanctus*, "consecrated with religious ceremonies, hence holy"; "sacred," from *sacrum*, "religious rite" (from *sacer*, "holy") + *sanctus*, "consecrated" (from *sancire*, "to make sacred by a religious act").

26. Kristeva, *Powers of Horror*, 3. I am indebted to my former graduate student, now Professor, Marc García-Martínez, of Allen Hancock College, Santa Maria, Califas, for bringing this passage to my attention after reading an earlier version of this chapter.

27. Carrasco, *City of Sacrifice*, 210; emphasis added.

28. Ibid., 191–192; emphasis in original.

Gallery Two

1. Rechy, *City of Night*, 285.

2. Rodriguez, *Days of Obligation: An Argument with My Mexican Father*.

3. One also notes, and not just in passing, that Rodriguez has anticipated (pre-ordained?) my reading of the Veronica in the Lupe Vélez chapter you just finished reading.

4. John Paul Gutiérrez, personal communication via e-mail, October 12, 2005. And no, Gutiérrez was *not* named after a pope.

5. At least he cops to his film-laced formulation under the thumb of Hollywood—see Richie Rodriguez's afterword to Lauren Greenfield's *Fast Forward: Growing Up in the Shadow of Hollywood*. http://www.amazon.com/exec/obidos/ASIN/0811844137/lauren greenfi-20/102-1344492-6350525?creative=327641&camp=14573&link_code=as1

6. For a recent scholarly view of Texas Ranger butchery and other, less highly charged findings, see Charles H. Harris III and Louis R. Sadler's *The Texas Rangers and the Mexican Revolution*.

7. Kaye, "Eye on Police Force," April 4, 1996.

8. The first version of this brief rant appeared in *Bad Subjects* 61 (2003), http://bad.eserver.org/issues/2002/61/nerricio.html (*sic*) (December 2, 2004). A CNN article and QuickTime video of this event are presently available (as of November 2005) at CNN at this address: http://www.cnn.com/US/9604/02/immigrant.beating/index2.html.

9. For more on the antics of this bizarre animated mannequin, be sure to munch on Chon A. Noriega's *Shot in America: Television, the State, and the Rise of Chicano Cinema*.

Chapter Five

1. A version of this chapter first appeared as "A Decidedly 'Mexican' and 'American' Semi[er]otic Transference: Frida Kahlo in the Eyes of Gilbert Hernandez," in *Latina/o Popular Culture*, edited by Mary Romero and Michelle Habell-Pallán (New York: NYU Press, 2002), 190–207.

2. Kahlo, *The Diary of Frida Kahlo*, 206.

3. For more on the artistic dynamics of the verge, see Nericcio, *Bordered Sexualities*.

4. Burciaga, "Last Dinner of Chicano Heroes," reprinted from the *Los Angeles Times*, May 3, 1988, with slight alterations by Carl Minzner. http://rescomp.stanford.edu/dorms/stern/zapata/Dinner.html (August 12, 2000). In his entry for "xicanismo/chicanismo" in the *Oxford Encyclopedia of Mesoamerican Cultures* (180–181), José B. Cuéllar sums up Burciaga's contributions to the Chicana/o *Dasein*, while also anticipating the dynamic XicanOsmotic processes: "Central among the outstanding artistic representatives of Chicanismo is José Antonio Burciaga, whose book *Drink Cultura-C/S* (1993) and murals *Mythology of Maize* and *Last Supper of Chicano Heroes* explore its core meanings. It is through a fine focus on Burciaga's written and painted work that we can grasp a broader understanding of Chicanismo . . . He reflects both its political energy and the ephemeral artistry by examining, in his words: 'the ironies in the experience of living within, between and sometimes outside, two cultures . . . Mexican by nature, American by nurture, a true "mexture" . . . the damnation, salvation, the celebration of it all.'"

5. *CLNET*, http://

clnet.sscnet.ucla.edu/ (October 22, 2005).

6. I have addressed this more fully in "Artif[r]acture," 79–109.

7. Goldstuck, "The Brothers Speak."

8. "Frida" is one of several experimental short stories by Gilbert Hernandez also collected in *Flies on the Ceiling*, 29–40.

9. This is no place for a flashback, but let the record show that Gould's genius gave the world, at least through its animated inheritors, a Speedy Gonzales wannabe, a "Mexican" character by the name of Go Go Gómez who was a master of disguise and a sidekick for detective Dick Tracy, along with an "Asian" gumshoe by the name of Joe Jitsu. The show was originally entitled *The Adventures of Dick Tracy* and then called *The Dick Tracy Show*; it was produced by Henry G. Saperstein's United Productions of America (UPA) Pictures in 1960. Ron Kurer, *Toon Tracker's Dick Tracy Show*, http://www.toontracker.com/tracy/dicktracy.htm (20 October 2005).

Go Go Gómez

10. Derrida, "Restitutions," 366; emphasis added.

11. Herrera, *Frida*.

12. Journalistic accounts of Gilbert Hernandez's literary roots repeat time and again the connection between the magic streets of his Palomar and those of a now-legendary Macondo invented by García Márquez. Jaime Hernandez, Gilbert's artist-brother, bursts our osmotic-sensitive sensors: "[He] read [García Márquez], but he didn't know about him till someone told him that they wrote similarly. It was really ironic: Gilbert had never read him, but people were telling him this. I think it was more being raised on the same wavelength" (cited in Goldstuck, "The Brothers Speak"). What García Márquez and Gilbert Hernandez do share is a fascination with the Latin American motherlands and the Latino mother tongue. In Gilbert Hernandez's own words: "The interest was always there. But I . . . refined it doing stories about the old country, doing stories about the old people, and the stories of Hispanic culture, particularly Mexican, I think it has me thinking about it every time I draw." On another note, for a first-rate recent critical consideration of Hernandez's Palomar series, see Charles Hatfield's "Heartbreak Soup," 2–17.

13. "A Fit of Pique over Border Patrol's Chic: What the Well-Dressed Agent's Wearing Isn't Made in the USA," Associated Press story, November 29, 2005. http://www.msnbc.msn.com/id/10256189/from/RL.1/

14. Groth and Fiore, *The New Comics*, 302.

Conclusion

1. Derrida, *Archive Fever*, 88.

2. Toole, *Confederacy of Dunces*, 101.

3. Baudrillard, "Orders of Simulacra," 119.

4. Marx, *Das Kapital/Capital*, 165.

5. Ashcraft, "Anime Eyes," http://www.wired.com/wired/archive/13.05/play.html?pg=4.

6. "c/s" is a tagger's mark that means *"con safos"*—"do not touch this tagger's mark," or "do so at your own risk."

BIBLIOGRAPHY

Abba, Rubin. *Images in Transition: The English Jew in English Literature, 1660–1830*. Westport, CT: Greenwood Press, 1984.

Acosta, Oscar Zeta. *The Revolt of the Cockroach People*. New York: Bantam, 1974.

Adorno, Theodor. *The Culture Industry: Selected Essays on Mass Culture*.

Adorno, Theodor, and Max Horkheimer. "The Culture Industry." In *Dialectic of Enlightenment*, 12–167. New York: Continuum, 1976.

Ali, Syed Ameer. *A Short History of the Saracens; Being a Concise Account of the Rise and Decline of the Saracenic Power and of the Economic, Social and Intellectual Development of the Arab Nation from the Earliest Times to the Destruction of Bagdad, and the Expulsion of the Moors from Spain*. London: Macmillan, 1924.

Althusser, Louis. "Ideology and Ideological State Apparatuses: Notes towards an Investigation." *La Pensée*, 1970.

Anger, Kenneth. *Hollywood Babylon*. New York: Bell Publishing, 1981.

Anzaldúa, Gloria. *Borderlands/la frontera: The New Mestiza*. San Francisco: Aunt Lute Books, 1987.

ARTFL Project. 1913 Webster's Revised Unabridged Dictionary. http://humanities.uchicago.edu/orgs/ARTFL/ (October 10, 2005).

Ashcraft, Brian. "Anime Eyes." *Wired* 13 (May 2005): 5. http://www.wired.com/wired/archive/13.05/play.html?pg=4

Baudrillard, Jean. "The Orders of Simulacra." In *Simulations*, 81–159. New York: Semiotext[e], 1983.

————. "The Precession of Simulacra." Translated by Paul Foss, Paul Patton, and Philip Beitchman. In *Simulations*, 1–49. New York: Semiotext[e], 1983.

Bazin, Andre. *Orson Welles: A Critical View*. New York: Harper and Row, 1978.

Beatty, Paul. *Joker, Joker, Deuce*. New York: Penguin Poets Books, 1994.

Bender, Steven W. *Greasers and Gringos: Latinos, Law, and the American Imagination*. New York: New York University Press, 2003.

Benjamin, Walter. "The Work of Art in the Age of Mechanical Reproduction." In *Illuminations*, 211–244. Translated by Harry Zohn. London: Fontana, 1992.

Berestein, Leslie. "Girl in Piñata Found during Border Check." *San Diego Union-Tribune*, Metro, November 12, 2004. http://www.signonsandiego.com/news/metro/20041112-9999-7m12pinata.html.

Berg, Charles Ramírez. *Latino Images in Film: Stereotypes, Subversion, and Resistance*. Texas Film and Media Studies Series. Austin: University of Texas Press, 2002.

Bhabha, Homi. *Nation and Narration*. London/New York: Routledge, 1990.

———. "The Other Question: Difference, Discrimination, and the Discourse of Colonialism." In *Out There: Marginalization and Contemporary Cultures*, edited by Russell Ferguson, 18–36. New York: New Museum of Contemporary Art, 1990.

Black, George. *The Good Neighbor: How the United States Wrote the History of Central America and the Caribbean*. New York: Pantheon, 1988.

Bogle, Donald. *Toms, Coons, Mulattos, Mammies, and Bucks: An Interpretive History of Blacks in American Films*. New York: The Viking Press, 1973.

Borges, Jorge Luis. "Borges and I." In *The Borges Reader*, edited by Emir Rodríguez Monegal and Alastair Reid, 278. New York: E. P. Dutton, 1981.

Brady, Frank. *Citizen Welles: A Biography of Orson Welles*. New York: Anchor Books, 1989.

Brasch, Walter M. *Cartoon Monickers: An Insight into the Animation Industry*. Bowling Green: Bowling Green University Popular Press, 1983.

Burciaga, José Antonio. "Last Dinner of Chicano Heroes." Reprinted from the *Los Angeles Times*, May 3, 1988, with slight alterations by Carl Minzner. http://web.archive.org/web/19970218075014/ http://rescomp.standord.edu/dorms/stern/zapata/Dinner.html

Aldama, Arturo. *Disrupting Savagism: Intersecting Chicana/o, Mexican Immigrant, and Native American Struggles for Self-Representation*. Durham, NC: Duke University Press, 2001.

Aldama, Frederick Luis. *Postethnic Narrative Criticism: Magicorealism in Oscar "Zeta" Acosta, Ana Castillo, Julie Dash, Hanif Kureishi, and Salman Rushdie*. Austin: University of Texas Press, 2003.

Althusser, Louis. "Ideology and Ideological State Apparatus." In *Lenin and Philosophy and Other Essays*, edited by Ben Brewster, 127–186. London: New Left Books, 1971.

Buel, J. W. *Heroes of the Dark Continent*. N.p., 1890.

Burt, Richard, and Jeffrey Wallen. "Knowing Better: Sex, Cultural Criticism, and the Pedagogical Imperative in the 1990s." *Diacritics* 29, no. 1 (1999): 72–91.

Carlson, Timothy. "'Love Goddess' Rita Hayworth Dead at 68." *Los Angeles Herald Exam*, May 16, 1987, n.p.

Carpenter, Gerry. *Musings on Dante's Inferno*, http://www.scifilm.org/musings2/musing964.html.

Carrasco, Davíd. *City of Sacrifice: The Aztec Empire and the Role of Violence in Civilization*. Boston: Beacon Press, 1999.

Cassuto, Leonard. *The Inhuman Race: The Racial Grotesque in American Literature and Culture*. New York: Columbia University Press, 1997.

Castellanos, Rosario. "Language as an Instrument of Domination." In *A Rosario Castellanos Reader*, edited and translated by Maureen Ahern, 250–253. Austin: University of Texas Press, 1988.

———. "Woman and Her Image." In *A Rosario Castellanos Reader*, edited and translated by Maureen Ahern, 236–244. Austin: University of Texas Press, 1988.

Chen, Tina. *Double Agency: Acts of Impersonation in Asian American Literature and Culture*. Palo Alto: Stanford University Press, 2005.

Cheyette, Bryan. *Between "Race" and Culture: Representations of "the Jew" in English and American Literature*. Stanford: Stanford University Press, 1996.

———. *Constructions of "the Jew" in English Literature and Society: Racial Repre-*

sentations, 1875–1945. Cambridge: Cambridge University Press, 1993.

Ciccone, Madonna. "Vogue." In *Songs Inspired by the Film "Dick Tracy."* Los Angeles: Epic Records, 1990.

Cisneros, Sandra. *The House on Mango Street.* New York: Vintage International, 1989.

Collet, Jean. "*Touch of Evil*, or Orson Welles and the Thirst for Transcendence." In *Touch of Evil: Orson Welles, Director*, edited by Terry Comito, 249–258. New Brunswick, NJ: Rutgers University Press, 1985.

Comito, Terry, ed. *Touch of Evil: Orson Welles, Director.* New Brunswick, NJ: Rutgers University Press, 1985.

Cruz, Penelope. "Salma Hayek: A One-of-a-Kind, Behind-the-Scenes Look at the Inner Life of One of Hollywood's Most Daring and Hottest—by a Photographer and Interviewer Who's Not Bad on the Big Screen Herself." *Interview Magazine* (April 2003), cited in Findarticles.com, Arts and Entertainment, Interviews, http://www.findarticles.com/p/articles/mi_m1285/is_3_33/ai_99165056 (October 5, 2005).

Cuéllar, José B. "Xicanismo/chicanismo." *Oxford Encyclopedia of Mesoamerican Cultures*, ed. David Carrasco, 180–181. Oxford: Oxford University Press, 2000.

Danbury Mint. "Guardian of Freedom." http://www.danburymint.com (March 23, 2006).

———. "María," by Kelly RuBert. http://www.danburymint.com/heirloom/product.asp?code=145 (March 23, 2006).

———. "Saluting John-John Doll." http://www.danburymint.com/heirloom/category.asp?id=52 (March 23, 2006).

Dear, Michael, and Gustavo LeClerc. "Tijuana Desenmascarada." *Wide Angle* 20, no. 3 (1998): 211–221.

Deleuze, Gilles, and Felix Guattari. *On the Line.* Translated by John Johnston. New York: Semiotext[e], 1983.

de Man, Paul. *Allegories of Reading: Figural Language in Rousseau, Nietzsche, Rilke, and Proust.* New Haven: Yale University Press, 1979.

de Orellana, Margarita. "The Circular Look: The Incursion of North American Fictional Cinema into the Mexican Revolution (1911–1917)." In *Mediating Two Worlds: Cinematic Encounters in the Americas*, edited by John King, Ana M. López, and Manuel Alvarado. London: BFI, 1993.

———. *Filming Pancho: How Hollywood Shaped the Mexican Revolution.* Translated by John King. London: Verson, 2003.

Derrida, Jacques. *Archive Fever: A Freudian Impression.* Translated by Eric Prenowitz. Chicago: University of Chicago Press, 1998.

———. "Circumfession." In *Jacques Derrida*, by Jacques Derrida and Geoffrey Bennington, 3–315. Chicago: University of Chicago Press, 1993.

———. *Limited Inc.* Translated by Sam Weber. Evanston, IL: Northwestern University Press, 1988.

———. *Memoirs for Paul de Man.* Translated by Cecile Lindsay et al. New York: Columbia University Press, 1986.

———. *Memoirs of the Blind: The Self-Portrait and Other Ruins.* Translated by Pascale-Anne Brault and Michael Naas. Chicago: University of Chicago Press, 1993.

———. *Of Grammatology.* Translated by Gayatri Chakravorty Spivak. Baltimore: Johns Hopkins University Press, 1976.

———. "Plato's Pharmacy." In *Dissemination*, translated by Barbara Johnson,

61–171. Chicago: University of Chicago Press, 1981.

———. "Restitutions." In *La Vérité en Peinture*. Paris: Flammarion, 1978. Translated by Geoff Bennington and Ian McLeod as *The Truth in Painting* (Chicago: University of Chicago Press, 1987).

Derrida, Jacques, and Geoffrey Bennington. *Jacques Derrida*. Translated by Geoffrey Bennington. Chicago: University of Chicago Press, 1993.

Desnoes, Edmundo. "Cuba Made Me So." In *On Signs*, edited by Marshall Blonsky, 384–403. Baltimore: Johns Hopkins University Press, 1985.

Dorfman, Ariel, and Armand Mattelart. *How to Read Donald Duck: Imperialist Ideology in the Disney Comic*. 2d ed., enlarged. Translated by David Kunzle. New York: International General, 1984.

Doughboy, Pillsbury. EBay.com. http://ebay.com (October 2, 2002).

Dyer, Richard. "Resistance through Charisma: Rita Hayworth and Gilda." In *Women in Film Noir*, edited by E. Ann Kaplan, 91–99. London: BFI, 1980.

Epstein, Robert. "Rita Hayworth Obituary." *Los Angeles Times*, San Diego County Edition, July 25, 1991, F4, F9.

Erman, Andrew L. *Blue Vaudeville: Sex, Morals, and the Mass Marketing of Amusement, 1895–1915*. Jefferson, NC: McFarland, 2004.

Fanon, Frantz. *Black Skin, White Masks*. Translated by Charles Lam Markmann. New York: Grove Press, 1967.

Faulkner, William. *Light in August*. New York: Vintage International, 1990.

Federal Theatre Project Collection. Library of Congress, *New Deal Stage*. http://memory.loc.gov/ammem/fedtp/fthome.html (May 12, 2005).

Feser, Edward, and Steven Postrel. "Reality Principles: An Interview with John R. Searle." *Reason Online*. http://reason.com/0002/fe.ef.reality.shtml (April 6, 2005).

Flaubert, Gustave. *Madame Bovary*. Rev. ed. http://www.univ-rouen.fr/flaubert/02manus/206 toilette/bro 6 269.htm, from Le Site Flaubert, http://www.univ-rouen.fr/flaubert/.

Fleming, Victor, dir. *The Wizard of Oz*. Film. Culver City, CA: Metro-Goldwyn-Mayer, 1939.

Foucault, Michel. "Contemporary Music and the Public." In *Politics, Philosophy, Culture: Interviews and Other Writings, 1977–1984*. New York: Routledge, 1988.

———. *Madness and Civilization: A History of Insanity in the Age of Reason*. New York: Vintage, 1973.

———. "The Masked Philosopher." In *Politics, Philosophy, Culture: Interviews and Other Writings 1977–1984*, 323–330. New York: Routledge, 1988.

———. *Remarks on Marx: Conversations with Duccio Trombadori*. Translated by R. James Goldstein and James Cascaito. New York: Semiotext[e], 1991.

Fregoso, Rosa Linda. *The Bronze Screen: Chicana and Chicano Film Culture*. Minneapolis: University of Minnesota Press, 1993.

———. "'Fantasy Heritage': Tracking Latina Bloodlines." In *MeXicana Encounters: The Making of Social Identities on the Borderlands*, 103–125. Berkeley: University of California Press, 2003.

Freud, Sigmund. *The Interpretation of Dreams*. Translated by James Strachey. New York: Bard, 1998.

Friedman, Lester D. *Hollywood's Image of the Jew*. New York: Ungar, 1982.

Friedwald, Will, and Jerry Beck. *The Warner Brother Cartoons*. Metuchen, NJ; London: The Scarecrow Press, 1981.

Fuentes, Carlos. *The Crystal Frontier: A Novel in Nine Stories.* Translated by Alfred MacAdam. New York: Farrar, Straus and Giroux, 1997.

Fusco, Paul, and Bernie Brillstein, dirs. *A Very Retail Christmas.* Television special. Los Angeles: Paul Fusco Productions, 1990.

Fussell, Paul. "Type-casting." In *Wartime: Understanding and Behavior in the Second World War*, 115–128. Oxford: Oxford University Press, 1990.

Gallop, Jane. "Encore, Encore." In *The Daughter's Seduction: Feminism and Psychoanalysis.* Ithaca: Cornell University Press, 1982.

Gerling, Daniel. "Tlaçolteotl Is Dead: The Wonderful, Horrible Life of Captain Bourke's Scatalogic Rites of All Nations." http://www.poopreport.com/Academic/Content/Gerling/gerling.html (March 22, 2006).

Gilman, Sander. *Difference and Pathology: Stereotypes of Sexuality, Race, and Madness.* Ithaca: Cornell University Press, 1985.

———. *The Jew's Body.* New York: Routledge, 1991.

Goebbels, Joseph. "The Good Companion." German Propaganda Archive, http://www.calvin.edu/academic/cas/gpa/goeb12.htm (October 12, 2005). Translated from "Der treue Helfer." In *Das eherne Herz*, 229–235. Munich: Zentralverlag der NSDAP, 1943.

Golden, Thelma. *Black Male: Representations of Masculinity in Contemporary American Art.* New York: Whitney Museum of American Art, 1994.

Goldstuck, Arthur. "The Brothers Speak." In *The Unlovely Love and Rockets Home Page* 1993, http://www.legends.org/za/arthur/losbros.htm (June 3, 2000).

González, Rita, dir. *The Assumption of Lupe Vélez.* Film. Los Angeles: Independent Film, USA, 1999.

Greenaway, Peter. *Prospero's Books.* Film. London, England; Amsterdam, The Netherlands; and Florence, Italy: Camera One, Canal+, Chanel Four Films, et al., 1991.

Greenfield, Lauren. *Fast Forward: Growing Up in the Shadow of Hollywood.* N.p.: Chronicle Books, 2004. (Hardcover published by Alfred A. Knopf/Melcher Media, 1997.)

Griffith, David W. *Birth of a Nation.* Film. Los Angeles: David W. Griffith Corporation, 1915.

Groth, Gary, and Robert Fiore. *The New Comics.* New York: Berkley Books, 1988.

Hadley-García, George. *Hispanic Hollywood: The Latins in Motion Pictures.* New York: Citadel Press, 1991.

Halleck, DeeDee. *The Gringo in Mañanaland.* Film. (1995). Frames of Reference: Reflections on Media film series. San Diego: Rockefeller and MacArthur film/video/multimedia, 2000.

Hamburger, Jeffrey. *The Vision and the Visionary: Art and Female Spirituality in Late Medieval Germany.* New York: Zone Books, 1998.

Haraway, Donna J. "A Cyborg Manifesto: Science, Technology, and Socialist-Feminism in the Late Twentieth Century." In *Simians, Cyborgs, and Women*, 149–181. New York: Routledge, 1991.

Harris, Charles H., III, and Louis R. Sadler. *The Texas Rangers and the Mexican Revolution: The Bloodiest Decade, 1910–1920.* Albuquerque: University of New Mexico Press, 2004.

Hatfield, Charles. "Heartbreak Soup: The Interdependency of Theme and Form." *Inks: Cartoon and Comic Art Studies* 4, no. 2 (1997): 2–17.

Heath, Stephen. "Film and System: Terms of Analysis, Part I." *Screen* 16, no. 1 (1975): 7–77.

———. "Film and System: Terms of Analysis, Part II." *Screen* 16, no. 2 (1975): 91–113.

Hernandez, Gilbert. *The Blood of Palomar: Volume VIII of the Complete Love and Rockets*. Seattle: Fantagraphic Books, 1991; the volume appeared in the U.K. as *Human Diastrophism: A Heartbreak Soup Graphic Novel* (London: Titan Books, 1989).

———. "'A Folktale' by Loup Garou." In *Flies on the Ceiling: Volume Nine of the Complete Love and Rockets*, edited by Gary Groth, 89–96. Seattle: Fantagraphic Books, 1991.

———. "Frida." In *Flies on the Ceiling: Volume Nine of the Complete Love and Rockets*, edited by Gary Groth, 29–40. Seattle: Fantagraphic Books, 1991.

Hernandez, Jaime. "Flies on the Ceiling." In *Flies on the Ceiling: Volume Nine of the Complete Love and Rockets*, edited by Gary Groth, 1–15. Seattle: Fantagraphic Books, 1991.

Herrera, Hayden. *Frida: A Biography of Frida Kahlo*. New York: Harper Perennial Library, 1991.

Hershfield, Joanne. "Dolores Del Rio, Uncomfortably Real: The Economics of Race in Hollywood's Latin American Musicals." In *Classic Hollywood, Classic Whiteness*, edited by Daniel Bernardi, 139–156. Minneapolis: University of Minnesota Press, 2001.

———. *The Invention of Dolores Del Rio*. Minneapolis: University of Minnesota Press, 2000.

Hobsbawm, Eric J. *Bandits*. Pageant of History series. New York: Dell, 1969.

Homer. *Odyssey*. Translated by Stanley Lombardo. Indianapolis: Hackett Publishing, 2000.

Horn, Maurice. *The World Encyclopedia of Comics*. New York: Chelsea House, 1976.

Irigaray, Luce. "How to Conceive (of) a Girl." In *Speculum de l'autre femme/Speculum of the Other Woman*, 160–167. Translated by Gillian C. Gill. Ithaca: Cornell University Press, 1985.

Ivins, William M. *Prints and Visual Communication*. Cambridge: Harvard University Press, 1953.

Jacobs, A. J. "The Complete Guide to Women: All About Eva." *Esquire*, May 2005, 98–103.

Jameson, Fredric. *The Political Unconscious: Narrative as a Socially Symbolic Act*. Ithaca: Cornell University Press, 1981.

Jelinek, Elfriede. *The Piano Teacher*. Translated by Joachim Neugroschel. New York: Weidenfeld and Nicolson, 1988.

Jenkins, Henry. "'You Don't Say That in English!': The Scandal of Lupe Vélez." http://web.mit.edu/cms/People/henry3/index.html (October 5, 2005).

Johnson, William. "Orson Welles: Of Time and Loss." In *Touch of Evil: Orson Welles, Director*, edited by Terry Comito, 235–248. New Brunswick, NJ: Rutgers University Press, 1985.

Joyce, James. *Ulysses*. New York: Modern Library/Random House, 1992.

Kaganoff, Benzion C. *A Dictionary of Jewish Names and Their History*. New York: Schocken Books, 1977.

Kahlo, Frida. *The Diary of Frida Kahlo: An Intimate Self-Portrait*. Edited by Sarah M. Lowe. New York: Harry N. Abrams, 1995.

Kamuf, Peggy, ed. and trans. *A Derrida Reader: Between the Blinds*. New York: Columbia University Press, 1991.

Katz, Jesse. "The Curse of Zapata: He Would Be a Great Movie; The 20th Century's

Purest Revolutionary. If only Hollywood could get over the fact he was Mexican: filmmaker Gregory Nava plans movie on life of Emiliano Zapata." *Los Angeles Magazine* 47, no. 12 (December 2002): 102–105.

Kaye, Jeffrey. "Eye on Police Force." *Police and Border Crossings*, April 4, 1996. http://www.pbs.org/newshour/bb/law/brutality_4-5.html (January 7, 2005).

Keller, Gary D. "The Image of the Chicano in Mexican, United States, and Chicano Cinema: An Overview." In *Chicano Cinema: Research, Reviews, and Resources*, edited by Gary Keller, 13–58. Binghamton, NY: Bilingual Review, 1985.

King, Louis, dir. *Charlie Chan in Egypt. Film.* Los Angeles: Fox Film Corporation, 1935.

Kirby, Dick, and Amy Ziering Kofman, dirs. *Derrida.* Documentary film. Los Angeles: Jane Doe Films, with Zeitgeist Films, 2002.

Kobal, John. *Rita Hayworth: The Time, the Place and the Woman.* London: W. H. Allen, 1977.

Korte, Tim. "Spielberg Production Sued Over Haircut." Associated Press, March 17, 2006. http://www.washingtonpost.com/wp-dyn/content/article/2006/03/17/AR2006031701690.html.

Krauss, Rosalind. *The Optical Unconscious.* Cambridge, MA: MIT Press, 1993.

Kricfalusi, John. "FAQ: R&S on a Napkin." Newsgroups: alt.animation.spumco. Subject: Re: R&S on a Napkin, http://pubweb.northwesternedu/ñavaho/renstimpy.html.

Kristeva, Julia. *Powers of Horror: An Essay on Abjection.* Translated by Leon S. Roudiez. New York: Columbia University Press, 1982.

Kunzle, David. "Introduction to the English Edition (1991)." In *How to Read Donald Duck: Imperialist Ideology in the Disney Comic*, by Ariel Dorfman and Armand Mattelart. Translation and updated introduction by David Kunzle, with appendix by John Shelton Lawrence. New York: International General, 1991. Originally published as *Para leer al Pato Donald* (Buenos Aires: Siglo Veintiuno Editores, 1986).

Lachman, Harry, dir. *Dante's Inferno. Film.* Los Angeles: Fox Film Corporation, 1935.

Lahr, John. "The Voodoo of Glamour." *New Yorker* 70, no. 5 (March 21, 1994): 113.

Lamb, Blaine T. "The Convenient Villain: The Early Cinema Views the Mexican-American." *Journal of the West* 14, no. 4 (1975): 75–81.

Leaming, Barbara. *If This Was Happiness: A Biography of Rita Hayworth.* New York: Viking, 1989.

———. *Orson Welles: A Biography.* New York: Penguin, 1985.

Lenburg, Jeff. *The Great Cartoon Directors.* Jefferson, NC: McFarland Press, 1983.

Lerner, Jesse. *Ruins.* Independent film, 1999. Screened as part of Cowboys, Indians, Divas, and Poets: A Re-vision of Mexican Mythologies film festival, New York: Subcine, 2002.

Lewis, Robert M., ed. *From Traveling Show to Vaudeville: Theatrical Spectacle in America, 1830–1910.* Baltimore: Johns Hopkins University Press, 2003.

Maltin, Leonard. *Of Mice and Magic: A History of American Animated Cartoons.* New York: McGraw-Hill, 1980.

Mankiewicz, Joseph, dir. *All About Eve. Film.* Los Angeles: 20th Century Fox Film Corporation, 1950.

Manring, M. M. *Slave in a Box: The Strange Career of Aunt Jemima.* Charlottesville: University of Virginia Press, 1998.

Martínez, Andrea. *La intervención norteamericana, Veracruz, 1914*. Colección Memoria y Olvido—Imágenes de México. Mexico City: Martín Casillas Editores: Cultura/SEP, 1982.

Marx, Karl. *Das Kapital/Capital*. Translated by Ben Fowkes. New York: Penguin, 1990.

Mazón, Mauricio. *The Zoot-Suit Riots: The Psychology of Symbolic Annihilation*. Mexican American Monographs 8. Austin: University of Texas Press, 1984.

McBride, Joseph. *Orson Welles*. New York: Viking Press. 1972.

McKimson, Robert, dir. *Cannery Woe*. Film (1960). In *Golden Jubilee 24 Karat Collection: Speedy Gonzales Fast Funnies*. Video compilation. Los Angeles: Warner Bros., 1985.

Mead, Robert G., Jr., "Images North and South of the Border: The United States and Latin America Today and Tomorrow." *Hispania* 57, no. 2 (1974): 321–328.

Melo de Remes, María Luisa. *Veracruz mártir: La infamia de Woodrow Wilson, 1914*. Mexico City: N.p., 1966.

Memmi, Albert. *The Colonizer and the Colonized*. Translated by Howard Greenfeld. Boston: Beacon Press, 1967.

Monter, E. William. *Frontiers of Heresy: The Spanish Inquisition from the Basque Lands to Sicily*. New York: Cambridge University Press, 1990.

Morella, Joe, and Edward Z. Epstein. *Rita: The Life of Rita Hayworth*. New York: Delacorte Press, 1983.

Nabokov, Vladimir. *Pale Fire*. London: Weidenfeld and Nicholson, 1962.

Naremore, James. *The Magic World of Orson Welles*. New York: Oxford University Press, 1978.

Nericcio, William Anthony. "Artif[r]acture: Virulent Pictures, Graphic Narrative and the Ideology of the Visual." *Mosaic: A Journal for the Interdisciplinary Study of Literature* 28, no. 4 (December 1995): 79–109.

———. "Autobiographies at *la frontera:* The Quest for Mexican-American Narrative." *The Americas Review: A Review of Hispanic Literature and Art of the USA* 16, no. 3–4 (Fall–Winter 1988): 165–187.

———. "Autopsy of a Rat: Odd, Sundry Parables of Freddy López, Speedy Gonzales, and Other Chicano/Latino Marionettes Prancing about Our First World Visual Emporium." *Camera Obscura* 1, no. 37 (1996): 189–237.

———. ed. *Bordered Sexualities: Bodies on the Verge of a Nation*. San Diego, CA, and Laredo, TX: Hyperbole Books, 2006.

———. "A Decidedly 'Mexican' and 'American' Transference: Frida Kahlo in the Eyes of Gilbert Hernández." In *Latina/o Popular Culture*, edited by Mary Romero, Michele Habell-Pallán, and Jaime Cárdenas, 190–207. New York: New York University Press, 2002.

———. "¿Nobel Paz?: A Pre- and Post-Nobel Survey Documenting a Mexican Writer's View of Mexico, the United States, and Other Assorted Matters." *Siglo Veinte: Critique in Cultural Discourse* 10, nos. 1–2 (Winter 1992): 165–194.

———. "Of Mestizos and Half-Breeds: Orson Welles's *Touch of Evil*." In *Chicanos and Film*, edited by Chon Noriega, 47–58. Minneapolis: University of Minnesota Press, 1992.

———. "Remembering: What Is Truth on the Border"/"Recuerdos: Cuál es la verdad en/de la frontera." In *Border Lives: Personal Essays on the U.S.-Mexico*

Border/Vidas fronterizas: La crónica en la frontera México–Estados Unidos, edited by Harry Polkinhorn et al., 77–114. Mexicali/Calexico, Mexico: Binational Press/Editorial Binacional, 1996.

———. "When Electrolysis Proxies for the Existential: A Somewhat Sordid Meditation on What Might Occur if Frantz Fanon, Rosario Castellanos, Jacques Derrida, Gayatri Spivak, and Sandra Cisneros Asked Rita Hayworth Her Name." In *Violence and the Body,* edited by Arturo Aldama, 263–286. Bloomington: Indiana University Press, 2003.

Netzloff, Mark. "'Counterfeit Egyptians' and Imagined Borders: Jonson's *The Gypsies* Metamorphosed." *ELH* 68, no. 4 (2001): 763–793.

Newstok, Scott L. "Touch of Shakespeare: Welles Unmoors *Othello.*" *Shakespeare Bulletin* 23, no. 1 (Spring 2005): 29–86.

Ngai, Sianne. "'A Foul Lump Started Making Promises in My Voice': Race, Affect, and the Animated Subject." *American Literature* 74, no. 3 (2002): 571–601.

Noriega, Chon A. *Chicanos and Film: Representation and Resistance.* Minneapolis: University of Minnesota Press, 1992.

———. *Shot in America: Television, the State, and the Rise of Chicano Cinema.* Minneapolis: University of Minnesota Press, 2000.

Nunokawa, Jeff. "Homosexual Desire and the Effacement of the Self in 'The Picture of Dorian Gray'." *American Imago* 49, no. 3 (Fall 1992): 311–321.

Obregón Pagán, Eduardo. *Murder at the Sleepy Lagoon: Zoot Suits, Race, and Riot in Wartime L.A.* Chapel Hill: University of North Carolina Press, 2003.

O'Connor, John J. "Review/Television; Santa Is Challenged in 'Retail Christmas.'" *New York Times,* December 24, 1990; http://query.nytimes.com/gst/fullpage.html?res=9C0CE2DA1038F937A15751C1A966958260.

Okely, Judith. "Deterritorialised and Spatially Unbounded Cultures within Other Regimes." *Anthropological Quarterly* 76, no. 1 (2003): 151–164.

Oliver, Kelly, and Benigno Trigo. *Noir Anxiety.* Minneapolis: University of Minnesota Press, 2003.

O'Neill, Brian. "The Demands of Authenticity: Addison Durland and Hollywood's Latin Images during World War II." In *Classic Hollywood, Classic Whiteness,* edited by Daniel Bernardi, 359–385. Minneapolis: University of Minnesota Press, 2001.

Osborne, Jim. "Hollywood Tragedy, the Suicide of Lupe Vélez." In *Snatch Sampler #2,* 76–82. San Francisco: Keith Green and Apex Novelties, 1977.

O'Shaughnessey, Edith. *A Diplomat's Wife in Mexico: Letters from the American Embassy at Mexico City, Covering the Dramatic Period between October 8th, 1913, and the Breaking Off of Diplomatic Relations on April 23rd, 1914.* New York: Harper and Brothers, 1916. This book appeared in Mexico as *Huerta y la Revolución vistos por la esposa de un diplomático en México: Cartas desde la embajada norteamericana en México que refieren al dramático período comprendido entre el 8 de octubre de 1913 y el rompimiento de relaciones que tuvo lugar el 23 de abril de 1914, junto con un resumen sobre la ocupación de Veracruz* (Mexico City: Editorial Diogenes, 1971).

Padilla, Génaro M. "The Recovery of Chicano Nineteenth-Century Autobiography." *American Quarterly* 40, no. 3 (1988): 294.

Panofsky, Erwin. "Style and Medium in the Motion Pictures." In *Film Theory and Criticism,* edited by Gerald Mast and Marshall Cohen, 289–302. New York: Oxford University Press, 1985.

Paredes, Américo. *With His Pistol in His Hand: A Border Ballad and Its Hero.*

Austin: University of Texas Press, 1958.

Pease, Donald E. "Borderline Justice/States of Emergency: Orson Welles' *Touch of Evil*." *CR: The New Centennial Review* 1, no. 1 (2001): 75–105.

Perry, Mary Elizabeth, and Anne J. Cruz, eds. *Cultural Encounters: The Impact of the Inquisition in Spain and the New World*. Berkeley: University of California Press, 1991.

Pettit, Arthur G. *Images of the Mexican American in Fiction and Film*. College Station: Texas A&M University Press, 1980.

Piedra, José. "The Game of Critical Arrival." *Diacritics* 19, no. 1(1989): 34–61.

Quirk, Robert E. *An Affair of Honor: Woodrow Wilson and the Occupation of Veracruz*. New York: W. W. Norton, 1962; 1967.

Ramírez, Gabriel. *Lupe Vélez: La mexicana que escupía fuego/Lupe Vélez: The Mexicana Who Spit Fire*. Mexico City: Cineteca Nacional, 1986.

Rechy, John. *City of Night*. Evergreen Black Cat Book. New York: Grove Press, 1963.

Retamar, Roberto Fernández. *Calibán: Apuntes sobre la cultura en nuestra América*. Appeared as "Caliban: Notes toward a Discussion of Culture in Our America," translated by Roberto Márquez. *The Massachusetts Review* 15, nos. 1–2 (1974): 7–72.

Rich, B. Ruby. "Mexico at the Multiplex Review." *The Nation*. Posted April 26, 2001, http://www.thenation.com/doc/20010514/rich (May 14, 2001, issue).

Richard, Alfred Charles, Jr. *Censorship and Hollywood's Hispanic Image*. Westport: Greenwood Press, 1995.

———. *Contemporary Hollywood's Negative Hispanic Image*. Westport, CT: Greenwood Press, 1995.

———. *The Hispanic Image on the Silver Screen*. Westport, CT: Greenwood Press, 1995.

Ringgold, Gene. *The Films of Rita Hayworth: The Legend and Career of a Love Goddess*. Secaucus, NJ: Citadel Press, 1974.

Rodriguez, Richard. *Days of Obligation: An Argument with My Mexican Father*. New York: Viking, 1992.

Rodríguez-Estrada, Alicia I. "Dolores del Río and Lupe Vélez: Images On and Off the Screen 1925–1944." In *Writing the Range: Race, Class, and Culture in the Women's West*, ed. Elizabeth Jameson and Susan Armitage, 475–492. Norman and London: University of Oklahoma Press, 1997.

Rogin, Michael. *Blackface, White Noise: Jewish Immigrants in the Hollywood Melting Pot*. Berkeley: University of California Press, 1996.

Rosaldo, Renato. *Culture and Truth: The Remaking of Social Analysis*. Boston: Beacon Press, 1989.

Said, Edward. Foreword to *Selected Subaltern Studies*, edited by Ranajit Guha and Gayatri Chakravorty Spivak, iii–x. New York: Oxford University Press, 1988.

———. "Jungle Calling." *Andy Warhol's Interview Magazine* 19, no. 6 (June 1989): 61–65, 112.

———. *Orientalism*. New York: Pantheon, 1978.

———. "Representing the Colonized: Anthropology's Interlocutors." *Critical Inquiry* 15, no. 2 (Winter 1989): 205–225.

Saldaña-Portillo, María Josefina. *The Revolutionary Imagination in the Americas and the Age of Development*. Durham, NC: Duke University Press, 2003.

Saldívar, Ramón. *Chicano Narrative: The Dialectics of Difference*. Madison: University of Wisconsin Press, 1990.

Saper, Wylie, ed. *Comedy: "An Essay on Comedy," by George Meredith; "Laughter," by Henri Bergson.* Baltimore: Johns Hopkins University Press, 1980.

Sarduy, Severo. *Written on a Body.* Translated by Carol Maier. New York: Lumen Books, 1989.

Searle, John. "Reiterating the Differences: A Reply to Derrida." *Glyph* 2 (1977): 198–208.

Segel, Harold B. *Pinocchio's Progeny: Puppets, Marionettes, Automatons, and Robots in Modernist and Avant-Garde Drama.* Baltimore: Johns Hopkins Univesity Press, 1995.

Seminario, Lee Anne Durham. *The History of the Blacks, the Jews, and the Moors in Spain.* Madrid: Playor, 1975.

Shohat, Ella, and Robert Stam. *Unthinking Eurocentrism.* London and New York: Routledge, 1994.

Simeon, Remi. *Diccionario de la lengua nahuatl o mexicana.* Mexico City: Siglo Veintiuno Editores, 2001.

Singerman, Robert. *Jewish and Hebrew Onomastics: A Bibliography.* New York: Garland, 1977.

The Sleepy Lagoon Case. Los Angeles: Mercury Printing Company, 1943.

Spines, Christine. "One from the Heart." *Premiere* (American edition, NY) 16, no. 1 (September 2003): 36; http://libproxy.sdsu.edu/login?url=http://proquest.umi.com/pqdweb?did=149319131&sid=1&Fmt=2&clientId=17862&RQT= 309&VName=PQD.

Spivak, Gayatri Chakravorty. "Who Claims Alterity." In *Remaking History*, edited by Barbara Kruger and Fred Mariana, 269–292. Seattle: Bay Press, 1989.

Starke, Leslie. *Starke Parade.* London: Max Reinhart, 1958.

Stevenson, Ralph. *The Animated Film: International Film Guide Series.* London: Tantivy Press, 1973.

Strain, Ellen. "Exotic Bodies, Distant Landscapes: Touristic Viewing and Popularized Anthropology in the Nineteenth Century." *Wide Angle* 18, no. 2 (1996): 70–100.

Stubbs, John. "The Evolution of Orson Welles's *Touch of Evil* from Novel to Film." In *Touch of Evil: Orson Welles, Director*, edited by Terry Comito, 175–193. New Brunswick, NJ: Rutgers University Press, 1985.

Sturtevant, Victoria. "Lupe Vélez and the Ambivalent Pleasures of Ethnic Masquerade." *The Velvet Light Trap* 55 (2005): 19–32.

SubCine. "Biography of Rita González." http://www.subcine.com/gonzalez.html (February 27, 2005).

Sweetman, Jack. *The Landing at Veracruz, 1914: The First Complete Chronicle of a Strange Encounter in April 1914, when the United States Navy Captured and Occupied the City of Veracruz, Mexico.* Annapolis: U.S. Naval Institute, 1968.

Taussig, Michael. *The Nervous System.* New York: Routledge, 1992.

Theweleit, Klaus. *Male Fantasies.* Translated by Stephen Conway et al. Minneapolis: University of Minnesota Press, 1987.

Thompson, Howard. Review of *Touch of Evil. New York Times*, May 22, 1958. http://movies2.nytimes.com/mem/movies/review.html? r=2&title1=&title2=TOUCH%20OF%20EVIL%28MOVIE%29&reviewer=Howard% 20Thompson&v id=50539.

Toole, John Kennedy. *A Confederacy of Dunces.* New York: Grove, 1980.

Truffaut, François. *The Films in My Life.* Translated by Leonard Mayhew. New

York: Simon and Schuster, 1978.

Urgo, Joseph R. "Menstrual Blood and 'Nigger' Blood: Joe Christmas and the Ideology of Sex and Race." *Mississippi Quarterly* 41, no. 3 (1988): 391–402.

Vanderwood, Paul J. *Disorder and Progress: Bandits, Police, and Mexican Development.* Lincoln: University of Nebraska Press, 1981.

Vanderwood, Paul J., and Frank N. Samponaro. *Border Fury: A Picture Postcard Record of Mexico's Revolution and U.S. War Preparedness, 1910–1917.* Albuquerque: University of New Mexico Press, 1988.

Vidor, Charles, dir. *Gilda.* Film. Los Angeles: Columbia Pictures Corporation, 1946.

Villanueva, Tino. *Scene from the Movie "Giant."* Willimantic, CT: Curbstone Press, 1993.

Virilio, Paul. *War and Cinema: The Logistics of Perception.* Translated by Patrick Camiller. London and New York: Verso, 1989.

Viscusi, Robert. "Coining." *Differentia: Review of Italian Thought* 1, no. 2 (Spring 1988): 7–42.

Walters, Barry. "John Kricfalusi: Creator of Ren and Stimpy." *San Francisco Examiner*, January 28, 1997.

Webster's Third International Dictionary. New York: G. and C. Merriam Company, 1951.

Webster's Third International Dictionary of the English Language Unabridged. Edited by Noah Porter. Springfield, MA: G. and C. Merriam Company, 1913.

Welles, Orson, dir. *Touch of Evil.* 35 mm film, 112 min. Venice, CA; Los Angeles, CA: Universal International Pictures, 1958. *Touch of Evil*, MCA (1987) VHS version; MCA is a subsidiary of Universal Studios. All rights reserved. *Touch of Evil: Restored to Orson Welles's Vision* was released October 31, 2000, on DVD by Universal Studios. All rights reserved.

Wilde, Oscar. *The Picture of Dorian Gray.* Illustrated by Tony Ross. New York: Viking, 2000.

———. *"The Picture of Dorian Gray" and Selected Stories.* New York: New American Library, 1962.

Williams, Lynda. "Skin Flicks on the Racial Border: Pornography, Exploitation, and Interracial Lust." In *Porn Studies*, edited by Lynda Williams, 271–308. Durham, N.C.: Duke University Press, 2004.

Williams, Patrick. *Gypsy World: The Silence of the Living and the Voices of the Dead.* Chicago: University of Chicago Press, 2003.

Woll, Allen L. *The Latin Image in American Film.* Los Angeles: UCLA Latin American Center Publications, 1980.

Wood, Andrew G. "Blind Men and Fallen Women: Notes on Modernity and Golden Age Mexican Cinema." *Post Identity* 3, no. 1 (2001): 11–24.

IMAGE CREDITS

All unattributed artifact photography is by the author and used by permission.

Front Matter

Page 3   "Equation #1," © copyright 2005 Guillermo Nericcio García; used by permission of the artist.

Page 3   "Outed Speedy," digital graphic art, © copyright 1993 Guillermo Nericcio García; used by permission of the artist.

Page 5   "The Typed Subject," digital mixed media, © copyright 1998 Guillermo Nericcio García; used by permission of the artist.

Page 6   Lomus.net, Dictionary Project, http://hallucinate.lomas.net/hallucinate.php?ref=hallucinate (October 10, 2005).

Backstory

Page 17   Original digital art, © copyright 2005 Guillermo Nericcio García. From the personal collection of the author.

Page 17   The source for the poster image is MoviePoster.com, http://www.movieposter.com/poster/A70-4561/Mandingo.html (January 3, 2005). Quotations from *Mandingo* come from IMDB, http://imdb.com/title/tt0073349/quotes (February 25, 2006).

Page 18   From the personal collection of the author.

Page 18   From the personal collection of the author.

Page 24   Photography © copyright 2004 Guillermo Nericcio García; used by permission of the artist. From the personal collection of the author.

Page 26   This is a photograph of a photograph of a postcard from Vanderwood and Samponaro's *Border Fury*, 174; used by permission of the authors. All book photography in *Tex[t]-Mex* is © copyright 2004–2006 Guillermo Nericcio García, and is used by permission of the artist.

Page 26   Another photograph of a photograph of a postcard from Vanderwood and Samponaro's *Border Fury*, 194; used by permission of the authors. All book photography in *Tex[t]-Mex* is © copyright 2004–2006 Guillermo Nericcio García, and is used by permission of the artist.

Page 27   The third photograph of a photograph of a postcard from Vanderwood and Samponaro's *Border Fury*, 160; used by permission of the authors. All book photography in *Tex[t]-Mex* is © copyright 2004–2006 Guillermo Nericcio García, and is used by permission of the artist.

Gallery 1

Page 32   From the personal collection of the author.

Page 33   Photocopied photograph of a page from an undated issue of *The Globe*, circa 1989, used as a class handout in Latin American studies courses at the University of Connecticut. From the personal collection of the author.

Page 34   "The Best and Worst Bodies on the Beach," © copyright 2004 Guillermo Nericcio García; used by permission of the artist. From the personal collection of the author.

Page 35   Undated advertisement torn from the pages of a *New Yorker* magazine, circa 1991. From the personal collection of the author.

Page 35   "The Best and Worst Bodies on the Beach," © copyright 2004 Guillermo Nericcio García;

Web site for the film, http://www.derri-dathemovie.com/info.html (November 15, 2005).

Page 103 Gerry Carpenter, *Musings on Dante's Inferno,* David Sindelar's Fantastic Sci-Fi Movie Musings, II, http://www.scifilm.org/musings2/musing964.html (September 29, 2005).

Page 104 *Cartelmania,* http://www.cartelmania.com/image.php?id=3730&imagen=http://www.cartelmania.com/images/c/junio2002/La_nave_de_Satan.jpg (January 11, 2005).

Page 104 http://web.archive.org/web/20050315152228/http://www.pc-fenster.de/ind4205.htm (April 5, 2005).

Page 105 Another Hollywood thrift-store find from the personal collection of the author.

Page 106 Publicity photos of Rita Hayworth from Gene Ringgold's *Films of Rita Hayworth.*

Page 106 These frames are from the Columbia/Tristar DVD version of the film released October 3, 2000.

Page 107 *The Best of the Movies,* http://www.thebestofmovies.com/files/The_Wizard_Of_Oz.jpg (October 12, 2005).

Page 109 Gary Cervantes, http://www.imdb.com/name/nm0148869/ (October 19, 2005).

Page 110 *Perfect People,* http://www.perfectpeople.net/picpage.php3/cpid=84166 (April 11, 2005).

Chapter Three

Page 111 From the personal collection of the author.

Page 112 I am grateful to Stephan Ramdohr for this marvelous screen grab; *Stephan's Alf-Page* (Germany), http://www.tvshows.de/alf/e-ep-049.htm (October 3, 2005).

Page 113 Carl Andreas, *Bundyology,* http://www.bundyology.com/ (October 20, 2005).

Page 114 Undated Web banner advertising by the General Electric Company. From the personal collection of the author.

Page 115 "Olivier's Nightmare," digital mixed media, © copyright 2005 Guillermo Nericcio García; used by permission of the artist.

Page 116 "Villains in Rehab," digital mixed media, © copyright 2005 Guillermo Nericcio García; used by permission of the artist.

Page 119 Oscar Wilde, *The Picture of Dorian Gray,* illus. Tony Ross (New York: Viking, 2000).

Page 121 "Mexicanesque Maus or Autopsy of a Rat" appeared on the cover of *Camera Obscura* 37 in 1998, © copyright 1997 Guillermo Nericcio Garcia; used by permission of the artist.

Page 122 "Portrait of Sophia Alessandra Nericcio's Eyes," © copyright 2005 Guillermo Nericcio García; used by permission of the artist.

Page 123 "The Typed Subject," digital mixed media, © copyright 1998 Guillermo Nericcio García; used by permission of the artist.

Page 125 © copyright 1995 Warner Bros., rescued out of the personal waste basket of the author.

Page 126 The image here reproduced is a digitized screen grab from *Golden Jubilee 24 Karat Collection: Speedy Gonzales™ Fast Funnies.*

Page 127 Vanderwood and Samponaro, *Border Fury,* 131.

Page 127 Photo on left: © copyright 2003 Galen R. Frysinger, http://www.galenfrysinger.com; used by permission; image on right: Speedy "Wallpaper" reproduction, *Cartoni Animati* (Italy), http://www.sfonditalia.it/CartoniAnimati.htm (October 12, 2005).

Page 128 Vanderwood and Samponaro, *Border Fury,* 13.

Page 129 The image here reproduced is a digitized screen grab from *Golden Jubilee 24 Karat Collection: Speedy Gonzales™ Fast Funnies.*

Page 130 The image here reproduced is a digitized screen grab from *Golden Jubilee 24 Karat Collection: Speedy Gonzales™ Fast Funnies.*

Page 130 The image here reproduced is a digitized screen grab from *Golden Jubilee 24 Karat Collection: Speedy Gonzales™ Fast Funnies.*

Page 131 Photograph of facsimile lobby card from the personal collection of the author.

Page 131 The image here reproduced is a digitized screen grab from *Golden Jubilee 24 Karat Collection: Speedy Gonzales™ Fast Funnies.*

Page 132 Facsimile reproduction of 1957 lobby card for *Tabasco Road.* From the personal collection of the author.

Page 132 The image here reproduced is a digitized screen grab from *Golden Jubilee 24 Karat Collection: Speedy Gonzales™ Fast Funnies.*

Page 133 "Che & Speedy," © copyright 2005 Guillermo Nericcio García; used by permission of the artist.

Page 136 From the personal collection of the author.

Page 142 State Archives African American Initiative, Missouri Secretary of State, Robin Carnahan, http://www.sos.mo.gov/archives/resources/africanamerican/guide/image005.asp (May 17, 2005). The Aunt Jemima ad is an original undated (circa 1950–1954) advertisement in the personal collection of the author. The smiling porter, brace yourself, is the "property" of The Cream of Wheat Corporation of Minneapolis, Minnesota, filing #6117 Cream of Wheat, 30 June 1930, with the United States Patent and Trademark Office, an agency of the United States Department of Commerce.

Page 142 Clipping from the personal collection of the author.

Page 145 Ren and Stimpy are © copyright Nickelodeon; these images derive from the *Spike TV Download Page,* http://www.spiketv.com/downloads/images/desktops/ren_and_stimpy/ren_and_stimpy2b.jpg (October 12, 2005).

Page 146 The images are © copyright 1992 Nickelodeon and MTV and are in the personal collection of the author.

Page 147 This panel is from the pages of *Love and Rockets,* © copyright 1989 Jaime Hernandez. Used by permission of the artist.

Page 147 © copyright 1989 Gilbert Hernandez. Used by permission of the artist.

Page 148 © copyright 1989 Gilbert Hernandez. Used by permission of the artist.

Page 149 "Speedy's Makeover," © copyright 1993 Rosina Talamantes and Guillermo García. From the personal collection of the author.

Page 151 "Autopsy of a Rat, Chapter 2," digital mixed media/photography, © copyright 1993, digital media, Guillermo Nericcio García; photography, Jamie Heather Fox-Rice; used by permission of the artists.

Page 151 Snapshot of the *Powerpuff Girls* home page, http://www.cartoonnetwork.com/tv_shows/ppg/index.html (August 24, 2005).

Page 151 MAC OSX screen grab from a WFTV Web site, an Orlando, Florida, ABC affiliate; http://www.wftv.com/news/4351937 (November 12, 2004).

Chapter Four

Page 153 Facsimile photograph from the personal collection of the author.

Page 154 J. Groen, *Lupe Vélez Web Site,* http://www.geocities.com/jocgroen2/ (April 8, 2003); also still live at http://web.archive.org/web/20021211064706/geocities.com/jocgroen2/pics.html

Page 159 *Palooka* was released on January 26, 1934, by Edward Small Productions as Reliance Pictures, Inc; its theatrical distribution was handled by United Artists; Henwood Cinema of Pennsylvania was responsible for its first release in video. Stills that appear in this chapter are fair-use screen grabs from the VCI Entertainment VHS edition of the movie, released in October 1998.

Page 160 From the personal collection of the author.

Page 160 From the personal collection of the author.

Page 161 From the personal collection of the author.

Page 161 From Modern Times, *Palace Classic Films,* http://www.moderntimes.com/palace/non_image/lupe37.jpg. (October 5, 2005). The image also appears on page 328 of Kenneth Anger's *Hollywood Babylon.*

Page 164 Anger, *Hollywood Babylon,* 340.

Page 165 *Lambiek Comic Shop Site,* http://www.lambiek.net/artists/o/osborne_jim.htm

Page 166 Studio "wallpaper," http://www.afterthe-sunset.com/wall_salma_1024.html (5 October 2005).

Page 166 Penelope Cruz, "Salma Hayek: A One-of-a-Kind, Behind-the-Scenes Look at the Inner Life of One of Hollywood's Most Daring and Hottest . . .," *Interview Magazine* (April 2003).

Page 167 Christine Spines, "One from the Heart," interview with Salma Hayek, *Premiere* (American edition) 16, no. 1 (September 2002): 36.

Page 168 Rita González, *The Assumption of Lupe Vélez* (1999, USA, 22 min.). The screen grab from *The Assumption of Lupe Vélez* is © copyright 1999 Rita González and appears here with the permission of the artist.

Page 169 Rita González, *The Assumption of Lupe Vélez* (1999, USA, 22 min.). The screen grab from *The Assumption of Lupe Vélez* is © copyright 1999 Rita González and appears here with the permission of the artist.

Page 169   The illustration of the *vera ikon,* or Veronica, pictured here is reproduced from the Web Gallery of Art, Virtual Museum, "St. Veronica with the Holy Kerchief," c. 1420, tempera on oak, 78 x 48 cm, Alte Pinakothek, Munich, http://www.wga.hu/frames-e.html?/html/m/master/veronica (October 5, 2005).

Page 172   From the personal collection of the author.

Gallery 2

Page 174   "Batman's Masked Hijo," digital mixed media, © copyright 2005 Guillermo Nericcio García. From the personal collection of the author.

Page 180   Lalo Alcaraz, "Brown Like Me," © copyright 2004; used by permission of the artist.

Page 181   From the personal collection of the author.

Page 182   "The Marquis de Sade Aghast as He Rides with Riverside County Sheriffs," digital mixed media, © copyright 2004–2005 Guillermo Nericcio García; used by permission of the artist.

Page 183   "Tracy Watson: Prelude to Pleasure," digital mixed media, © copyright 2004 Guillermo Nericcio García; used by permission of the artist.

Page 183   Lalo Alcaraz, *La Cucaracha* (April 1, 2005); used by permission of the artist.

Page 183   From the personal collection of the author.

Page 184   Newspaper clipping from the personal collection of the author.

Page 184   Left: http://news.bbc.co.uk/1/hi/entertainment/1201949.stm; right (May 4 2005): http://story.news.yahoo.com/news?tmpl=story&u=/050405/photos_en_afp/050405021005_nfphh3pz_photo2.

Page 184   Vanderwood and Samponaro, *Border Fury,* 13.

Page 185   "Horsing Around With Abby," digital mixed media/newspaper clipping, © copyright 2005 Guillermo Nericcio García; used by permission of the artist.

Page 186   From the personal collection of the author.

Page 187   Frito Bandito 1970 television commercial screen grab from Billy Ingraham, *TV Partyboom,* http://www.tvparty.com/ (August 21, 2005).

Page 187   T. Danno, *The Frito Bandito: Featuring Tex Avery,* http://64.41.109.149/school/bandito.html (November 1, 2005). This image derives from an animation cell that is the property of Mr. Danno and is used with his permission.

Page 188   From the personal collection of Miguel-Ángel Sória; used by permission of the archivist.

Page 189   From the personal collection of Miguel-Ángel Sória; used by permission of the archivist.

Chapter 5

Page 192   "Aztlán Osmosis," mixed-media digital montage, © copyright 2000 Guillermo Nericcio García; used by permission of the artist.

Page 192   "XicanOsmosis #1," © copyright 2004 Guillermo Nericcio García. The digital art contains original cell photography from the archive in the Yale School of Medicine, http://info.med.yale./edu/cellimg/Adenovirus.GIF (August 4, 1996).

Page 193   *Parábola óptica* (1931), Manuel Álvarez Bravo. This image is reproduced from *Manuel Álvarez Bravo: Aperture Masters,* 1987.

Page 193   *Fe ciega* (1995), Adam Sergio Rodriguez, www.mercado.com/arte/artists/rodrigez/blind.gif (November 11, 1996). All reasonable efforts were made to contact the artist; no response was forthcoming. The image appears here under the fair-use provision of the U.S. Copyright laws.

Page 196   From the pages of *Escritos de Carlos Mérida sobre arte: El muralismo,* ed. Xavier Guzmán, Alicia Sánchez, et al. (Mexico City: Serie Investigación y Documentación de las Artes, 1987). Queries to the publisher have not as yet been answered.

Page 197   This mural detail derived from a poster in the personal collection of the author.

Page 198   CLNET, http://clnet.sscnet.ucla.edu/ (October 22, 2005).

Page 198   "Aztlán Web Equation #2," digital mixed media, © copyright 2005 Guillermo Nericcio García; used by permission of the artist.

Page 200   Gilbert Hernandez, "Frida," in *Flies on the Ceiling: Volume Nine of the Complete Love and Rockets.* Used by permission of the artist.

Page 201 Gilbert Hernandez, "Frida," in *Flies on the Ceiling: Volume Nine of the Complete Love and Rockets*. Used by permission of the artist.

Page 202 Gilbert Hernandez, "Frida," in *Flies on the Ceiling: Volume Nine of the Complete Love and Rockets*. Used by permission of the artist.

Page 202 Gilbert Hernandez, "Frida," in *Flies on the Ceiling: Volume Nine of the Complete Love and Rockets*. Used by permission of the artist.

Page 202 Detail from Frida Kahlo, *The Little Deer* (1946), oil on Masonite, 8 7/8 x 11 7/8 in.; in collection of Mrs. Carolyn Farb. Image source: Hendrik Asper, http://asper. maruanaja.nl/art/artgallery/L003M_Frida. Kahlo_The.Wounded.Deer_1946.jpg (May 12, 2005).

Page 203 Gilbert Hernandez, "Frida," in *Flies on the Ceiling: Volume Nine of the Complete Love and Rockets*. Used by permission of the artist.

Page 203 Rex Carlton, *The Brain That Wouldn't Die* (signage, detail), in *Daddy-O's Drive-In Dirt: The History Behind the Movies and Shorts on Mystery Science Theater 3000*, http://www.mst3kinfo.com/daddyo/di_513 .html (May 30, 2001).

Page 204 Gilbert Hernandez, *The Blood of Palomar: Volume Eight of the Complete Love and Rockets*. Used by permission of the publisher.

Page 204 Left to right: Frida Kahlo, *The Broken Column* (1944), Museo Dolores Olmedo Patiño, http://www.arts-history.mx/museos/mdo/ okahloin2.html (October 23, 2001); Gilbert Hernandez, two panels from *Blood of Palomar* (1987), india ink on paper, courtesy Fantagraphic Books; Pablo Ruiz Picasso, *Don Quixote and Sancho Panza* (1955), detail of the cover of *Les Lettres Françaises*, 1955; http://users.ipfw.edu/jehle/ cervante/csa/artics92/lo_re.htm (March 4, 2006). The Web site is a facsimile of an article by A. G. Loré, "A Possible Source for Picasso's Drawing of Don Quixote," that appeared in *Cervantes: Bulletin of the Cervantes Society of America* 12, no. 1 (1992): 105–110.

Page 205 "My Abuela Reads Comic Books and I Stand in Her Shadow, Silent," digital mixed media, © copyright 2005 Guillermo Nericcio García and Billy Nericcio; used by permission of the artists.

Conclusion

Page 208 Brian Ashcraft, "Anime Eyes," *Wired* 13, no. 5 (May 2005), http://www. wired.com/wired/archive/13.05/play.html? pg=4

Page 210 "Cherished Friends," illustration © copyright 1993 William Anthony Nericcio; used by permission of the artist.

Page 212 Toontracker, Home of the Lost Cartoons, http://www.toontracker. com/tracy/dicktracy.htm

INDEX